Yekaterinoslav-Dnepropetrovsk Memorial Book
(Dnipropetrovsk, Ukraine)

Translation of
Sefer Yekaterinoslav-Dnepropetrovsk

Original written in Hebrew

Edited by Zvi Harkavi and Yaakov Goldburt

Published by Yekaterinoslav-Dnepropetrovsk Society

Jerusalem-Tel Aviv 1973

Published by JewishGen

**An Affiliate of the Museum of Jewish Heritage - A Living Memorial to the Holocaust
New York**

Yekaterinoslav-Dnepropetrovsk Memorial Book (Dnipropetrovsk, Ukraine)
Translation of *Sefer Yekaterinoslav-Dnepropetrovsk*

Copyright © 2018 by JewishGen, Inc.
All rights reserved.
First Printing: December 2018, Kislev 5779
Second Printing: March 2019, Adar II 5779

Translation Coordinator: Marilyn Levinson
Editors: Zvi Harkavi and Yaakov Goldburt
Translators: Yocheved Klausner and Sara Mages
Layout: Joel Alpert
Cover Design: Rachel Kolokoff Hopper

Published by JewishGen, Inc.
An Affiliate of the Museum of Jewish Heritage
A Living Memorial to the Holocaust
36 Battery Place, New York, NY 10280

"JewishGen, Inc. is not responsible for inaccuracies or omissions in the original work and makes no representations regarding the accuracy of this translation. Digital images of the original book's contents can be seen online at the New York Public Library Web site."

The mission of the JewishGen organization is to produce a translation of the original work and we cannot verify the accuracy of statements or alter facts cited.

Printed in the United States of America by Lightning Source, Inc.

Library of Congress Control Number (LCCN): 2018965011

ISBN: 978-1-939561-71-8 (hard cover: 292 pages, alk. paper)

JewishGen and the Yizkor-Books-in-Print Project

This book has been published by the **Yizkor-Books-in-Print Project,** as part of the **Yizkor Book Project** of **JewishGen, Inc.**

JewishGen, Inc. is a non-profit organization founded in 1987 as a resource for Jewish genealogy. Its website [www.jewishgen.org] serves as an international clearinghouse and resource center to assist individuals who are researching the history of their Jewish families and the places where they lived. JewishGen provides databases, facilitates discussion groups, and coordinates projects relating to Jewish genealogy and the history of the Jewish people. In 2003, JewishGen became an affiliate of the **Museum of Jewish Heritage - A Living Memorial to the Holocaust** in New York.

The **JewishGen Yizkor Book Project** was organized to make more widely known the existence of Yizkor (Memorial) Books written by survivors and former residents of various Jewish communities throughout the world. Later, volunteers connected to the different destroyed communities began cooperating to have these books translated from the original language— usually Hebrew or Yiddish—into English, thus enabling a wider audience to have access to the valuable information contained within them. As each chapter of these books was translated, it was posted on the JewishGen website and made available to the general public.

The **Yizkor-Books-in-Print Project** began in 2011 as an initiative to print and publish Yizkor Books that had been fully translated, so that hard copies would be available for purchase by the descendants of these communities and also by scholars, universities, synagogues, libraries, and museums.

These Yizkor books have been produced almost entirely through the volunteer effort of researchers from around the world, assisted by donations from private individuals. The books are printed and sold at near cost, so as to make them as affordable as possible. Our goal is to make this important genre of Jewish literature and history available in English in book form, so that people can have the personal histories of their ancestral towns on their bookshelves for themselves and for their children and grandchildren.

A list of all published translated Yizkor Books in the project with prices and ordering information can be found at:
            http://www.jewishgen.org/Yizkor/ybip.html

Lance Ackerfeld, Yizkor Book Project Manager

Joel Alpert, Yizkor-Book-in-Print Project Coordinator

JewishGen
Yizkor Book Project

This book is presented by the
Yizkor Books in Print Project
Project Coordinator: Joel Alpert

Part of the
Yizkor Books Project of JewishGen, Inc.
Project Manager: Lance Ackerfeld

These books have been produced solely through volunteer effort
of individuals from around the world. The books are printed and
sold at near cost, so as to make them as affordable as possible.

Our goal is to make this history and important genre of Jewish
literature available in English in book form so that people can have
the near-personal histories of their ancestral towns on their bookshelves for themselves and for their children and grandchildren.

Any donations to the Yizkor Books Project are appreciated.

Please send donations to:
Yizkor Book Project
JewishGen
36 Battery Place
New York, NY 10280

JewishGen, Inc. is an affiliate of the
Museum of Jewish Heritage
A Living Memorial to the Holocaust

Preface for the Translation and Publication

My interest in Yekaterinoslav began when I learned that three members of my Yanofsky family had travelled to that city in the early part of the twentieth century. My great-grandfather Isaiah Yanofsky managed a brewery, his daughter Hannah became a midwife, and my grandfather Mendel studied in a gymnasium, was imprisoned for Marxist activities and emigrated to the United States in 1913.

The person who truly brought this book into being is Lance Ackerfeld. He explained to me the fundraising requirements and methods, he helped select the translators, and answered any questions I might have. My deepest thanks to Mr. Ackerfeld.

I wanted not only to have the Yizkor book translated, but to learn as much about the city as I could. The following sources helped me to understand this dynamic city's life and the tragedies it faced due to pogroms, revolutions, and the Civil War following the Russian Revolution of October 1917.

1. Miriam Weiner Routes to Roots Foundation. This is a good source to learn what documents are available in the Dnipro archives, and therefore what a researcher might find.

2. Gerard Surh's paper entitled "Ekaterinoslav City in 1905: Workers, Jews and Violence."

3. The Joint Distribution Committee Archives documenting the Civil War in Yekaterinoslav. I have accessed these records both on-line, and by visiting the archives in New York City.

4. American Relief Association Archives. The ARA worked closely with the Joint in bringing aid to Yekaterinoslav.

5. Dr. Bogen "Born A Jew" describing his relief work in Yekaterinoslav during the Civil War.

6. Dr. Roman Serbyn "The First Man-made famine in Soviet Ukraine 1921-1923."

7. "Ekaterinoslav One Family's Passage To America A Memoir in Verse by Jane Yolen.'

The chapters that follow provide a window into the past, and a chance to understand the lives of our ancestors.

Marilyn Levinson

October 2, 2018

Geopolitical Information:

Alternate names: Dnipro Дніпро [Ukr, since 2016], Dnipropetrovs'k [Ukraine, until 2016], Dnepropetrovsk [Russia, since 1926], Ekaterinoslav [Russia, before 1926], Yekaterinoslav [Yiddish], Jekaterynoslaw, Iekaterinoslav, Dniepropietrowsk [Polish], Dnjepropetrowsk, Dniepropetrovsk, Dniepropetrovsk, Ekaterinoslav, Jekaterynoslaw, Keterinoslav, Sicheslav [Russia, 1917-18], Secheslav, Siczeslaw

Period	Town	District	Province	Country
Before WWI (c. 1900):	Ekaterinoslav	Ekaterinoslav	Ekaterinoslav	Russian Empire
Between the wars (c. 1930):	Dnepropetrovsk	Dnepropetrovsk	Ukraine SSR	Soviet Union
After WWII (c. 1950):	Dnipropetrovs'k			Soviet Union
Today (c. 2000):	Dnipropetrovs'k			Ukraine

Jewish population in 1897: 41,240

Dnipro, Ukraine is located at 48°27' N, 34°59' E
240 miles ESE of Kiev, on the Dnieper. Ukraine's fourth-largest city.

Notes: Russian: Днепропетровск, formerly Екатеринослав. Ukrainian: Дніпро / Дніпропетровськ. Yiddish: קאַטערינעסלאָוו

Nearby Jewish Communities:

Nizhnedneprovsk 5 miles NE

Ihren' 10 miles E

Novomoskovs'k 15 miles NE

Dniprodzerzhyns'k 17 miles W

Synel'nykove 26 miles ESE

MAP OF UKRAINE IN 2014

Explanation for the Design Cover of the Yekaterinoslav-Dnepropetrovsk Memorial Book

"For the dead and the living, we must bear witness."
— Elie Wiesel

Reading through the Yekaterinoslav-Dnepropetrovsk Memorial Book will eventually bring you to the horrific events and atrocities that occurred in this Jewish community throughout the years, but particularly during the Holocaust.

With a Jewish population of over 100,000 people in 1939, a vibrant community was decimated by the Nazis, with a total of about 50,000 Jews murdered in Dnepropetrovsk during the occupation.

But reading this memorial book will also take you back to a Jewish community filled with active, educated, and intellectual people. With this cover, I wanted to remember that dynamic life and the individual people that once filled that community.

The front cover illustration is a collage of photos from the interior of the book. The back cover is a map of Yekaterinoslav-Dnepropetrovsk from 1885 (public domain) showing life as it was before the atrocities.

On the front cover, at the center of the collage, is the Great Synagogue in Ekaterinoslav, representing the central part of life that the synagogue played in all Jewish communities throughout Europe. Surrounding the synagogue, are the portraits of the people that made Yekaterinoslav-Dnepropetrovsk their home and brought life to this once energetic and thriving community.

The individual people of Yekaterinoslav-Dnepropetrovsk represented on the cover:

R'Efraim ben Yoel–Zelig Strod: One of the most loyal and devoted activists of Ekaterinoslav Zionism. **Hadassa Rachel Birman**: Daughter of Asher Yitzchak Wolfowitz. A strong and active Zionist. **Rabbi R'Dober-Zev-Wolf Kozhvenikov**: A dear man and a "doer of good deeds" – no needy person was turned away from his door. **Rabbi Levi–Yitzhak Schneurson**: In addition to his scholarship in Torah, he was very knowledgeable in Kabala and Chabad Hassidism He was pious and God–fearing and of good qualities. **Rabbi Yehuda Leib Levin**: A great luminary, who preserved and guarded the glowing embers of the Torah, a figure of a rabbi of the old days.

R'Moshe Karpas: A leader of the Community in Ekaterinoslav; a well-known philanthropist in Russia; a great donor to Zionism and Eretz Israel. **Eliyahu Orshanski:** The great journalist, and one of the first researchers of the Russian Jews. **Mechl Maidanski**: One of the most famous and devoted community workers in Ekaterinoslav during many years. **Menachem Ussishkin**: One of the world leaders of the Zionist movement. **Moshe ben Shmuel Bruk**: One of the exceptional leaders of the Ekaterinoslav community and the Jews in Southern Russia. **Dr. Shmaryahu Levin**: The third rabbi in Ekaterinoslav appointed by the authorities and one of the most outstanding. **Sergei Paley**: One of the first Jewish engineers in Ekaterinoslav and manager of large business enterprises in town. **Dr. Yakov Dolzhanski**: One of the well-known and important activists in Ekaterinoslav. **Shlomo Braslavski**: One of the most active and energetic persons in the Zionist movement in Ekaterinoslav, in the first decade and a half of the 20th century. **Moshe Duchan**: Respected lawyer and Zionist. **Israel ben Baruch Idelson**: One of the prominent leaders of the Tze'irei Zion movement and the Zionists in Ekaterinoslav. **Moshe Rissin**: A righteous and honest man, speaker of truth, "pure of hands and pure of heart", innocent, and modest. **Zalman Yupit**: One of the active members of the Zionist underground in Ekaterinoslav. **Avraham Gutman**: One of the devoted, loyal and active Zionists during the difficult years of the early Soviet rule in Ekaterinoslav. **Dov ben Yakov–Nathan Admoni:** A proud Jew and a devoted Zionist. **Yehuda Avisar (Kozlovski)**: Active member of the Jewish self–defense in town.

I hope this cover helps us to remember what made Yekaterinoslav-Dnepropetrovsk one of the greatest Jewish communities in Russia. And we must never forget the horrors this community and its beloved people endured.

Rachel Kolokoff Hopper

Notes to the Reader:

We apologize ahead of time for the poor quality of images in the book. Often these images had been scanned from the original Yizkor books which were of poor quality to begin with, being copies of old photographs. Each transfer results in loss of quality. We have done the best we could given the original material and the resources and technology at hand. Even though images often appear of higher quality on computer screens, that does not transfer to high quality images in print. A reader can view the original scans on the web sites listed below.

Within the text the reader will note "{34}" standing ahead of a paragraph. This indicates that the material translated below was on page 34 of the original book. However, when a paragraph was split between two pages in the original book, the marker is placed in this book after the end of the paragraph for ease of reading.

Also please note that all references within the text of the book to page numbers, refer to the page numbers of the original Yizkor Book.

The original book can be seen online at the NY Public Library site:

http://yizkor.nypl.org/index.php? then scroll down to Dnepropetrovsk

or at the Yiddish Book Center web site:

https://www.yiddishbookcenter.org/collections/yizkor-books/yzk-nybc314110/harkavi-zvi-goldbourt-sefer-yekaterinoslav-dnepropetrovsk-ha-kehilah-ha-yehudit

In order to obtain a list of all Shoah victims from the town, the reader should access the Yad Vashem web site listed below; one can also search for specific family names using family name option. These lists are continually updated by Yad Vashem, so it is worthwhile to periodically search these lists.

There is much valuable information available on this web site, including the Pages of Testimony, etc.

http://yvng.yadvashem.org

A list of this book and all books available in the Yizkor-Book-In-Print Project along with prices is available at:

http://www.jewishgen.org/Yizkor/ybip.html

Title Page of Original Yizkor Book

ספר

יקאטרינוסלאב - דנפרופטרובסק

(הקהילה היהודית מהיווסדה ועד היום)

העורכים: הרב ד"ר צבי הרכבי, יעקב גולדבורט

הוצאת ארגון יוצאי יקאטרינוסלאב – דנפרופטרובסק בישראל

בסיוע משפחת אפרים סטרוד ז"ל

ירושלים — תל-אביב תשל"ג

Translation of the Title Page of Original Yizkor Book

Yekaterinoslav-Dnepropetrovsk Book

Editors: Dr. Zvi Harkavi, Yaakov Goldbur

Published by Yekaterinoslav-Dnepropetrovsk Society in Israel

Published in Jerusalem-Tel Aviv 1973

Table of Contents

Family Notes

[Page 5]

From the Editors

Translated by Yocheved Klausner

A. Finally, we can say that we have completed our job; the devotion to our aim assisted us, with God's help, to conclude the project.

We considered it our duty to preserve the history of this important town of the magnificent Russian Jewry from which we originate – in particular after the Holocaust, as the Germans and their helpers annihilated over fifty thousand of our brothers and sisters, may God avenge their blood.

A very large amount of material was researched for the purpose of writing this book: thousands of items, documents, books, and newspapers mainly in the three languages – Hebrew, Yiddish and Russian. But due to the limitations of time and space, much material had to be left out – as the saying of our sages: learn and leave some for others. We hope the rest of this important material will be published elsewhere.

The Ekaterinoslav Jews were unique. A special type of Russian Jew has grown there: a Jew full of energy, who worked hard for his own progress and the progress of the town and its surroundings, and absorbed much from the Russian culture, at the same time preserving his Judaism proudly, as an individual as well as a member of his community (see on this subject the words of Shlonski, in his conversation with the editors of this book).

This young "Potiomkin Town" (as opposite to his "villages") received and accepted Jews who, in the course of 150 years grew to a large number, absolute as well as proportional, among the general population. The town became a center of commerce, heavy industry and mining, with a strong labor movement (Petrovski and his friends). Two power stations – of the biggest in the world – were erected on the Dnieper. On the eve of the Holocaust, 100,000 Jews lived there out of 500,000 residents. Today, as its population is gradually growing, it again includes several tens of thousands of Jews, but they are scattered among the general population, without a traditional community. Yet they have, thank God, a prayer house, a ritual slaughterer and a Jewish cemetery.

It was a great Jewish town, with many great rabbis. There was R'Chone'le z"l, who preceded the great rabbi Y. L. Levin (our last rabbi, died as the Chief Rabbi of Moscow); R'Binyamin'ke z"l, a Lithuanian genius in the knowledge of Halakha (Jewish Law); R'Bere–Wolf z"l from the Chabad Hassidic movement, influential and educated, an "out of this world" Tzaddik. After them came Rabbi Pinchas Gellman z"l – a genius, a great speaker in three languages, a

Zionist, a great leader, the head of the Yeshiva, a dreamer; he died young. Then there was Rabbi Levi–Yitzhak Schneurson z"l, a charismatic personality, worthy of the title ADMOR, who would sacrifice his soul for the sanctification of the Torah; as an important rabbinic personality, he was persecuted by the Soviet regime: was arrested and exiled, and died in exile; as his writings are being published today, one discovers his special method in the framework of Chabad Hasidism; he was the father of the ADMOR of Lubavitch – a great man of the Jewish people; the memories of his wife Rabbanit Chana z"l – 100 pages in Yiddish – are waiting to be published.

There was the Talmud Torah and several cheders in town and, the "crown" of all this – the Yeshiva, where the Gaon Rabbi Chaim–Oizer Grodzenski z"l – the Rabbi of all the Jews in Exile – taught regularly. Rabbi Grodzenski came to Ekaterinoslav as a refugee during World War I. In time, they erected in Ekaterinoslav a religious–Hebrew–Zionist Teachers College.

And there were also Jewish high–schools, and a modern Cheder [cheder metukan = improved cheder] and P. Cohen (Kagan)'s high–school relocated from Vilna; and private teachers of Hebrew; and in the Gentile's schools they also had special lessons of "God's Religion" for the Jewish pupils, among the teachers being Dr. S. Levin and Bragin; and on the eve of the February revolution, the first Institute of High Technical Studies in the Diaspora – the Jewish Polytechnic – was erected.

In Ekaterinoslav, the first Jewish armed self–defense was founded, and Yitzhak Shimshelewitz (later Ben–Zvi) was one of its weapons providers; Po'alei Zion was founded, and Borochov prepared his "Platform" (I had the privilege to help bringing his remains from the Jewish cemetery in Kiev – which was to be closed – to be buried in Eretz Israel).

Many Jewish personalities grew up, visited or lived in Ekaterinoslav, some of them remained to work there. The town was known in literature, in research and in the press, and by the valued deeds of its Jews. The brilliant jurist Eliyahu Orshanski came from Ekaterinoslav; his tombstone was created by Antokolski himself.

[Page 6]

Jewish artists lived there. Newspapers, pamphlets and books were printed in three languages. We shall mention the publication Аргонавты edited by Alexander Karpas.

Zionism took hold there since the times of the First Aliya, and an attempt was made to build settlements in the Golan, the Achva village. From there, Ussishkin led the Zionist movement in Russia and in the world; Dr. S. Levin, the "appointed" rabbi, was a great Zionist, and the famous teacher Ch. A. Zuta spread Hebrew–Zionist education. During the Soviet rule, the Zionist underground acted with great devotion; the poet Chananya Reichman dedicated his poem to this movement – a song to the keepers of the fire.

Here lived the famous philanthropist, my grandfather R'Moshe Karpas z"l, leader of the community and supporter of its educational and cultural institutions, a great donor to Zionism and Eretz Israel.

And there was in Ekaterinoslav also the Bund movement and other Jewish parties, as well as the "Ekaterinoslav Circle" of the Soviet Yiddish writers, headed by Peretz Markish, may God avenge his blood.

A fundamental document describing the Holocaust in town – the diary of the physician Dr. Rosa Leikina z"l – is the heart of this book.

The book is available to the 200 families in Israel who made Aliya from Ekaterinoslav–Dniepropetrovsk and to all the former residents of our town throughout the world, as well as for others – individuals or institutions.

After two congresses in Tel Aviv and two in Jerusalem (in Martef Hashoah on Mount Zion and at Yad Vashem), a plot in the JNF Martyrs Forest and radio broadcasts – the Ekaterinoslav–Dniepropetrovsk book is a par excellence memory to our town.

The indexing of the book enables bibliographical research.

We extend thanks to all those who supported and encouraged us – by participating in writing, donations and advice, and we shall mention in particular: Mrs. Rachel–Hadassa Birman Баьушка Екатеринославского Сионизма aged 96 (we wish her to 120!), the physician Dr. Arie Ben–Gefen, the poet Avraham Shlonski, Member of Knesset Aharon Becker and Mr. Yakov Strod, General Consul of Thailand.

Z. H.

With God's Help,
in the United Jerusalem,
end of 5732 (1972)

B. There are only few Memorial Books for the communities destroyed during World War II by the Germans in the Soviet Union – for various reasons. The main reason was that the Landsmanshaften (the organizations of former residents of the town) – the main factors in the publication of memorial books – have not developed in our country: the immigrants from Russia during the second and third Aliya became immediately and totally involved in the life of Eretz Israel and showed little interest for their original places of residence, and during the period between the two World Wars there was very little Aliya from the Soviet Union. In America as well, there was no reason to establish new organizations, and the existing ones stopped their activities. In the twenties and thirties there was almost no Aliya from the Soviet Union, contrary to the situation in Poland and Lithuania.

Another problem was the lack of historic–archival material concerning the Russian communities, and the lack of possibility to use the little material that was available, especially from the time between the two world wars.

In spite of all these difficulties, the former Ekaterinoslav–Dniepropetrovsk residents in Israel – and they are not many – considered their duty to publish a memorial book of their community, one of the youngest in Russia, which in a short time became one of the biggest and most important. The task was to gather what we found, to save from oblivion details that had not been recorded before, thus building a memorial to the beautiful and active community, for the coming generations.

It was not an easy task, and the editors met with many difficulties. Yet we hope that the reader of the "Ekaterinoslav–Dniepropetrovsk Book" will find a true picture of the life of the local community, of the persons who acted there and the problems they had to meet.

I. G.

[Page 7]

Efraim Strod z"l

Translated by Yocheved Klausner

Efraim Strod z"l

R'Efraim ben Yoel–Zelig Strod, one of the most loyal and devoted activists of the Ekaterinoslav Zionism, was born in 1873 in Pinsk. In 1900 he moved to Ekaterinoslav and continued to work in his trade, printing. In time, he bought a printing shop of his own, and then another, named Издтельство, one of the biggest in town. As an owner of two modern printing shops he employcd a considerable number of workers. Apart from his professional expertise and organizing and managing abilities, he knew the secrets of good human relations and managed to create a very good working relationship with his employees. There were no strikes in his plants. In difficult days, during and after the revolution, he was attentive to the needs of his workers and provided for them products that were not to be found in the market. As a religious man he kept the Commandments, and his workers, including the Christians (who were the majority of the workers in the printing shop), did not work on Sabbath. So, the shop was closed two days a week, Saturday and Sunday (the official day of rest) – which was unusual in those days.

[Page 8]

Mr. Efraim Strod, who was a member of Hovevei Zion while still in Pinsk, joined the Ekaterinoslav Zionists as soon as he arrived. He performed successfully and with devotion the various tasks that were assigned to him. His home was a Zionist home, hospitable and open to all. He helped, openly as well as secretly, all those who addressed him; his hand was open to the needy, and they were many. In 1915, with the flow of Jewish war refugees from the Russian Western borders, he dedicated his time and energy to helping them.

After the February 1917 revolution, his Zionist activity increased even more. He was a member of the local Zionist Committee and participated in all its activities. He recruited new members to the movement and took an active part in the elections to the various institutions, in collaboration with the other leaders – Moshe Bruk, Emanuel Brustein, the Rabbi, Avraham Berezovski and others. He was also one of the founders and organizers of a group preparing to make Aliya, but unfortunately the group was not able to accomplish the task.

During the difficult years that came after the short period of freedom, he was among the founders and managers of the co–operative Kalkala, whose purpose was to provide to its members the necessary products at the time of severe limitations and prohibitions on free trade. Even in those hard times, he found the means to help his friends to overcome the hardships.

In 1922 he left the Soviet Union and in 1923 he arrived to Eretz Israel together with his large family: his sons Mordechai, Yoel z"l and Yakov and his daughter Sara (Shapira). His age and his health did not enable him, however, to fulfill his dream – to be a farmer on the soil of his fatherland, therefore he opened, in partnership with his sons, a printing shop in Tel Aviv. He introduced many innovations (for example, he was the first to use linoleum in advertising announcements). Here, as well, the working relations were correct – no strikes or other trouble. The printing shop is now managed by his son Yakov Strod, the honorary consul of Thailand, in partnership with his grandson Adee.

Efraim Strod continued his charity work and his support activity in Tel Aviv, and responded to any call from national projects, as a loyal and devoted Zionist that he was.

He died in Tel Aviv at a ripe old age on 13 Sivan 5718 (1958), after a long and fruitful life, an active life full of good deeds.

[Page 9]

Verses of Memories
by Hanania Reichman
Translated by Jerrold Landau

More than just once, my memories of my childhood paths move
To you, a major city in Jewish Ukraine,
I return to your past, Ekaterinoslav,
And live in it anew – stage after stage.

The world war, without end streamed to you
Our brethren from the border – refugees from the threat of the sword,
Their Jewish character, populist, alive,
Strengthened their protectors, "Judaized" the reality.

Let my memory testify: please return, please transport
Me to my school, whose roots were from Vilna!
It too was forced to wander when the war broke out
And it granted us a warm, Hebrew corner.

The Jews lived in the center of town.
I never sensed a different population in my surroundings.
Even in my school filled with students
I felt myself in a "city of Jews."

*

In 1917, there shone
The brief shine of freedom also on the "City Yekaterina."
During that "spring"[1] I was a young lad
But I will never forget the days of drunkenness.

Waves and waves of people streamed to the expanse of the city
A procession of free people – with their flags above them
For the Jews, this was also a sublime holiday:
The banner of Zion fluttered among all the flags of freedom.

Every heart opened up to think: "The turn of the blood and sweat has passed
The Marseillaise broke forth from the masses celebrating
But this song did not keep from our mouths
The echo of another hymn: We then sung Hatikva.

[Page 10]

Woe, how quickly did that spring in Russia disappear!
All flowers of freedom were trampled in the Andralamusya dance
A pall pervaded the city and the roads
The civil war caused destruction everywhere.

A terrible dance of demons: gangs, Makhno[2], Petlyura
The conquest of the "Whites" – and again a dictatorship...
Every step of man on the ground, of the blood of man –
And the Jews has such a great part in the blood!

*

The victory of the "Red Government" stopped the surge of pogroms.
However, in the meantime, upon every freedom was decreed: "Halt!"
Dictatorship grew – and a giant shield
Of stifling and muteness was created by the oppressive regime.

We Zionists as well went underground
Where the Hebrew eternal flame shone its hidden light.
In the shadow of isolation, redemption was given to the soul:
We merited to obtain "Freedom within slavery."

We were voluntarily confined in a prison or a "ghetto"
But the foreign government had no veto power there.
Daily, we lived a two–faced life
The life of an "Anoos"[3] outside, and the life of a free person internally.

*

Daily my eyes saw the pages of the Soviet newspaper,
However, I did not desire to read its news.
I felt no feelings of a citizen with the strangers
We were situated in the north, we dreamed of the east.

With trembling, my eyes read a different type of periodical
A creased booklet was passed from hand to hand –
In which every person, fearful and active,
Found snippets of news from the Land of Israel.

Somewhere in a district city, was printed and collated
The pages of these booklets in a clandestine printing house.
From there, hidden in a pocket, a briefcase, a suitcase,
They wandered afar – to the destined place.

[Page 11]

The entire state was surrounded by the underground.
We were one cell, formed into a framework.
And a secret connection, hidden and concealed,
United the cells, connected them to the headquarters.

*

We read every line, we looked at every number.
We recited the "Shehecheyanu" blessing with every new thing.
We looked for an increase in population
We greeted each wave of aliya with joy.

I remember, for example, the satisfaction
With which I read a small detail on the statistics of development:
The number of automobiles that the census office
Registered in Tel Aviv throughout a single day.

We followed the changes in the homeland
And on the variety of streams in the labor settlements.
For example, we wondered about the difference between a chalutz
Who was a member of a group, versus a member of a kibbutz.

*

The Tz. Tz.[4] faction was set up through a schism,
It still hesitated about the text of its program.
Against the Tz.Tz. Marxist–leftist stream
The Tzeirei Tzion stream was designated as "labor."

We aspired to make the nation productive
We dreamed of a just and progressive regime.
But we dismissed a class struggle as misleading:
We believed that unity is a national imperative.

However, a debate had broken out on various details
Over sharp wording and nitpicking formulations.
Reports of the deliberations were also sent to us
Describing the internal battles in full detail.

After each convention (in Kiev of Moscow)
Every chapter of Tz. Tz. was invited:
"To take a stance in every battle!"
And all members did not care about the hours of effort
Needed to delve into the depths of every difference of opinion.

[Page 12]

Each group sat for nights, diligently pouring over the program
Clarifying each and every detail, explaining – how and why:
What is the statue of public and private property?
And how does it connect with social justice?

On what basis should one participate in colonization?
How can "petite bourgeoisie" actualize laborization?
How many apprentices should a working artisan be permitted to hire –
Without being considered idle, Heaven forbid?

After the debates – we summarized and voted
Proud that the movement consulted with us
And all members were so careful with their opinions
As if their voices were decisive in the entire adjudication.

*

The polishing of the "foundation lines" (Tezises in the vernacular)
Hurt the heart with the dearth of deeds,
However, aside from battles, there were also deeds:
The guarded remnants followed the remnants of the "properties."

The remnants escaped to the underground
Every organizational flag, every sign and frame –
Thus they were saved, from the times of public existence
Signs of Hechalutz, Tarbut, and Macabee.

Physical activity and sport –
A matter so "neutral"
It is possible to exercise in an informal fashion.
A more complex issue – the organization of language study
Even that enjoyed fine success.

With various distractions, we maintained a network
Of courses in Hebrew and knowledge of the homeland.
We organized classes, flexible and wide–branched,
Encompassing many students – youth and children.

There were many students – but the teachers were a handful
They worked for years with strength and diligence.
And the youth who made aliya to the Land did not embarrass them:
Most of them brought their knowledge of their language with them.

[Page 13]

All daily contract was slowly woven,
A chapter of love in a struggling family.
And during the complex battles, everyone felt in every detail
An active participant in general – and not a grain of dust.

As I survey that praiseworthy era with the eyes of my spirit,
I recall with satisfaction a bundle of small events.
A group of stubborn people held to their beliefs,
Existing like a remote island in the sea.

Now, when I recall the atmosphere of our lives,
The "scenery" of our experience is sevenfold dear to me.
And from the depths of my heart, is still not erased
The memory of festive evenings and the echoes of hours of joy.

Even the holidays went down to the underground with us.
Even there, you, the light of the holiday, did not hide your rays!
We celebrated every festival in a closed private residence
(In an intimate, family environment).

Every celebration was opened with some "words of Torah"
And the crowd of celebrants listened intently.
The openings of the parties "disseminated Zionism"
Not like our way here – without a semblance of embarrassment.

Then came the turn of song. The group became aflame.
We opened with the song, "Hava Nagila, Hava..."
And then we sung the rest of the repertoire –
Its sweetness cannot be imagined – its warmth cannot be described!

Blessed art though, song of our people! You warmed and enthused
Every modest celebration, every gathering.
And the owners of the voices – how did their souls enjoy
Every new tune that infiltrated there.

*

The Chanukah festival was significant to us.
The name Antiochus did not only symbolize the past:
Even in his Russian incarnation, his heirs attempted to decree
Assimilation upon Israel, a desecration of its holy things.

[Page 14]

Of course, the festival of Purim was dedicated to "our Haman":
Arrows of mockery were sent to the enemies of our time.
An oral newspaper, satirical and mocking
Dealt with every "Haman" and wonderfully beat him.

Hymns with great color and uniqueness were composed
And verses of the times in feuilleton style.
We dedicated light parody to every festival.
An imitation of the Haggadah, and imitation of the Megillah.

The central synagogue, which was nicknamed the Choral
As I remember its name, I recall its Simchat Torah
We celebrated among the many – around it or inside it
(This holiday still demonstrates its power in Russia).

There were also regular events – according to the mood,
There were also memorials – according to the calendar:
We marked the 20th of Tammuz – the memorial of the giant of our generation[5]
The 11th of Adar – Tel Hai and Trumpeldor.

*

We will also not forget the culinary folklore:
Every holiday reminded you that you were a Jew – not a lion.
Every holiday had its treats – according to the commandments of the season:
Here there are latkes according to tradition – and here hamantashen.;

Here there are treats of matzos, the food of Passover –
And other delicacies that every mouth discussed[6].
Everything that was included in the baking tradition
Prepared by "our fine couples" for everyone who was hungry.

"Our fine couples" – I have not yet noted
That in that reality, there was also a romantic side
Our common lot created "underground couples" –
And more than once romance created a covenant for life.

*

My activity was both on the surface and descriptive:
In the committee of Tz. Tz. and the youth movement.
Regarding the faction, I confess my sin:
When I joined Tz. Tz. – I had not yet reached the age of eighteen.

[Page 15]

The youth did not always meet behind closed doors:
They desired to break through all fences in nature and health.
We were attracted afar, to nature and landscape,
None of these were lacking in the in the city with a beautiful riverbank.

Along the length of the "Prospekt" the path wound upward
The tram "Place of the Paths – Cathedral Yard"
(Vakzal–Sobornaya: Belgian Line, Green Tram:
It was different from afar from the red "City Line".)

Here is the "Pol Museum"[8] filled with Ukrainian antiquities,
(Again, a hidden memory passes before me from my memory:
My school went to visit there often during my childhood
And a Hebrew expression could be heard among the antiquities.)

The "Potemkin Garden" is on the riverbank
We often wandered around there for an entire day in groups.
Or sometimes, discreetly in an organized group of friends
Of the Zionist youth, under the protection of the trees of the garden.

And for those who desired, due to modesty and calmness
On the Dnieper, opposite the garden, the pleasant Bogomolov Island
Boats floated to the island from a jetty in the garden –
And there was nothing better than its groves for a secret discussion.

[Page 16]

It is obvious that they kept a watchful eye
On everyone whom they thought was suspicious and was on the "black"
list.
And many friends had a basis
To be suspicious of an informer (nicknamed "Sek–Sot).

I will describe the arrangement: in the form of "not there"
You get of the tram – and again jump on the tram,
But in the opposite direction – and hasten to the meeting
In a roundabout manner – to "confuse the informer".

*

Every underground gathering studied, in some form
They kept secrets in writing with the help of a coder.

When letters were received in coded writing
Only the "experts" knew how to delve into them.

And the expert, "the coder" sat patiently –
Occupied for many hours in the secret work.
Using the key to decipher, complex and wisely,
Hidden in a deep secret – summarized in verses of a poem.

The number of letters, in accordance with their order in the section,
Translated into letters of the alphabet –
Or the essence of the counting was a secret writ,
And letters were sent in the language of numbers.

At that time, there was no concept of an "electronic brain."
The memory of a lad such as I was sufficient.
Through the power of practice, the memory was trained
To read the hidden language well, even without the help of a dictionary.

*

The rookies passed a form of "conspirational course."
The worked on in in groups in a sufficiently naïve fashion.
A counsellor in the form of an "interrogator" taught them to "interrogate":
To know how to "lie" without signs of recognition.

[Page 17]

The questionnaire was interpreted in any form of interpretation,
To determine what and how to "respond to a heretic"[9].
However, when the time came for an actual test
We discovered that the course was not practical.

In the realm of "vigilance" – there was no shortage of curiosities.
Several lads displayed a sense of inventiveness and initiative.
Between hidden plans and solutions to problems,
I recall a form of a "patent": removal of evidence.

Between "YE V O S M" (that is the youth movement)
A strange menu opened: binging on mail.
With the clear aim: anything that was swallowed
Will be erased when the arm of the "G P U"[10] searches.

He practiced every day. It is said that he already reached
The pinnacle of swallowing exercises.
But he fattened himself with written and printed material for naught:
In his house, a search was never conducted.

*

Only very few were no caught in the net.
But then, the hand of Stalin had not yet ruled over the informers.
Most of my friends were sent to jail or were deported –
"In exchange to their punishment" … to Palestine, the Land of Israel.

I was also imprisoned – then I found a wonder:
Complete freedom of speech… specifically in the jail.
Only there could I remove the muzzle from my mouth –
Without fear of imprisonment: for I was already a prisoner.

Regarding any "forbidden" topic, we conducted a debate there.
This was a paradox of the sealed spirit:
In the land of dictatorship and absence of civil rights
Only prisoners' merit free debates.

*

A miracle of liberation occurred – and a miracle of travel also came:
I set sail to the Land of Israel from Odessa…
But to this day, my heart beats with emotion
From the sparks of memory of those days.

[Page 18]

My words have been very long: my pen has conducted a convention here
Of memories of the past that burst through from oblivion.
But I desire to state a few more words:
Not about the past, but rather about the future.

Decades have past – years of blood and burning fire
Years of destruction in the Diaspora, years of wonder in the homeland.
All parts of the nation of merited the light of the miracle
Except for a large group of "Jews of silence."

We know: the stream still whispers somewhere over there –
But at times it seems that the hope has ceased.
And suddenly – in the darkness of the fearful days
Of this tragic tribe – a wonderful vision is displayed.

Jewish youth arise: demonstrating for their existence
After a surge of assimilation, the likes of which there never was.
An eternal spark lives, that same eternal light,
That is the answer to "who is a Jew."

They again drink with thirst from that wellspring
At the end, they will recite the Shehecheyanu blessing

The life of the hidden Jews will no longer be wanton
They will eventually be redeemed, their eternity will not fail them.

    The borders of Russia will open! And from there, speedily
Our eyes will witness a stream of aliya!
And you will yet merit to contribute to the growth of its waves
You too, Dnipropetrovsk – Yekaterinoslav!

Tel Aviv
5731 – 1970

Translator's Footnotes

1. Referring to the February revolution, and the time between the February Revolution and the October (Bolshevik) Revolution. See https://en.wikipedia.org/wiki/February_Revolution

2. See https://en.wikipedia.org/wiki/Nestor_Makhno

3. See https://en.wikipedia.org/wiki/Anusim

4. Tzeirei Tzion, or Young Zion.

5. Referring to Theodore Herzl.

6. A play on words here. There have been many in this poem, lost in translation, but this one is worth noting. Passover is "Pesach", and a mouth that discusses in "Peh Sach."

7. See https://en.wikipedia.org/wiki/Zalman_Shneur

8. See https://en.wikipedia.org/wiki/Dmytro_Yavornytsky_National_Historical_Museum_of_Dnipro

9. A take–off from Pirkei Avot 2:14.

10. See https://en.wikipedia.org/wiki/State_Political_Directorate

[Page 21]

The Jews in Ekaterinoslav–Dniepropetrovsk

by I. Goldbrot

Translated by Yocheved Klausner

Assistance with Russian characters by Yefim Kogan

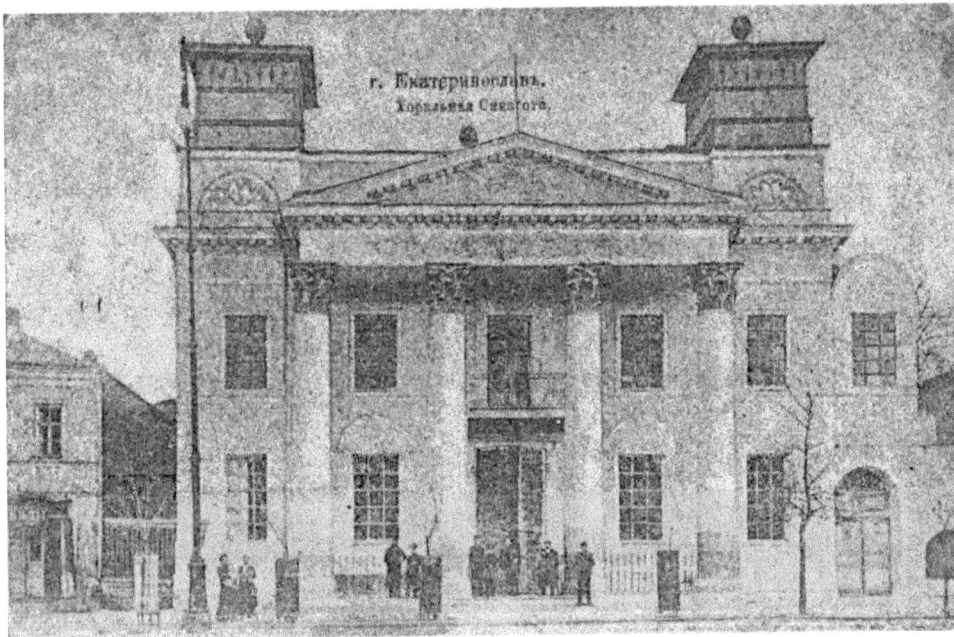

The Great Synagogue in Ekaterinoslav

A. The First Half of the Nineteenth Century

1.

The name of the town Ekaterinoslav – popularly called Katerinoslav – was changed in 1926 to Dniepropetrovsk, after Petrovski, a former factory–worker, chairman of the executive committee of the Supreme Soviet, the Ukrainian Republic. Ekaterinoslav was founded in 1778, by Prince Potemkin, one of the aides of Queen Ekaterina II, and he named the town after her.

The town was founded in another location, and in 1783 it was transferred to the place it is today, on the West bank of the big river Dnieper. Its founders meant it to be the capital of the region, which had just been conquered from the Turks and was called Novo–Russia, therefore they prepared a beautiful city–plan, with wide paved roads, piazzas etc. The entire region is rich in grains, the soil is fertile and yields large crops. In addition, iron mines were discovered near the town, in Krivoy–Rog, as well as anthracite mines in Donbas. As the railroad was built, connecting Ekaterinoslav with the Great Russian cities on one hand and with the iron and coal mines on the other hand, factories, of the largest in the country, were erected in town. The lumber and grains commerce flourished, the town developed quickly, and the population grew. And since Ekaterinoslav was situated within the limits of the "Pale of Settlement" – where there was no limitation to the settlement of Jews – the number of Jews in town grew as well, and in the course of a few years the Jewish community in town became one of the biggest in Russia.

[Page 22]

2.

The Jewish population in Ekaterinoslav

		% of population	
In 1802	376 persons		According to the Gov. records[1]
1825	880 persons		Id.
1847	1,699 persons		Id.
1857	3,565 persons		Leshtzinski: "Jews in Ukraine"
1897	40,971 persons	37%	Gov. census in 1897
1910	69,000 persons		Jewish Statistical Association
1926	62,100 persons	27%	Gov. census in 1926
1939	100,000 persons	20%	Estimate
1959	52,800 persons	8%	1959 census

3.

It is fair to assume, that Jews began to settle in Ekaterinoslav as soon as it was founded. Prince Potemkin did all in his power to advance its growth and development. There he established the government institutions and built his palace, and the Jews, who were closely associated with the government offices and naturally served as his providers, entrepreneurs, merchants etc. were among the first to settle in town. In addition, Jews who had useful occupations were invited to settle in town, and sometimes help was promised for that purpose.[2]

Novo–Russia attracted Jews due to the opportunity to make a good living. As early as 1776, a group of Jews from Balta asked for permission to relocate to Novo–Russia and for aid to accomplish that.[3] This was even before this region was declared, according to the 1791 law, open for Jewish settlement, which encouraged Jews to leave crowded places and seek to settle there.

The first Jews came to Ekaterinoslav from Western Ukraine, then from Lithuania and Belarus. One of the first was Moshe Stanislavski, who raised a large family in town. The majority of settlers chose to live in the section of the town that was close to the River Dnieper. This river served as a major channel of communication, for the transport of wares, in particular lumber from the North, as well as for people. The Ekaterinoslav Jews made a living by collecting taxes, small businesses, pubs, providing for the army and government institutions, and craftsmanship. Some of them managed to get rich. The Jews had a big share in the lumber commerce, as Ekaterinoslav was the last station of the lumber rafts from the North; they also erected and managed sawmills.

Most of the Jews kept Jewish tradition; their language was Yiddish, interspersed with some Russian words. The children received their education in the Cheders, the melamdim [teachers] coming mostly from Lithuania. A Community Committee [Kahal] managed the community, until it was dissolved in 1844. The Kahal managed the community institutions – the cemetery, the Kashrut matters, and the sustenance of the rabbi and the dayanim [judges in the religious court]. One of its functions was also collecting the government taxes and recruiting young men to the army. After the Kahal stopped functioning, the community was represented by the "Jewish Society" Еврейское Общество – actually the rabbi and several of the leaders managed all the needs of the community.

The major income of the community, as in other places, was from the meat tax. This was used to pay the salary of the rabbi and the judges, to support the synagogue, the mikveh [ritual bath] and the Talmud Torah, to help the poor etc. Since the meat tax was not enough to cover all the expenses, donations were also collected. The first cemetery was in the Novia Kardaki suburb; it functioned until the forties of the 19th century and some 1,000 persons were buried there. The oldest gravestone that was still legible (in the eighties) was from 1831.[4]

In the first half of the 19th century – including the 39 years of the reactionary rule of Nicolai I, the Jewish community in Ekaterinoslav developed slowly. Its growth was due partly to natural increase and partly to the immigration from Lithuania and Belarus, and in a small measure to Jewish settlers in the colonies of Southern Russia (begun in 1846), who did not succeed to take roots in their villages and relocated to the cities, among them Ekaterinoslav.

[Page 23]

The Ekaterinoslav Jews participated actively in the economic life of the town, in close relationship with its Christian residents. They obtained permission to enroll their children in the government schools, and in 1851[5] the first Jewish student enrolled in the local high–school. At first only the rich sent their children to the general schools, but in time their number grew, in 1865 their number was 39 and in the 1882–1883 school year it reached 153.[6] One of the first graduates of the Ekaterinoslav high school, who was allowed to enroll at the university and became a medical doctor was Eliezer Eingorn,[7] who later served as doctor in Berditchev. The Jews were usually very good students and received medals. Many parents, however, did not send their children to the high schools, out of fear that they might become distanced from Jewish learning. Those parents engaged Jewish private teachers, and after several years of study the sons joined the parents' businesses.[8] The daughters received their education at the government schools or at home. The children of the less well–to–do families learned in the private cheder, in the Talmud–Torah (founded in 1857) and in the Jewish government school Казённое Еврейское Училище, opened in the early fifties.

B. The Time of Alexander II

4.

The ascent of King Alexander II to the throne, the reforms in the life of the country, liberation of the farmers, abolishment of several of the limitations imposed on the Jews – all this heralded a new era in Russia and brought new development to the region in general and Ekaterinoslav in particular. The Jews took an active part in the developing economical life. In addition to their former occupations, they were very active in the grain trade, part of which was directed to export. Following this development, the authorities started building flour mills, the largest of them being owned by Jews. In the early seventies, the town was connected to the state railroad network, a fact which gave an additional push to the economic development of Ekaterinoslav, and again the Jews took a considerable part in the expansion of the commercial connections of the town.[9]

In the sixties and seventies, several of the important community institutions were established: The "Great Synagogue" on the "Jewish Street" Еврейская улица which later turned into the "Choral Temple" with a permanent cantor and chorus; the Jewish Hospital, at first with 20 beds, which expanded fast; a Home for the Aged (in 1880) built thanks to Yitzhak Stanislavski's donation;[10] free accommodation for guests etc. In 1871 the Association Maskil–El–Dal[11] was founded, its function being to give support to the poor, in particular those who came from other places, so that they would not wander in the streets of the town. Several private Jewish schools were also founded at that time.

The area, where the Ecaterinoslav Jews lived, was a place of new settlements, mostly free of prejudice, a place that encouraged private initiative and provided a good chance to attain material success. The Jews that arrived there were energetic, adapted quickly to the new conditions and their economic situation improved constantly. They created a new type of a proud and self–conscious Jew, who kept his connection with Judaism and at the same time adapted to world–manners and the Russian culture. The new community leaders introduced several changes and improvements in the community institutions, in the Cheder and Talmud Torah curriculum, in the aid–to–the–poor association etc. Among them we should mention: I. Berezovski, A. Targovitzki, Ch. Levanda, M. Meidanski, I. Stanislavski, P Stein and others, and in particular Eliyahu Orshanski, who, in spite of his short life, has become one of the outstanding leaders of the Russian Jewry.[12] These leaders, in addition to working for their own community they responded, together with others, to the call of other localities and collected for them donations from the Ekaterinoslav Jews. For example, in 1860 money was collected for the victims of the Syria pogroms,[13] in 1869 for the Jews who suffered from hunger in various places in Russia[14] etc. Therefore, as the members of that generation would say, the Ekaterinoslav community was one of the advanced communities in Southern Russia, where "the spirit of freedom prevails."[15]

The main problems of the community were schooling for children and help for the poor, and these matters received special attention. The curriculum was improved in the cheder and in the private schools that were opened, as well as in the Talmud Torah, where the poorer children learned; children were helped with clothing and shoes, etc. Often, disputes arose between the innovators and the more conservatives. The number of poor people was significant, since constantly many people came to town from Lithuania and Belarus to look for parnasa [livelihood], but not all were lucky; many needed the help of the community institutions.

[Page 24]

It is enough to mention, that in 1878, 429 families (2051 souls) received help, and an 1882 their number reached 500 families (2,625 souls).[16] Many resources were devoted to that goal.

The relationship with the other residents and with the authorities was, in those days, quite correct, and some of the ruling leaders and high–level employees demonstrated a proper and considerate attitude toward the Jews in town. The Ekaterinoslav Jews sent their representatives to the town council and the court of justice, as judges or jurors.

The first "appointed [by the authorities] Rabbi" was Mr. Gavriel Safranski, who, as related by the members of his generation, did not have a large education and was not very active in the community. After his death in 1877, Mr. Zev Nachum Shakhor (who had been his aide) was elected Rabbi and served in this position until 1898. He was more involved in the life of the community, which grew to about 10,000 souls.[17] The Ashkenazic rabbi of the town was Rabbi Binyamin Zev Sakheim 1872–1913, and the Hassidic rabbi was Rabbi Dov–Zev Kuzivnikov (died in 1928). There were eight registered synagogues,[18] and the income from the meat tax reached in 1880 15,000 Rubles.

C. The Time of Alexander III

5.

In 1881, at the beginning of the rule of King Alexander III, pogroms broke out against the Jews of Southern Russia. Ekaterinoslav was spared that year. In 1882 there was an attempt to organize a pogrom, but thanks to measures taken by the authorities it was prevented.[19] The pogroms that took place in neighboring localities and the refugees that came from those places, caused, naturally, sorrow and fear among the Jews in town. Money was collected and sent to the victims of the pogroms.[20] But the incitement and provocations against the Ekaterinoslav Jews did not cease. It found easy ground – the many laborers who had come from all parts of Russia, to work at the new railroad and the bridge over the Dnieper.

The disturbances began on 20 July (by the Julian calendar) 1883. As a parade passed through the streets, a clash was staged between a Jewish shopkeeper and a Christian young boy and a rumor was spread that the boy was killed by the Jew. Immediately the workers who participated in the parade, joined by many of the town residents, began attacking the shops and stands of the Jews, and the Jewish apartments along the streets of the town, robbing and destroying anything that was in their way. The police were not strong enough to stop them and the army arrived only late afternoon and began acting. However, the pogrom continued the next day, and only by the end of the second day, after the army used guns and several hooligans (about 15 people) were killed and several were wounded the pogrom stopped. It should be mentioned, that the Christian public was remarkably indifferent, and very few came to the aid of the victims or gave them shelter. This shameful day was mentioned even in the general press. The Ekaterinoslav Jews were seized by fear and many left town temporarily; a great amount of property was robbed; mostly the poor suffered. None of the Jews was killed; there were some wounded; the synagogue on Kazatzia Street was destroyed.[21]

As published in the Report of the Aid Committee, 657 families (2,870 souls) asked the Committee for help, mostly small businessmen and craftsmen. The damage was estimated at 600,000 Rubles.[22] 300 apartments were destroyed and robbed.

Immediately an Aid–Committee was organized, headed by I. Brodeski and the first local donations were collected. Soon donations arrived from other places as well, and a total of 17,000 Rubles was collected. The municipality gave 5,000 Rubles and supplied bread for the needy.[23] All this help was not sufficient for the needs of all the victims; several families left town and immigrated to America, some made plans to make Aliya to Eretz Israel. Thanks to the efforts of the authorities, the situation calmed down, the economic life recovered, and the Jewish community returned to normal.

6.

The 1880s and 1890s, the years of the reactionary rule of King Alexander III, brought limitations and new restrictions to the Russian Jews, and the Ekaterinoslav Jews also suffered from the increasing Anti–Semitism and the negative attitude of the authorities. In spite of that, they continued to participate in the economic development of the town, which turned into an important center of commerce and industry, thanks mainly to the new railroad (1884) that crossed the town and connected the Krivoy–Rog region, the center of iron mining, with the anthracite mines in Donbas. In addition to the grains and lumber commerce, the Jews participated in the development of industry, in particular the food industry. They owned the big flour mills, sawmills, tobacco factories, printing shops, oil industry, candies, mineral water etc. They opened large stores, owned houses, were doctors, lawyers, accountants, shop managers etc. Many were tailors, cobblers, ironsmiths, locksmiths, painters, glaziers, bakers, workers in the sawmills and the tobacco factories, and wagon owners, who mainly transported the lumber from the rafts to the sawmills.[24] This way the Jewish settlement in town grew, and it absorbed Jews expelled from Moscow and from Rostov on the river Don, as Jews were forbidden to live in those places.[25] Many lived in apartments situated on the main streets, and the number of Jews in Ekaterinoslav increased, reaching over 20,000.

[Page 25]

These facts – the growth and development of the community, the increase of anti–Semitic feelings, the national spirit that spread among the Jews, the young intelligentsia that more and more came to recognize its nation and its origins – caused public activity in various areas. The existing institutions expanded, a new wing was added to the hospital,[26] the Talmud Torah was enlarged,[27] the activity of the Maskil Ladal Association was renewed in 1889.[28] Women's groups were organized to help needy children in the Talmud Torah and other schools. The limitations on the number of Jewish students accepted in government schools, together with the growing desire of Jewish parents to give their children an extended education were among the reasons that several new Jewish schools opened in town; in some of them a trade was also learned.[29] The Jewish public supported these schools, by helping needy children with tuition.

Various other aid and support societies were founded as well. In 1888, the Organization of Jewish Aides in commerce was founded;[30] in 1893 the Association for helping Jewish teachers and students;[31] 1n 1898 the Society to help the poor[32] – Еврейской Благотворительное Общество. They also collected money for the various needs of the community. Some of the donors were instrumental in building and maintaining the important institutions of the community. Here are some of the names: M. Doleinik, M. Karpas Tavrovski, M. Maidanski, I. Stanislavski, and the ladies: Tavrovski, Yampolski, Vitalin, Karpas, Nemirovski, Stein and others.[33]

The government took interest in the affairs of the community and, to its request, the management of the "Great Synagogue," Правление хоральной синагоги received the task to care for all community institutions: hospital, Talmud Torah, synagogues, help for the poor, cemetery etc. Representatives of the above institutions joined the Synagogue management and together they constituted the executive board of the community.[34]

7.

The Hovevei Zion movement slowly took hold in Ekaterinoslav. It was founded in 1884 and in time it expanded and increased its activity. The most active leaders were Ch. Levanda and S. Stanislavski, helped by the well–known preacher Tzabri–Hirsh, who settled in Ekaterinoslav. The Ekaterinoslav delegates to the Droseknik congress in 1887 were Binyamin Zvi Scheinfinkel, and to the Odessa congress in 1890 were Avraham Harkavi, Mechl Maidanski and Avraham Perl.[35] A delegation visited Eretz Israel with the purpose of buying land.[36] All the time they collected money for the settlement of Eretz Israel.[37]

In the course of the years, the influence of the Russian culture increased. The reasons were, mainly, the economic relations with the neighboring localities, which were conducted exclusively in Russian, as well as the increasing number of school pupils, who brought home the Russian language. The number of readers of Russian books increased as well, and the Yiddish language, while still used, albeit far less than before, absorbed more and more Russian and Ukrainian words. Many of the educated and well–to–do Jews distanced themselves from Judaism and demonstrated clear signs of assimilation. Their interests were, on one hand, personal interests and success in life above all, and on the other hand the questions of the Russian people and general politics, totally unrelated to Judaism and its problems. During that period, there were many cases of conversion to Christianity.

However, a group with a strong national inclination, among the young intelligentsia as well as the general public was slowly taking shape. They cared for the national content of the public life and fought for civil rights in the government and municipal institutions. The share of the Zionists in these endeavors was constantly increasing, especially after 1881, when M. Ussishkin came to Ekaterinoslav and directed the entire Zionist work in town. Much attention was given to schooling and education and the first "improved cheder" [cheder metukan] was opened in 1899, under the direction of Ch. A. Zuta.[38] In 1895 a Hebrew library was opened with the support of Ussishkin, in addition to the existing library, which was managed by the merchants. Money was collected for Zionist purposes and lectures on various national subjects were organized often. Together with Ussishkin, who was a delegate to the First Zionist Congress, worked Messrs. I. Berezovski, A. Harkavi, Levinski,

Ch. Levanda, S. Stanislavski, B. Spivak and others, and later they were joined by the engineer M. Bruk.

[Page 26]

Due to the limitations imposed on the registration of Jewish children to the general high-schools, the community founded Jewish private Zionist high-schools – the high-school for boys directed by Yona Wechsler and the high-school for girls directed by Yaffa Yudkowitz. An important feat was the erection of a tombstone on the grave of the leader A. Orshanski, made by the known sculptor Ginzburg.[40]

D. The Time of Nicolai II
8.

The first years of the rule of Nicolai II were a continuation of the rule of the former king. The attitude of the authorities toward the Jews did not change much, neither did the relationship with the other residents of the town; so that the life of the Ekaterinoslav Jews went on, more or less, as before. The economic progress increased in the entire region and the Jews enjoyed it as well. Within the community, the influence of the national circles increased.[40] They realized that the "appointed rabbi," who represented the community vis-a-vis the authorities, must be a man of national consciousness – and Rabbi N. Z. Shakhor was not suitable. Therefore they intended to appoint another rabbi, and a conflict erupted at election time; finally in 1898 Dr. Shemaryahu Levin, a known Zionist and a talented speaker, was elected.[41]

The general Russian census that took place in 1897, gives us a clear picture of the demographic and economic situation of the Ekaterinoslav Jews. There were 40,971 Jews in town, 20,864 men and 20,107 women – 37% of the general population. In the course of 20 years the community has grown rapidly and has become, considering the number of souls, one of the largest in Russia. Of this number, 12,114 men and 3,046 women were independent providers (with 24,819 dependents): 4,531 were merchants, including 432 women, 2,969 worked in the clothing industry, helped by 4,415 dependents, 1,714 were in private service and helpers in shops, including 1091 women, 657 were occupied in woodwork and 771 in metal works. We find here a creative group, occupied not only in commerce but also in craftsmanship and light industry. A considerable number of people were involved in the dress industry, wood and metal. There were also the liberal professions: doctors, lawyers, accountants, pharmacists, employees in banks and commercial associations. Some of the Jewish companies employed non–Jewish workers, with a considerable turnover and production.[42] Jews owned many of the shops, as well as houses in the central parts of the town. They also founded commercial companies with the aim to by–pass the government rules that restricted their activity in the mining industry.

The development of the Jewish crafts and commerce caused a problem of credit, and this was solved by founding a credit fund for craftsmen and small business men;[43] its founder and manager until the day he died was the engineer Moshe Bruk. In time, this institution grew and helped its members by providing the necessary credit and saving them from exaggerated interest.

At the end of the 19th century, 12 registered synagogues were active in Ekaterinoslav, 3 Talmud Torah schools with 500 pupils, and several Chadarim with 885 pupils. In addition to that there was a Yeshiva and 16 private schools for boys and for girls.[44]

9.

During the first years of the 20th century, under the rule of Nicolai II the attitude of the local authorities toward the Jews did not change much; it depended mainly on the personality of the district governor. If he was an honest man, not under the influence of the anti–Semites, it was possible to advance the community matters and develop its institutions. But if he was an anti–Semite, it was difficult to care for the many needs of the community. Luckily for the Ekaterinoslav Jews, several liberal governors were in office during that time, and it was possible to develop the existing institutions and establish additional ones.[45] However, the anti–Semitic incitement among the Christian public did not stop, and was expressed in 1904 by the attack of hooligans on the Ekaterinoslav Jews, which was suppressed by the police.[46]

[Page 27]

The general revival before the Japan war was felt also among the Ekaterinoslav Jews, who participated in the political movements. In 1903, one of the first Hovevei Zion organizations was founded. It was strong and specially oriented, helped by the activity of Yitzhak Shimshelewitz (in the future Ben–Zvi, the second president of the State of Israel), who resided in town at the time and was one of the founders of its self–defense. After the split in the party, the second in importance was the "Jewish Workers' Socialist Party." The Jews participated in the activity of the socialist parties in town, whose members were mainly laborers, among them organizers, speakers, and printers of announcements and proclamations. Outstanding among them was David Braginski, born in Kremnotcheg who, in 1901–1903 was very active as the representative of the "Social–Democrats," and organized strikes and other activities against the rulers, until he was arrested.[47]

The house in Ekaterinoslav where Ussishkin lived

In the Jewish street, in opposition to the process of assimilation, the power of the Zionist movement increased, under the leadership of M. Ussishkin.[48] The movement recruited new members and sympathizers, collected donations, printed propaganda booklets and managed in 1900 to organize a regional assembly of the representatives of the Zionist associations in Ekaterinoslav and surroundings.[49] The right hand of M. Ussishkin was M. Bruk (his brother–in–law); after Ussishkin relocated to Odessa, he directed the Zionist activity.

The public activity, guided by the national circles together with the "appointed Rabbi" Dr. S. Levin (who was elected for another term), expanded. In 1901 they organized in Ekaterinoslav the first congress of the Jewish teachers in Russia;[50] a new building was built for the Jewish hospital, of 100 beds;[51] a vocational section was added to the Talmud Torah school; a placement bureau was opened by the "Society for the Aid of the Poor;"[52] an orphanage was opened and the soup kitchen for the poor was enlarged.[53] In general, much attention was given to helping the poor and improving the educational institutions of the community. Natural increase added yearly more than one thousand souls,[54] in addition to many who came from other locations; many of those were forced by the living conditions to ask the community for help. The income of the community was mainly from the meat tax – 137,000 Rubles yearly, starting from 1901, instead of 87,000 Rubles before that.[55] Many donations were received from the Jews in town.

[Page 28]

Although the Ekaterinoslav Jews were only 40% of the general population in town, their mark on the economic life was considerable, due to their energetic economic activity (centered around the main street of the town, the "Prospect"), the influence of the Jews from the neighboring localities and the connection with various institutions and commercial companies. As a result, the town seemed "full of Jews." The contact with the non–Jewish population was mainly in the area of economics, and part of the Jewish intelligentsia, merchants and industrialists would meet with their Christian colleagues at the various common Societies, institutions, charity events and other public gatherings. The Jewish influence in the local press merits mentioning as well; many of the reporters, editors and writers were Jewish and readers even more. The press discussed the Jewish problem in general and showed interest in the affairs of the Community and its institutions.

10.

The war with Japan did not affect the Ekaterinoslav Jews specifically, except for the young men recruited to the army and sent to the front. The general revival in the country in 1905, after the defeat in this war, included the Ekaterinoslav community. The Jews sent a telegram to the chairman of the Ministers' Council, asking to grant the Russian Jews the same rights as the rest of the population.[56] The Jews in the Municipal Council resigned, as did the Jewish members in other municipalities.[57] The agitation among the public increased – everybody expected changes to occur; the Jewish young people, together with the others, demonstrated this quite openly. They began discussions on the subject of self–defense, collected money and acquired arms.

Soon, however, disappointment came. On 20 July 1905, following wild incitement, rioters attacked, and the Jews defended themselves. There were some wounded, but the authorities intervened immediately and the riots were stopped.[58] This, however, did not happen after the declaration known as the "Manifesto" on 17 October (by the Julian calendar) 1905. This time the riots were organized; they started on 21 October 1905. Following the "patriotic" parade through the central streets of the town, the rioters attacked Jewish homes and shops, robbed and destroyed, and murdered Jews. The defense forces, including members of various parties, as "The Jewish socialist labor party," Poalei Zion" "The Bund" and many private individuals, were more–or–less ready. They organized groups armed with light arms (revolvers), who immediately began chasing the rioters from the streets.[59] Later, however, as the army intervened and began to shoot at the members of the defense groups, they had to stop their activity,[60] giving the rioters a free hand to continue destroying and killing, on 22 and 23 October. Only when the army received a clear order to stop the riots, the pogrom was stopped. Over 100 Jews were killed (the exact number is not known), over 200 were wounded. Over 300 shops were robbed, a large number of houses and apartments were destroyed, some of them burned down entirely.[61] The censor did not allow publication of the pogrom in the press, except for a short notice – therefore many details are missing.[62]

The damage was great. The poor suffered in particular, since they remained without any means of sustenance. Few of the Christians helped the Jews; however, we should mention a group of young factory workers who defended the Jews living in their neighborhood and blocked the rioters.[63] A committee was formed, to aid the victims and donations were received from Russia and abroad, as well as from Ekaterinoslav people. A total of 297,500 Rubles was collected, including 52,000 from Ekaterinoslav.[64] Out of fear, many of the Ekaterinoslav Jews left town, some immigrated to America, some made Aliya to Eretz Israel. The rioters were tried and found guilty, but were pardoned by Nicolai II...

In spite of the difficult blow, recovery took little time. The Jews invested a great deal of energy in the project of recovering their economic life. This did not happen, however, in the area of the relationship with the representatives of the authorities. Anti–Semitism was felt in the attitude toward Jews, in the various municipal and other public institutions.

[Page 29]

עקאטערינאסלאוווער וואהל-קרייז.

№ 10.

דער צעטל

פון יודישען נאציאנאלען וואהל-קאמיטעט.

1. משה בן שמואל ברוק, אינזשינער, יעקאטערינאסלאוו, אלעק־
סאנדראווסקי ה. № 25

2. אלעקסנדר בן משה גאלדשטיין, מיטגליד פון ציוניסטי־
שען צענטראל קאמיטעט אין רוסלאנד, פעטראגראד, קא־
מענאסטראווסקי פ־. № 9 ה. № 47

3. דוד בן יצחק שמארגאנער, פריסיאזני פאווערעני, יע־
קאטערינאסלאוו קאזאטשיע № 12

4. אליעזר בן מאיר קאפלאן, אינזשינער-טעכנאלאג, פעטרא־
גראד,זאנאראדני פראספעקט 1/3, פארזיצענדער פון צ. ק
פון צעירי-ציון.

ЕКАТЕРИНОСЛАВСКІЙ ИЗБИРАТЕЛЬНЫЙ ОКРУГЪ

№ 10.

СПИСОКЪ

Еврейскаго національнаго избирательнаго комитета.

1. Брукъ Моисей Самуиловичъ, инженеръ г. Екатеринославъ, Александровская ул, д. № 25.

2. Гольдштейнъ Александръ Моисеевичъ, членъ центральнаго комитета сіонистской организаціи въ Россіи, г. Петроградъ Каменноостровскій проспектъ 9 кв. 44.

3. Шморгонеръ Давидъ Исааковичъ, присяжный повѣренный Екатеринославъ, Казачья ул. д. № 42.

4. Капланъ Лейзеръ Мееровичъ, инженеръ-техногъ г. Петроградъ Загородный проспектъ 1/3 Предсѣдатель Ц. К. «Цеирей-Ціонъ»

List of representatives to the election of the Founding Assembly, Ekaterinoslav District

The Ekaterinoslav election committee

No. 10

The list

Of the Jewish National Election Committee:

1. Moshe ben Shmuel Bruk, engineer, Ekaterinoslav, Alexandrovski H. No.25.

2. Alexander ben Moshe Goldstein member of the Zionist Central Committee in Russia,

Petrograd, Kamenastravski P. NO. 9 H. No. 47.

3. David ben Yitzhak Smorgoner, Prisiazhni Pavereni, Ekaterinoslav Kazatcha No. 12.

4. Eliezer ben Meir Kaplan, Engineer Technologist, Petrograd, Zanarodni Prospect 1/3.

Chairman of C.K. of Tze'irei Zion

The "Black Century" groups – "The Two–Headed Eagle" Двуглавый Орёл, who were supported by the regime, attacked Jews in the streets and in various public places, beating, wounding and robbing. Complaints to the authorities did not help; the mayor himself was a known "Jew–hater" and supported the gangs. The conflict with the authorities and the fight for equal rights in Ekaterinoslav continued until the breakout of World War II. The authorities interfered in the activity of many community institutions, limited the registration of Jewish students in high–schools etc. Since Jews filled important functions in the economic life of the town, no wonder that often representatives of the economic circles demanded from the authorities to stop the persecutions.[65]

11.

One of the important questions facing at the time the Jewish population in Russia, naturally including Ekaterinoslav, was the participation in the elections to the Russian Parliament – the Duma – Государственная Дума. In spite of the leftist propaganda asking not to participate in the elections and in spite of the demand of the authorities not to join the activity of the left, it was decided to participate in the elections, in order to ensure the election of liberal delegates, and perhaps succeed in sending a Jewish delegate to the Duma. Indeed, a Jewish delegate from the Ekaterinoslav District was elected to the first Duma, Mr. M. Sheftel from Petersburg. A Jewish delegate from the Ekaterinoslav District was elected to the second Duma as well, but there was no connection between his election and his being Jewish.

In the course of those years, the local Zionist Movement developed, headed by Mr. M. Bruk, after M. Ussishkin left Ekaterinoslav in 1906. Bruk was helped, in addition to the former Zionist activists by S. Braslavski, A. Berezovski, Dr. I. Dolzanski, I. Motzkin, who were later joined by T. Vidrin, Z. Wlodarski and others. The "appointed rabbi," elected to this post in 1904, was active as well, after Dr. S. Levin relocated to Vilna. He helped the community, especially from the national aspect, and developed the Jewish institutions. Much of his attention was given to the young people – to teach them Judaism, and he founded a special association for the distribution of the Hebrew culture among the Jewish youth[66] and the association Agudat Sefat Ever was established as well.[67] In Ekaterinoslav they organized the Tzeirei Zion movement, one of the first and strongest in Russia, and its representative, Daniel Wechsler, participated in the first Tzeirei Zion congress in Lodz in 1912. The Zionists organized lectures and banquets, distributed Zionist literature and collected money for JNF, for other Zionist causes and for the party.

After the years of elation, part of the Jewish public, as other circles in the country, became indifferent to the Jewish cause and distanced themselves from Jewish values. The important matter was the individual and his needs;

as a result, the number of conversions among the youth increased again, especially in view of the new, more severe limitations and restrictions concerning the acceptance of Jews to the universities. The Jewish leaders fervently opposed this tendency, and published in the press an "open letter to the youth," signed by 80 high–school graduates, expressing their great indignation and opposition to those who "leave their nation in order to enter the university."[68]

[Page 30]

In these conditions of persecution and conflict with the authorities, the community continued to develop its institutions. New ones were added, thanks to the contributions of the Jews in town, who donated money and property. Women's organizations cared for the societies of aid for the poor, the children, the sick and the orphans. The JCA delegation helped those who wanted to emigrate. Outstanding in this work were: Dr. Bolokhovski, Dr. Goldberg, Silberberg, L. Rotenberg, D. Smorgoner, A. Shapira and others. The community affairs were taken care of by a council of representatives of the important synagogues in town, which met from time to time and was recognized by the authorities.[69] In 1908 Rav Pinchas Gellman was elected as the rabbi of the community and was soon accepted and beloved by the members of the community. He expanded the "Little Yeshiva" that functioned in town; the Yeshiva moved to a new building and went through a series of changes,[70] and Rabbi Levi Yitzhak Shneurson was elected by the Hasidim. There were several other rabbis in the suburbs and also dayanim [judges in the religious court].

12.

During this period of persecutions by the authorities and fights for the basic civil rights of the Jewish people, the First World War broke out. The Russian population, including the Jews, took side with the government; the Ekaterinoslav Jewish community organized a special collection for the needs of the war, and presented the money to the Czar when he visited in town.[71] In addition, many private donations were collected for institutions and organizations connected with the war. Life in Ekaterinoslav generally continued its regular course. Jewish soldiers were recruited and sent to the front; some of them fell in battle, some were wounded, some received medals. Many Jewish refugees arrived in town – whether because they left their own places when the fighting got close, whether for fear of the Russian army. Others were evacuated from their places by the army "for security reasons." Several important personalities were among the refugees, as Rabbi Ch. E.

Grodzinski from Vilna, and several educational institutions were transferred to Ekaterinoslav, as the Jewish High–School directed by P. Cohen from Vilna and others. The economic situation of most residents improved due to the orders from the army and many of the providers and entrepreneurs made a great deal of money.

But the attitude toward the Jewish population changed rapidly, due to the persecutions in the places occupied by the Russian army and the many accusations and libel spread by the anti–Semitic circles. In June 1915, the evacuees from the Kovno and Kurland districts began arriving to Ekaterinoslav and the community did everything to help. The young people, in particular, devoted strength and energy to organize the refugees. The local aid committee, headed by Mr. Silberberg and Mr. Rotenberg, collected large sums of money. Money was received also from the central committee for the aid of the Petrograd refugees. The refugees received apartments and medical care and managed to find work, the children were accepted in the local schools or new schools were opened for them, etc. It was also necessary to care for the so-called "guarantors" (community leaders in Galicia, who were arrested and sent to Russia, where they were demanded to "guarantee" for the "good" behavior of the members of their community, who were kept in Ekaterinoslav under the supervision of the authorities).[72] The exact number of Jewish refugees in Ekaterinoslav is not known, because it changed constantly, but in 1915, 5,700 souls were registered at the committee for receiving help.[73] It is probable that their number was really higher, since many had arrived on their own and did not ask for help.

In general, due to the economic situation and the lack of laborers, the refugees found work quite soon after their arrival. The craftsmen among them opened shops and the professionals worked, with much success, in their professions. The Yiddish language, with the Lithuanian accent and without many Russian words, was heard again in the streets of Ekaterinoslav. The number of people in the synagogues grew, Yiddish songs were heard – and the Ekaterinoslav young people met and were impressed by this Jewish public.

With the refugees came various leaders and activists who had an extended Hebrew education, as the teachers of Cohen's high–school and Hebrew and Yiddish writers, who soon began to take part in the local community work. The party leaders, the "Bund," Poalei Zion and others increased the power of their parties; this was strongly felt during the 1917 revolution. Among the refugees who came to Ekaterinoslav it is worth mentioning Dr. Yosef Hazanowitz, the founder of the National Library, who continued his activity of collecting books and helping the sick and died in "The Home for the Aged,"[74] and the well–known Yiddish writer Ch. Tzemerinski (R'Mordche'le), who died there in 1917.

[Page 31]

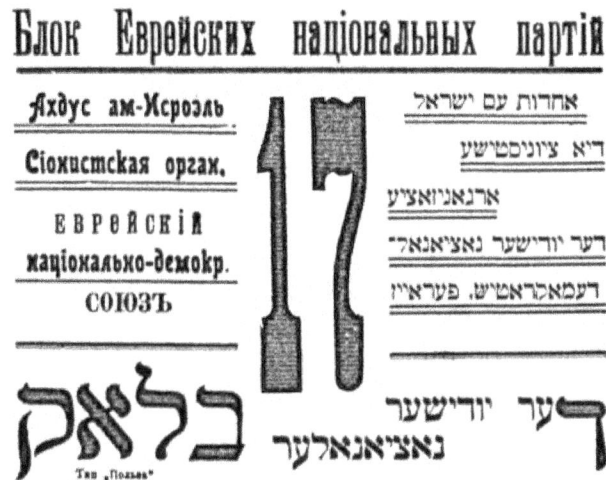

כרוז גוש המפלגות הלאומיות היהודיות לבחירות למועצה העירונית ביקאטרינוסלאב ב-1917

Announcement of the Block of Jewish National Parties before the elections to the Municipal Council in Ekaterinoslav in 1917 (Russian and Yiddish)

Achdut Am Israel
The Zionist organization of the Jewish National Democratic Party
The Jewish National Block

In the course of the war, due to the increased orders from the army and the general economic development of the region, the Ekaterinoslav Jews reached important economic positions in town and a considerable part of commerce and industry was in their hands. A report from 1915 shows that the Jews owned 84 factories, among them sawmills, flour mills, iron industry, bricks manufactory etc. The number of workers was 3,700 laborers and clerks; the Jews among them 645 workers and 250 clerks.[75] The Jews owned many large stores as well.

The community work continued energetically. Various cultural activities took place, as Hovevei Sfat Ever,[76] lectures, concerts of Jewish music etc. The political parties worked clandestinely in spite of the prohibitions and acquired new members. The Zionists expanded their cultural activity – lectures, book distribution and money collection. In collaboration with the "Society for Jewish education" schools for the refugee children were opened and evening lessons for adults and youth were organized.[77] With the "Society for the preservation of health" ОПЕ they gave medical help, organized day–care centers for children and other necessary medical support.[78] Children enrolled in Cohen's high-school, as well as in Rabbi Gellman's Yeshiva.

E. The Revolution, 1917–1919

13.

The Ekaterinoslav Jews received the February 1917 revolution with joy and sympathy, as did all the Russian Jews, hoping and believing that it will mark the end of persecutions and begin a time of freedom, and it will be possible to develop Jewish life in town and in the country. All parties began appearing freely in public, with assemblies, congresses, lectures, books and recruiting new members: The General Zionists and Tzeirei Zion, the Bund, Poalei Zion, the Jewish Socialist Worker's Party ("Seim"), the Popular Party "Volkspartei" and after some time the religious–national party Achdut [Unity]. The non-Jewish parties – the "Social–Democrats" and the "Social–Revolutionaries" and some of the "Kadets" – made efforts to recruit Jewish members and sympathizers. Of all these parties, the most active – immediately gaining the support of the Jewish population – were the "Zionists" and with them the "Tze'irei Zion" headed by Israel Idelson (the future I. Ben–Yehuda, an Israeli minister) and with him I. Ritov, B. Idelson and others. They opened clubs, organized Hevrew lessons and published a magazine in Russian:

Известия Екатиринославского Районного Сионистского Комитета Еврейский Путь

(The way of the Jews "The District Zionist Committee in Ekaterinoslav").

They also published several propaganda booklets in Hebrew, Russian and Yiddish.

The studying youth was organized in Hatekhiya, the students in Hekhaver. In April, the District Committee was assembled, its members being the representatives of the local committees of the Ekaterinoslav and Tabrina districts. The "Bund" was very active as well, in particular among the Jewish workers and the refugees; one of its leaders was Fischman. The "Bund" published a journal in Russian Наше Слово [We have spoken] and in Yiddish "Der Internatzional." Poalei Zion was also active, headed by Zalman Ostrovski. The "Jewish Socialists Worker's Party" published in Yiddish Der Kempfer [the fighter]. The publicity was conducted mostly in Russian; the leftist parties used Yiddish as well, especially among the refugees, who participated in the party activity.

[Page 32]

Many Jews participated in the establishment and management of the new institutions and some of them were elected to the municipal executive committee.[79] Jewish employees occupied important and responsible positions in the various government institutions; this increased the self–consciousness of the Ekaterinoslav Jews, who began to feel free and of equal civil rights; the spring and summer of that year, 1917, seemed most beautiful in the life of the Ekaterinoslav Community!

The community was still managed by its former leaders. The financial situation of its many institutions was difficult; the income from the meat–tax decreased, because its sale decreased due to the war and high prices. Due to inflation the number of donations decreased as well, although the need to ask help from the community remained the same.[80] In general, the importance and status of the community diminished, and in public appearances the power of the parties' spokesmen became much greater.

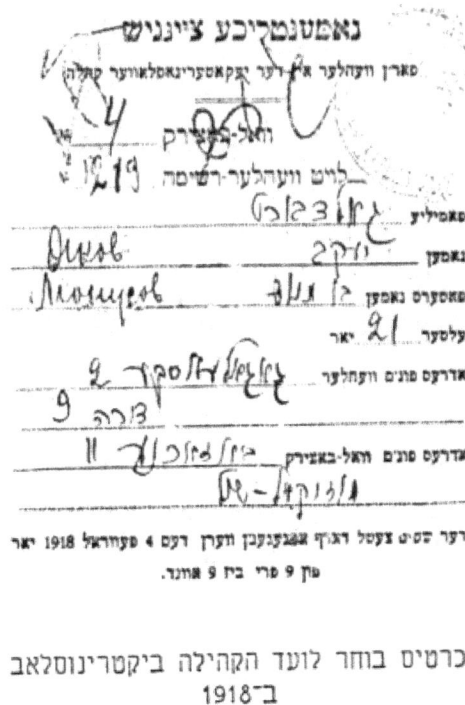

כרטיס בוחר לועד הקהילה ביקטרינוסלאב
ב־1918

Photo–copy of an "elector's card" to the community council in Ekaterinoslav, 1918. The card was issued to Yakov Goldbart, Gogolevska St. 2, apt. 9

In that year, the community established a new institution, the "Private Polytechnic," which opened its school–year at the end of January 1917. The idea to open such an institution came from Jewish leaders in Petrograd, who wanted to help young Jewish high–school graduates, who could not enroll in the learning institutions due to the limitations and restrictions. The graduates of this Polytechnic would be granted the title Engineer, after they passed the government exams. Ekaterinoslav was chosen for this project because it was an important industrial and Jewish center, and it was the location of a government Polytechnic which gave it the possibility to get help from its professors and use its laboratories.[81]

The elections to the various new institutions – municipal council. Parliament, community – were an important matter on the agenda of the Jewish public; this caused dispute and conflict between the parties, especially between the Zionists and the leftist parties, which accused the Zionists of being the representatives of the bourgeoisie and in opposition to the laborers and the democratic Russia.

The desire of the Zionists and the Tze'irei Zion movement was to create a national list for the elections of the town and country institutions and elect Jewish delegates. This idea was not accepted by the leftist parties, which in most cases joined the general leftist parties.[82] Of the 97 members elected to the municipal council, 19 were Jews, 9 of them from the Zionists and Tze'irei Zion and the rest from other parties.[83] A list of Jewish candidates representing the District, headed by M. Bruk was presented to the Parliament elections; none of the persons on the list was elected. At the elections to the Community Committee, held on 17 February 1918, the Zionist list had success; Moshe Bruk was elected as the president of the community and P. Cohen, principal of the high–school and representative of the Volkspartei was elected as the head of the executive committee.

The relationship with the general population was tolerable, and anti-Semitic occurrences were few. Ekaterinoslav was a city of laborers, class-conscious, far from reactional influence. During the autumn months, due to the instability of the regime, the situation deteriorated, and the Ukrainian movement, which contained many anti–Semitic elements, began to take shape in town. Since the tradition of self-defense was strong among the Jews of Ekaterinoslav, various defense groups were organized by the "Association of the Jewish Soldier," the "United Jewish Socialist Party," and also small groups of the "Bund" and Poalei Zion. These defense groups, some of them having their commanding offices in special buildings given by the authorities, were however disarmed in March 1918, because they were not accepted by the Soviet Regime, and because the anarchist groups (which included many Jews) demanded it.[84]

[Page 33]

A considerable and important change occurred in the social structure of the Jewish community in Ekaterinoslav. The former leaders – the well–to–do, the liberal professionals etc. – were replaced by the party leaders, whose representatives were elected to the management of the various institutions. There was a sharp conflict between the Zionists and the leftist parties; the Zionists were accused of being the representatives of the bourgeoisie, supporters of the imperialism etc. In general, the great majority of the Jewish public sympathized with the Zionists and supported them.

14.

After the Bolshevik revolution at the end of 1917, the transfer to the rule of the Workers Councils and the army passed quietly in Ekaterinoslav. Following a short period of well–being in 1917, life became difficult in particular for the poor people. The range of commercial relations and common craftsmanship work was reduced, economic life in general slowed down and the livelihood of many families was cut off. It was difficult to get provisions, especially food. At the same time the town suffered from a typhoid epidemic and the regular aid organs were short in money and unable to help. Considering the situation, the community was not disassembled by the authorities; on the contrary, it was allowed to collect money from the rich families in town in order to reinforce its institutions, and the community indeed did so.

In the spring of 1918, the Soviet regime was ended by the German army, which invaded the Ukraine, and the Ukrainian regime began. First was the rule of the "respublika" – the "Rada" – then of the Hetman Skoropadaski. The town itself was occupied by the Austrian army – easier than with the German army. During that short period, summer and fall 1918, the economic situation improved, commercial, industrial and craftsmanship activity was renewed, there was enough food and a calm atmosphere reigned, since the army would not allow robbing and hooligan attacks. The community institutions renewed their work and so did the political parties, except for the leftist parties; the Zionists collected money, distributed literature and published one issue of "Volkswort." The Ekaterinoslav Jews participated in the elections to the Ukrainian Jews conference which took place in Kiev.

Still, in spite of the fact that daily life was normal and it was possible to travel from place to place, people did not feel entirely secure. The army performed from time to time inspections and checkups, and even arrests; worry and anxiety expecting the coming days was great, in particular after the allies' victory on the Western Front and the revolution in Germany, as it was assumed that the Austrian army would leave town.

And the question arose again: what is going to happen? Will there be pogroms? The Ukrainian influence increased, and the communist party also gained power, with the support of the workers. The self–defense consciousness in Ekaterinoslav being strong, defense groups were established when the foreign army began to leave: one by the "United Jewish Socialist Party" (after the 1905 tradition) and the other by the community committee. Both groups were strong, unified and armed, and headed by experienced leaders. In time, other groups formed and helped, by Poalei Zion, the "Bund", Tzeirei Zion, Mensheviks and students. A security committee coordinated the activity of all these groups and the municipality provided the budget. Patrols were seen in town, securing the various institutions; it gave the residents a feeling of security.[85]

After the Germans left, Petliura came to power, but he ruled only for a short time. The Ukrainians' behavior toward the Jews was fair, maybe because their local commanders were not anti–Semitic. Fear increased when the "anarchist" Machno was several days in town, burned the market place, robbed stores and homes and left a few victims. These were days of distress and lack of food, commerce was slow, prices and inflation rose.

[Page 34]

15.

At the beginning of 1919, the Soviet army entered Ekaterinoslav, and a new period began for the Jewish community there. The activity of all parties and organizations was suspended. The institutions were managed by the local rulers – the executive committees of the workers and soldiers. Residents – especially Jews – were asked to contribute considerable sums to the municipal council. Many Jews who could not pay were arrested, although not the leaders, since they found hiding places. It was difficult to obtain food and the black market flourished, but the authorities managed to catch some of them and punish them. Fear was in the air, in particular after the news about the activity of the "white Army" in the Caucasus and the attacks on the Jews in the Western Ukraine towns and villages. Panic struck the Ekaterinoslav Jews when they heard the Gregoriev's gangs were approaching the town, but the Soviet army chased him away.

In the spring of 1919, the "Whites," under General Denikin's leadership, advanced through Southern Russia and occupied many towns. Many of Ekaterinoslav's Jews expected that this army would free them from the Soviet rule, which became more and more of a burden – Denikin's soldiers had not yet begun their own pogroms. In the beginning of June 1919, the Soviets left Ekaterinoslav following the pressure of Denikin's army, which occupied the town.

As soon as Denikin's army reached town, while the soldiers were still marching festively on the main street, the Cossacks began robbing the shops. Soon they went to the Jewish homes, especially by night, taking all they could. They killed seldom, but rapes were common. In general, it was quiet during the day, it was possible to walk through the streets, the shops that have not been robbed were open – but the nights were horrible. The only weapons against the rioters were the loud shouts calling for help. Sometimes the shouts would drive the robbers away from the house, but help would come very seldom – the demands for help from the commander of the town remained without answer. This situation lasted several weeks, and only after the robbing spread through the parts of the town where many Christians lived, and several officers were bribed, the Cossacks were taken out of the town.

The few months of Denikin's rule were difficult times for the Ekaterinoslav Jews. The robbing and killing in town and in the neighborhood (the Cossacks would take Jews out of the trains and kill them), the fear of the day of tomorrow – all this weakened the public and economic life of the Ekaterinoslav Jews. The attraction of communism was strong, on the hope that under its rule they would be left alone, and their lives would be safe. This feeling was especially strong among the leftist parties and some of the Tze'irei Zion. The Zionists tried to become active again and the temporary center in Rostov tried to renew the activity in the region formerly occupied by Denikin, but the result was insignificant. Several families left town, some to Odessa, some to Rostov, on the way to the Caucasus and some to Crimea, hoping to get a chance to leave the country and go abroad.

During the rule of Denikin's "white Army" the town was occupied for several weeks by Machno. Although there was not a real pogrom, robbing and senseless murders were common. The residents of the town stayed in their homes, it was difficult to obtain food and fear was great. Soon after the town was liberated from Machno's gangs, Denikin's army left and in order to defend the Jewish settlement in town against various gangs in the neighborhood the Jewish defense groups organized again and acquired defense weapons. The communist workers armed themselves and assumed the duty of defending the town, until the Soviet army came, and so Ekaterinoslav finally came under the rule of the Ukrainian Soviet government.

F. The Soviet Rule

16.

The situation of the town was still challenging – it did not yet recover from the robbing and rioting of Machno's people. The limitations and prohibitions of the new regime, in particular in the economic area, added to the difficulties, and naturally the Jews were the ones who suffered most. The peasants from the villages did not bring the food products to town, because the authorities confiscated them for the use of the army. The large stores, the factories and many of the workshops were nationalized and public help was discontinued. Many people, especially from among the well–to–do, remained without a livelihood.

[Page 35]

The new offices that were opened by the authorities employed many people – Jews filled important and responsible jobs in the municipal and regional offices; however, many were left without a job. One of the ways to obtain minimal food products was by barter: clothes and other objects in exchange for food. In spite of the danger of such procedure – the authorities forbade it and punished heavily – this type of commerce was common, and Jews have taken a considerable part in it.

A great change occurred in the economic structure of the Jewish population. Most of the rich people lost their wealth. Many left the town, whether from fear of arrest or in order to find employment in other places. Liberal professionals – doctors, engineers, lawyers – lost their importance and honor and were replaced by members of the communist party or of the unions.

Jewish public life stopped almost entirely. The community institutions – schools, hospitals etc. – were managed by the municipality; only synagogues and cemeteries remained under the former management, and the few community workers who were still in town were in charge of them.

In 1921, many residents began to leave Ekaterinoslav. The first were the refugees, who were allowed to return to their former homes: Lithuania, Poland or Belarus villages; many of the formerly wealthy people and public activists left as well. On the other hand, residents of the neighboring villages came to live in town, out of fear of the gangs and loss of livelihood sources. A small number of families emigrated and went to America or to Eretz Israel. In 1920 the number of Jews in Ekaterinoslav was 72,230, out of the general population of 167,200.

Of the Jewish parties, the "Bund" was still active somewhat, before it merged with the communist party, as well as Po'alei Zion Left, who in 1920 still published their journal Der Gedank [The Thought].[86] The communist influence in the Jewish Street was very strong, especially among the young people. They joined the party, partly out of idealism and partly out of anger at the acts of the Ukrainians and the Denikin army against the Jews.

In spite of the watching eye of the Evsektzia ["the Jewish section"], the Zionists – especially Tze'irei Zion and the youth movements – continued their work, albeit on a much smaller scale: lectures and Hebrew lessons were given, and booklets and newsletters were obtained from Kharkov and Kiev, the two centers with which there was still constant contact. Ekaterinoslav delegates participated in secret meetings, where news about Eretz Israel was discussed. An important topic of these meetings was the influence of communism on the youth and several actions were taken against it – trips, various sports etc. Local guides, as well as guides who came from other places volunteered for this work, which continued almost to the end of the Twenties.[87]

Although in 1920 some arrests were made, the mass–arrests – from Tze'irei Zion, Hano'ar Hatzioni, Hashomer Hatza'ir, Maccabi – came in 1924 and the following years. The verdicts were mostly exile to Siberia or other far–away places, or arrest in special "political prisons." Some were lucky, and their verdict was changed to a permit to make Aliya. The suffering of the arrestees was great – some died in prison, some came out ill and weak.[88]

As in other places, the Evsektzia opened Yiddish schools for the Jewish pupils. Newspapers in Yiddish were published (The Communist World, The Communist), as well as some books, especially school–books.[89] In 1922, the year of hunger, a one–time newsletter was published, Zu Hilf [to help]. In general, the Russian language ruled in the Jewish street and home, and only part of the old generation used Yiddish.

[Page 36]

It is worth mentioning, that by learning Yiddish in school, the use of the language was preserved among part of the young generation.

Due to common work, common interests and party activity, the Jewish and non–Jewish youth became close and the number of mixed marriages increased. Traditional customs and laws were observed only among the old people. Yet there was Kosher slaughtering, Matzot were baked for Passover, and Mishna and Talmud lessons were given in the synagogues – the authorities did not forbid that.

17.

The "New Policy," announced in 1921, which permitted commerce and workshops, enabled many to reestablish their economic situation and earn a living, in some cases even get rich again. Many Jews opened their shops again, craftsmen enlarged their workshops and some former industrialists rented from the government factories and produced food and household objects. But before the entire public could recover, the great hunger of 1921–1922 came, in the entire Southern Russia and the Volga region.

It was a very difficult time. In the villages there was no food, and the government was not able to provide the people's necessities. Bread became very expensive, and the lower classes were not able to buy it. With the hunger came epidemics – typhoid fever and cholera – which left many dead. According to the report of "The London Committee of the Ukrainian Jews" in 1921 2,025 Jews died and in 1922 3,677, which meant 30 pro mil.[90] This committee, through its representative Dr. B. Hanis was in close contact with the local committee, which, aided by several sub–committees, gave help to the needy. A soup kitchen was opened, food packages were provided, and a loan fund was created. These actions saved many people.[91] Some people received food packages from relatives abroad – all this helped overcome the hunger.

The JOINT organization helped as well. After obtaining the necessary permit, it allocated large sums for repairing the hospital and renewing its equipment, and a new clinic was opened. Several children's homes were opened as well under the management of the local JOINT, but they were soon transferred to the management of the authorities. Hunger and epidemics caused many people – those who could – to leave town; many died, and the 1923 census showed in Ekaterinoslav 50,240 Jews, out of a population of 167,000.[92]

Due to the changes in the economic structure of the Ekaterinoslav Jewish society under Soviet rule and growing unemployment, the Evsektzia and cooperation leaders decided to establish Jewish cooperatives in various areas of work – "Collectiv"s – of tailors, hatters and others. Although the beginnings were modest, these cooperatives developed well; they obtained their budgets from "Ort," "JCA" and the government. The tailors' cooperative, for example, grew from 10 to 70 members and in 1924 it had a considerable number of employees.[93] Jewish workers were hired by the various large factories and became permanent workers there.

In the twenties, there were no severe persecutions against the Jews; but valuable objects in the synagogues (and in the churches) were confiscated – officially in order to help those suffering from hunger. The Big Synagogue was taken from the Jewish community and used as a "Workmen's Club;" again, this was the fate of several churches as well (many of the Ekaterinoslav Jews signed a petition to cancel this decree). Anti–Semitism was deeply rooted among the Ukrainians; there was also envy of the Jewish employee, who was usually lucky and received packages from his relatives abroad. The regime fought all that.

Lodging conditions were not bad; ownership of small houses – 2 or 3 apartments to rent – was permitted. The number of liberal professionals among Jews grew: doctors, engineers, attorneys, teachers; most of them were under the influence of communism and distanced themselves from Judaism.[94] On the other hand, much attention was given to the development of the "Yiddish" culture: The Yiddish Theater visited often, there were concerts of Jewish music and lectures of various Jewish writers.[95] News from abroad was rare, mostly from contact with family relatives and friends.

[Page 37]

In the twenties and thirties, some tourists visited Ekaterinoslav, mostly from the USA, and brought news from there, often untrue.

The government census of 1926 gives us a clear picture of the many changes in the social and economic structure of the Ekaterinoslav Jews. Of a general population of 233,000 souls, 62,100 (27%), were Jews, as follows: laborers in factories and small industry – 6,397; clerks – 8,477; liberal professions – 425; commerce – 2,194; craftsmanship – 3,469; without a profession – 2,146; unemployed – 4,819. There was mass transfer from occupation to occupation, therefore the number of unemployed and those without a profession was large.

During the late twenties, with the termination of the "New Policy," the Jews were again the main victims. The high taxes and the fines and arrests due to failing to pay them hit a large part of the Jewish population and the number of unemployed rose again. A new concept appeared – "people without rights." On the other hand, with the introduction of the "five–year program" new jobs became available and many obtained work in the newly built factories.

Following propaganda, many Jews relocated to Birobidjan; one of the groups settled in the "Waldheim" kolkhoz.[96]

Traditional Judaism weakened. Synagogues were confiscated, or closed by the authorities, some following the "demand of the professional unions" or another "Jewish group." Finally, very few remained in the community, led by Rabbi L. I. Shneurson, and they took care of the cemetery, kosher slaughtering, matzot for Passover, circumcising the children etc. Rabbi Shneurson worked hard to preserve some of the Jewish tradition – finally in 1940 he was exiled to Alma Alta in Kazakhstan and died there in 1944.

No other public activity existed. Due to the restrictions and many arrests, all Zionist activity ended. Of the former leaders, some simply stopped their activity, some left own, some died, some were arrested and exiled. Assimilation was strong and mixed marriages prevailed.

During the thirties, the economic situation of the Ekaterinoslav Jews improved. Almost all worked; some earned a very good living. The town grew and developed fast, and many people, including Jews, came to live there and found work in the factories and offices and, according to an estimate, in 1939 the number of Jews rose to 100,000.[97]

In order to increase the amount of foreign currency and obtain the gold kept by the population, the Soviet government established the special "Torgsin" stores, where it was possible to obtain, in exchange for foreign currency or gold, many products not to be found in the regular stores. The authorities exploited this situation, and as soon as someone paid with foreign currency or gold, as advertised, they would hunt him and under threat of arrest would blackmail him and extort all the gold he had. Many Jews, who really did not have gold, were arrested and exiled.[98]

G. The Holocaust

18.

At the beginning of the war against the Germans, Ekaterinoslav was far from the front. No detailed news could be obtained, in particular not about the attitude of the Germans toward the Jews in the occupied areas. As the front came nearer, the authorities began to prepare evacuation, and at the same time news arrived about the murders in the occupied areas. The government institutions began to leave town – the large factories, the party institutions and many workers with their families. The evacuation took place in panic and disorder and it was accelerated by the attack of the German air force in June 1941. The evacuation was to the East – the factories mostly to central Asia and Ural and the families to the Caucasus. Many Jews, who were connected with the factories and institutions, as well as the families of the soldiers left town with them. But some, remembering the German occupation in 1918, decided to stay and not leave their homes. However, as evacuation time approached, the panic grew and so did the number of those wanting to leave. Since it was very difficult to get on a train, many left on carts and horses, but the Germans caught them. Some managed to return to town, others fell into the hands of the Ukrainians and were murdered.[99]

After Ekaterinoslav was bombed several times, it was occupied by the Germans on 25 August 1941. As soon as this happened, the anti–Semitic attitude, especially of the Ukrainians, became open. Jews were attacked, especially in the parts of town far from the center. People informed on their Jewish neighbors, whether in order "to get even" or in order to rob the property. The Germans joined in the attacks and rapes. Soon the German authorities ordered the Jews to wear on the sleeve "the yellow star of David" On 8 October a new order was issued, that the Jews must transfer to the German command 30 million Mark, a fine for having "robbed the property of the Ekaterinoslav residents." In order to collect such a large sum, it was necessary to open a special office. The office was opened on Kharkovskaya Street 3, and was headed by Att. Garnburg. The money was paid through a bank order. The first payment was on 10 October; but only part of the residents managed to transfer the money.[100]

[Page 38]

On Hol Hamo'ed Sukkot the Jews were ordered to gather on 13 October in the Univermag department store, on the Prospect in the name of Karl Marx, "in order to be transferred to a safe place, for their own protection." They were ordered to take with them valuables and food. Many believed and went. As they arrived, however, the things they brought were taken from them and they were led by the brutal Ukrainians, who beat them and wounded them, to the South–West of town, to a ravine behind the School of Transport and shot by machine–gun. This Aktzia continued the next day as well, and in order to muffle the sound of shots and the bitter cries, an orchestra played all the time.[101] Very few were able to save themselves from the pit, where they fell when being shot. Some escaped to the villages, only to be caught by the Germans. We don't have exact numbers of the Jews that were murdered in those two days, the local residents give an estimate of 18,00 – 20,000 victims.[102] To those murdered in this Aktzia, we must add those who were caught by the Germans in the Caucasus, where they were evacuated, and those who died of hunger and epidemics in Central Asia and Ural. We will probably never know the number of members of the Ekaterinoslav community who fell d in the course of the Second World War!

It is probable that even after the Aktzia a few people survived in town – several doctors, women and children. Some were saved by hiding in the villages, although not many residents were ready to help them hide (it is true that this was very dangerous to those who provided hiding places). Some did it for money, some out of human feelings and so several of the Ekaterinoslav Jews, mostly women and children, were saved.[103]

On 25 October 1943 Ekaterinoslav was liberated from the Germans. The town was partly ruined, but people were beginning to return. The Jews were not welcomed back, except for high government employees, doctors and engineers. In many cases the returnees were met with open hatred by the population. They spoke about "the Jews who were not slaughtered yet" Недорезанные Евреи and there were cases where they were attacked, especially when they began to demand back their robbed homes and property. It was also not easy to obtain the former positions, and the authorities were not ready to hire Jews in prominent positions.[104] Anti–Semitism was strong, since the German propaganda added to the anti–Jewish feelings that had existed before.

The first year after liberation was a difficult year. Rumors were spread, that the general population plans attacks against the returning Jews, but the authorities intervened, and order was maintained. In spite of the difficulties and the open hatred, the Jews returned, and their number increased; many villagers moved to the city, where it was easier to find work. Ekaterinoslav developed fast during those years.

19.

Slowly, Jewish life continued and adapted to the new conditions. In the only synagogue that the authorities "gave" to the community, on Иорданская street, prayers were held regularly, and on holidays, in particular Rosh Hashana and Yom Kipur, it was full of people. In 1946, Rav I. S. Levin was elected rabbi of Ekaterinoslav and he served until 1953, when he relocated to Moscow.

[Page 39]

The horrors of the war and the losses of the Russian Jewry caused an increase in national feelings among the Jewish youth. At the concerts of Jewish music, the halls were full and the interest in national values increased. Several community leaders helped the rabbi in fulfilling the religious needs,[105] as taking care of the cemetery, kosher slaughtering, baking matzot for Passover, etc. A permit was received from the authorities to build a fence around the place where the Jews were murdered and erect a modest memorial stone, saying (in Russian): "Here fell in 1941, murdered by the Germans, Russian citizens,"[106] without mentioning that they were Jews... Every year on Tish'a BeAv [the 9th day in the month of Av, the Memorial Day of the destruction of the First and Second Temple in Jerusalem], Ekaterinoslav Jews gathered to memorial prayers. In 1958, the cemetery was taken by the authorities in order to enlarge the airport, and the Jews were allowed to transfer the remains of their relatives to the new cemetery, not far away. The remains of rabbi Pinchas Gellman were transferred by the community.[107]

In 1952, the year of "the doctors' libel–trials," life was very difficult. The non–Jewish residents, in particular the Ukrainians spread various rumors, the hatred was great, and the Jewish community lived in constant fear and distress. Most difficult was the situation of the Jewish doctors in the hospitals. People did not seek their help, spread rumors that the Jewish doctor intended to kill them etc. etc.[108]

Today Ekaterinoslav is one of the largest cities in the Soviet Union. The 1959 census showed 661,000 residents, 52,800 of them Jewish. By the 1970 census, the number of residents rose to 863,000. The economic situation of the Ekaterinoslav Jews is good, they are clerks, doctors, engineers, attorneys, teachers and university professors. There are also craftsmen and a small number of laborers working in the factories in town. Assimilation increased greatly. The Russian language is used in the street and at home; very few, of the old generation, still use Yiddish.[109]

But there is no public Jewish life in Ekaterinoslav. The few who still keep our tradition are taking care of the synagogue and provide the religious needs. There is a limited interest in the Yiddish language; some of the Yiddish writers are from Ekaterinoslav. The Ekaterinoslav Jews know – not much – about Israel and the happenings here and about life abroad in general. The news comes from various sources.

During the recent years, as time are changing, national feelings increased in town, in particular among the young people and the intelligentsia, who show interest in the fate of our people and the State of Israel. Another factor in this process is the "traditional" Ukrainian Anti–Semitism, as well as the unofficial ban on Jews as managers or university graduates. We believe that this community, in the past so alive and active, will revive and contribute to the life of our nation.

Footnotes

1. Еврейская Энциклопедия, Т. 7, Екатеринослав

2. Регесты И Написи, Петербург 1910, 2328б 2397

3. С. Станиславский, Восход, 1887, 7

4. Недельная Хроника Восход 1887, 18

5. Недельная Хроника Восход 1883, 7

6. Недельная Хроника Восход 1883, 7

7. Недельная Хроника Восход 1883, 7

8. Ямпольский, Еврейская Старина 1911, 4

9. Вестник Русских Евреев, 1871, 20

10. Рассвет, 1880, 8

11. 38, 1880

12. See further: *Hamelitz*: the Orshanski list

13. Рассвет, 1860, 11

14. День 1869, 27

15. Ямпольский, Еврейская Старина 1911, 4

16. Недельная Хроника Восход 1882, 47

17. Рассвет, 1881, 6

18. Рассвет, 1881, 14

19. Рассвет, 1881, 47

20. Русский Еврей 1882, 7

21. Недельная Хроника Восход 1883, 30, 31, 34, 39

22. Недельная Хроника Восход 1883, 32

23. *Hamelitz* 1883, 20

24. *Hamelitz* 1888, 13

25. *Hamelitz* 1892, 51/52

26. *Hamelitz*, 1888, 43

27. *Hamelitz*, 1890, 26

28. *Hamelitz*, 1890, 6

29. *Hamelitz* 1890, 24

30. *Hamelitz* 1888, 25

31. *Hamelitz* 1895, 38

32. *Hamelitz* 1898, 98

33. *Hamelitz* 1880 4, 1892, 12

34. *Hamelitz* 1892,42

35. Dr. Y. Klausner, From Katowitz to Basel 8, 35, 237

36. Dr. Y. Klausner, From Katowitz to Basel 36, 247

37. See the article of Dr. Y. Klausner The Zionist movement in Ekaterinoslav

38. T. A. Zuta, The Road of a Teacher

39. Недельная Хроника Восход 1890, 43

40. Недельная Хроника Восход 1893, 25

41. Недельная Хроника Восход 1898, 23

42. Еврейская Энциклопедия, Т. 7, Екатеринослав

43. Восход 1904, 17

44. Справочная книга Опе, Петербург, 109 2

45. Dr. S. Levin, Memories of my life, Vol. 3 216

46. Восход 1904, 17

47. David Braginski, Jewish Workers Publishing, Philadelphia 1942

48. Восход 1901, 4

49. Будущность, 1900, 29

50. Восход 1901, 42

51. Восход 1901, 53

52. Будущность, 1901, 53

53. Восход 1902, 28

54. Рассвет, 1908, 3

55. Будущность, 1901, 1

56. Восход 1905, 7

57. Восход 1905, 25

58. Хроника Еврейской Жизни, 1905, 29

59. Дальман, Октябрьские дни в Екатеринославе, Серп 1907

60. Дальман, Октябрьские дни в Екатеринославе, Серп 1907

61. Хроника Еврейской Жизни, 1905, 45

62. Дальман, Октябрьские Дни в Екатеринославе, Серп 1907

63. Рассвет, 1907, 50

64. Die Juden Pogromen in Russland. Berlin 1910, 40 26

65. Рассвет, 1908, 17

66. Рассвет, 1910, 19

67. Рассвет, 1910, 12

68. Рассвет, 1913, 31

69. Рассвет, 1913, 22

70. Рассвет, 1912, 7

71. Рассвет, 1915, 6

72. Рассвет, 1915, 20

73. Еврейская Жизнь, 1915, 23

74. Еврейская Жизнь, 1916, 35

75. Рассвет, 1915, 20

76. Еврейская Жизнь, 1915, 26

77. Еврейская Жизнь, 1915, 20

78. Еврейская Жизнь, 1916, 31

79. Еврейская Жизнь, 1917, 12/13

80. Рассвет, 1917, 17/18

81. See further, on The Jewish Polytechnic

82. Рассвет, 1917, 4/5

83. Рассвет, 1917, 6/8

84. See further on The Defense in Ekaterinoslav 1918–1919

85. See further on The Defense in Ekaterinoslav 1918–1919

86. Jewish Publications in the Soviet Union, Jerusalem

87. S. Milstein, Struggles of a Generation, 233

88. B. Berekovski, Manuscript

89. Jewish Publications in the Soviet Union, Jerusalem

90. Report from the Association of Ukrainian Jews in London, 23, 44

91. Report from the Association of Ukrainian Jews in London

92. See further the article of S. Teslitzki on the activity of the JOINT in Ekaterinoslav

93. *Der Roiter Nadl*, 1927, 8 (Yiddish)

94. I. Meshorer, Manuscript

95. Id. Id.

96. I. Levavi, Jewish Settlement in Birobidjan 93, 163 (Hebrew)

97. Sewe further, Translation of the article by Ortenberg

98. I. Meshorer, Manuscript

99. S. Levkowitz, Manuscript

100. See the translation of the article by Leikina

101. S. Levkowitz, Manuscript

102. Id. Id.

103. See the translation of the article by Leikina

104. I. Meshorer, Manuscript

105. Id. Id.

106. B. Berekovski, Manuscript

107. Id. Id.

108. S. Levkowitz, Manuscript

109. Id. Id.

[Page 41]

The Zionist Movement in Ekaterinoslav

The Time of Hibat Zion

by Dr. Israel Klausner

Translated by Yocheved Klausner

A.

The pogroms that, beginning in 1881 have struck the Jews of southern Russia like an unexpected storm did not spare Ekaterinoslav and surroundings. In July 1883 the pogrom in town lasted two days. In the fall of the same year and then in 1884 and 1886 pogroms occurred again, albeit in a somewhat smaller measure. These pogroms, as well as the attitude of the authorities caused panic and a desire to flee from the country and confronted the Jewish population with the problem of emigration. The Jews of Ekaterinoslav and the Jewish villages around it sought to immigrate to Eretz Israel and settle there, and in 1884 they sent a delegation to Eretz Israel to explore the possibilities of settlement.[1]

In the month of Shevat 5654 [1884], an Association of Hovevei Zion with the aim of supporting the emigrants was founded.[2] It was at first a small association; however the number of members soon increased. Binyamin–Zvi Sheinfinkel, the secretary and general leader of the Association in Ekaterinoslav, wrote in early 1885 in reply to questions asked by Shaul Pinchas Rabinowitz (SPR), the secretary of the Hovevei Zion Association in Warsaw that the Association had more than 200 members, almost all from the poorer classes; their monthly income was about 40 Rubles, yearly about 500 Rubles. Of the donations for the settlement of Eretz Israel collected on the eve of Yom Kippur, Avraham Harkavi sent to the editorial Board of the newspaper Hamelitz 136 Rubles. The number of members grew steadily and it was hoped that well–to–do people will join as well, especially after the central committee of the movement would be founded.[3] As part of the festivities in honor of Moses Montefiore, held all over Russia and throughout the Jewish world with the occasion of his 100th birthday on 7 Marcheshvan 5645 [1884], the Ekaterinoslav Association held a festive banquet as well, during which many new members joined and about 100 Rubles were collected.[4] At the beginning of 1885 the Association decided to send 100 Rubles to the management of Hovevei Zion.[5] On 17 Adar 5645 [1885], B.Z. Sheinfinkel wrote to the management that the number of members was 400, most of them from the poor classes but there were also some "average Balei–Batim" ["house owners", well–to–do]. According to his estimate, the annual income of the association was at least 600 Rubles.[6] The list of 51 Associations at the time and their income, recorded by SPR, stated that the Ekaterinoslav Association had 400 members with an income of 1,200 Rubles per year.[7] In another article, published in the newspaper Jüdische Presse (1885, No. 11), probably by SPR as well, the income is estimated as 1,500 Rubles. This was an exaggeration. During one year and a half, from the Katowice Conference to the end of April 1886, the Ekaterinoslav Association sent a total of 404 Rubles.[8] In that year it was decided to convene small assemblies of Zionist organizations in neighboring districts, and the Ekaterinoslav Association joined the associations of Rostov and Bardiansk, that were scheduled to assemble in Rostov.[9] In the Hovevei Zion convention in Druzegnik in the month of Tamuz 1887, the Ekaterinoslav Association was represented by B.Z. Sheinfinkel.

B.

Farmers in the Jewish colonies in the Ekaterinoslav district and the other southern districts, who witnessed the repeated pogroms, desired to make Aliya to Eretz Israel and settle there. They hoped, that the "well–known philanthropist" [the Baron Edmund De Rothschild] or the Hovevei Zion organization would help them achieve the goal to settle in Eretz Israel. The Magid [preacher] of Chaslawitch, R'Yehuda–Zvi Yevzerov, who traveled in 1866 and 1867 through the districts of Ekaterinoslav and Tavira as a delegate of Hovevei Zion encouraged the people in their aspirations to make Aliya. He told his listeners, that Hovevei Zion will help: any settler, who has 1,000 Rubles, will receive from the organization a loan of 1,500 Rubles.

Some of the Ekaterinoslav Jews joined the Aleksandrovsk organization. Delegates were sent to Eretz Israel, but one of them spoke ill of Eretz Israel and by his influence some members left the association. Those who remained, however, intended to realize the plan of buying land in Eretz Israel before Pesach 5648 [1888]. Nine members from Aleksandrovsk ordered 11 plots of land and seven members from Ekaterinoslav ordered 5 plots. There was still need of members who would be ready to invest 70,000 Rubles. At this point the Association addressed the Hovevei Zion management, asking help in finding additional members–settlers. The management gave them an address: B.Z. Sheinfinkel, Ekaterinoslav. Additional members were not found and the deal was called off.[10]

[Page 42]

C.

Slowly but surely, the Ekaterinoslav Hovevei Zion organization grew and developed. In 5647 [1887] the number of members reached 700. Between January and October that year, the association sent 500 Rubles to the central treasury of the organization; on Yom–Kippur eve 5648 [1887], 164 Rubles were collected and sent to Dr. Y.L. Pinsker; it sent 50 Rubles to a family from Caucasia who went to Eretz Israel, and 25 Rubles to a young man (Levitas). In private houses there was not enough room for the assemblies that took place, therefore the Association decided, as did other similar associations, to build its own synagogue, Ohel Moshe [Moses' Tent] in honor of Moses Montefiore, which would serve as a place to hold the meetings, as well. This opened the way for intensified activity and also provided some more funds.

One of the members, who used the name Hamabit [the onlooker, the observer] wrote a complaint in the newspaper Jüdishes Volksblatt (published in Petersburg by Alexander Zederboim), arguing that the Association was not doing enough. The Association – asked the Observer – existed several years, and what did it accomplish? Did it help the Jews in Eretz Israel? The same "observer" also replied, explaining that the Association cannot really do much: the members are few, most of them of low income; it was true that here were several rich families in town, but these kept to themselves. The only ray of light that the observer saw was the synagogue Ohel Moshe.

Avraham–Yakov Bruck, member of the Ohel Moshe committee, replied. It was true, he said, that at the beginning the Association was weak, but in time it strengthened and grew to 700 members. Bruck thought that the sums collected and transferred to the settlement of Eretz Israel were not to be underestimated, and hoped that the building of the synagogue would indeed help further the activities.[11]

Ohel Moshe did help. The Hebrew teacher Zvi–Hirsh Maslanski, who came from Pinsk to Ekaterinoslav in 1888, brought a true spirit of life to the synagogue. Together with Chaim Levanda, brother of the writer I. L. Levanda and with the writer Shimon–Yehuda Stanislavski he made Ohel Moshe the center of Hovevei Zion.[12] The idea of settlements in Eretz Israel spread in town, not only among the lower classes but also among the rich and enlightened. In the month of Tevet 5649 [1889], the Magid of Chaslavitch, R'Yehuda–Zvi Yevzerov visited in town. The newspaper Hatzefira reported that a large audience came to listen to his beautiful sermons, and that his words had a deep effect on the enlightened, who decided to support the settlement of Eretz Israel. The community gave him a present – a silver cup with an inscription.[13] Maslanski, who became more and more respected for his influential speeches, often spoke at Ohel Moshe. He gained the respect of young people as well, following his establishment of the Benei Zion Association in town. Zvi Maslanski spoke at the celebration of completing the writing of a Torah Scroll by the donations of the Ohel Moshe members, and on that occasion the Hovevei Zion members collected money for the support of the Yisud Hama'ale colony in Eretz Israel. He spoke on other occasions as well – for example eulogies for Rabbi Eliashberg from Boysk (5649) and R'Shmuel–Yosef Foenn (5651). The Benei Zion Association that he founded in 5651 [1891] developed beautifully. When he left town in 5653 [1893], the Hovevei Zion group presented him with a letter of thanks, where they expressed their appreciation of his activity.[14]

In 5649, the Hovevei Zion Association in Ekaterinoslav sent money to the central committee but did not participate in the Vilna Convention – perhaps because the invitation arrived too late. Several groups in the South received invitations too late, and therefore participated only partly.[15] In the founding assembly of "The Association for supporting Jewish Farmers and Craftsmen in Syria and the Holy Land," with the permission of the authorities, as well as at smaller meetings prior to the official meeting in Iyar 5650 [1890], three delegates from Ekaterinoslav participated: Avraham Harkavi, Michel Maydanski and A. Perl.

Michel Maydanski participated in a trip to Eretz Israel of a group of people under the leadership of Rav Shmuel Mohliver. After they returned from the Holy Land, Rav Mohliver, Maydanski and Dr. Yosef Chazanowitz reported to the Odessa Committee on the situation of the colonies and of their own activity. As candidates for the Executive Committee of the Odessa Association in Jaffa they proposed Z. Tyomkin, I.A. Ben–Tovim and Y.M. Pines, and their candidates were accepted.

D.

The longing of the Ekaterinoslav Jews to establish a settlement in Eretz Israel did not cease. The Poltava Hovevei Zion Association began realizing a settlement program by lottery, and some of the Ekaterinoslav Jews bought lottery tickets through Zvi Shimshelewitz. However, the plan did not succeed and had to be cancelled.[16]

[Page 43]

In 5650 [1890], when in Russia a movement for Aliya and settlement began, the Ekaterinoslav Jews were among the first to organize on a large scale. About forty middle–class families from Ekaterinoslav and Aleksandrovsk formed an Association by the name of Tzemach David with the purpose of establishing a settlement in Eretz Israel. In the spring, they sent two delegates to "explore the land;" later, in the fall of that year they sent another two, among them the rich I.S. Dolnik. Another Association, of rich people, was founded in Ekaterinoslav on the first of the month of Sivan 5650, with the purpose of buying jointly land, manage it during five years through administrators and then make Aliya and settle on the land. This association was founded by six people, among them Mordechai Ben Hillel Hakohen; it was supposed to include only twenty families, each contributing 5,000 Rubles. They named the association Agudat Achim [Brothers Association]. Six months later, a delegate of the Association, Nemirovski, was sent to Paris, asking the Baron Rothschild to lend them money to buy the land, but Rothschild was reluctant to help the rich. The Association then sent Nemirovski to Eretz Israel to buy land. He contacted the engineer Y. Seidner and together they looked for land. When he returned on Passover 5651, Nemirovski proposed to buy for the Association 60,000 Dunams, but he soon received a message from Seidner that he bought 120,000 Dunams in the Golan Heights, soil of better quality and that he intended to sell it. He went again to Paris and persuaded Rothschild to buy the entire plot and sell parts of it to the various associations.

The representatives of the Tzemach David association, who came to Eretz Israel in Elul 5650, bought from Yehoshua Chankin 11,000 Dunams in Emek Chefer [Wadi Hawarit]. They intended to found a colony by the name of Tzemach David. However, it turned out that the land had not been in the possession of Chankin, and it was later sold to a Greek. In Sivan 5651 1891], Chankin proposed to Tzemach David to buy land in the Valley of Jezreel [Emek Yizre'el]. I.S. Dolnik gave Chankin a check of 90,000 Franks as well as a private loan of 1,000 Pounds (about 35,000 Franks) for one week. Other associations invested money as well, for the purchase of land in Emek Yizre'el. In the summer of 5651, as the prohibition of Aliya and purchase of land became effective, Chankin as well as the Hovevei Zion executive committee in Jaffa went through a serious crisis. Chankin had used Tzemach David funds to buy land in Hadera and could not return the loan, since the Hadera people had not paid him. Neither did he return the private loan that he had received from Dolnik. One hundred families in Ekaterinoslav feared the loss of their money. In the beginning of 1892 Dolnik traveled to Istanbul and met Chankin there, but he could not save the loan. The purchase of the land was cancelled.

קטע מההסכם על חלוקת האדמה שנקנתה בגולן

Part of the agreement of dividing the land purchased in the Golan Heights [names and areas]:

Thursday 28 Tamuz 5656 [1896]

Twenty three families possessing 493 Desyatin [1 desyatin = 2.7 acres] which equal to 5916 Dunams of land in Syria (Golan and Bashan), bought by the Paris Committee for the Society *Agudat Achim* Ekaterinoslav. Below are the twenty-three families and the land.

Evidvarski	50 desyatin	Huberman	10
		Geiger	25
Reshawitz	10	Kizneshker	15
Vedvedovski	30	Gabrilowitz	25
Kalamatzev	30	Goldfein	20
Levinski	30	Riedak	10
Sulemenke ?	20	Pindros	13.5
Spector	25	Laydaske	15
Kossotzevske	25	Kremer	10
Raletzkaren ?	30	Kantzewitz	20
Wishnay ?	??		

[Page 44]

In the summer of 5651, a group of 20 families from Ekaterinoslav, who made Aliya and lived temporarily in Jaffa, sent a delegation to Trans–Jordania. In Russia, the occupation of these families was farming and cattle growing, and they desired to continue this occupation in Eretz Israel. The delegates returned and announced that it would be worthwhile to purchase the land that they had seen, and the Baron's administrator Ottowjecki tried to help.

As mentioned before, Rothschild had taken upon himself to buy from the Agudat Achim the large area of 120,000 Dunams in the Golan Heights, since the association did not need such an extensive area and was looking for partners. When the restrictions on Aliya were made public, almost all members left the association. Seidner found a buyer for part of the land, 25,000 Dunams – the Shavei Zion Association in New–York. The Hovevei Zion association in England bought 10,000 Dunams. Other settlement associations on Russia – Byalistok and Homel – have shown interest in purchasing land in the Golan Heights, but there arose a problem in registering the land in the name of the buyers. The Baron tried to obtain from the authorities' permission to buy and sent his representative, Eliyahu Scheid, to Istanbul for that purpose, but with little success. The government did not allow immigrants who were foreign citizens to settle on the land. In the spring of 5653 [1893] Scheid went again to Istanbul, paid a great deal of money and succeeded in many of the Baron's assignments, but did not obtain the annulment of the settlement restrictions for new immigrants. Still, 300–400 families of immigrants were allowed to settle on the land they had bought. Scheid hoped that he would be able to overcome the restrictions and announced his victory. The "Eretz Israel Committee," founded in Paris by the Baron, with the purpose of selling land to the associations, was out of work since the associations have been dissolved and new ones have not been founded. Agudat Achim and Shavei Zion in New–York and Hovevei Zion in England convened in Paris on 20 Tevet 5654 and decided to demand from the Baron to promise that the prohibition would be cancelled in six months, and if this could not be achieved then the land in the Golan will not be bought. Shavei Zion and Hovevei Zion in England cancelled their purchase. Only the Ekaterinoslav Agudat Achim remained; it could not abandon the deal because it had invested 40,000 Franks as an advance deposit and naturally it did not want to forfeit it.

In the winter of 5655 [1895], Scheid obtained in Istanbul permission to bring 200–300 families from Russia to Trans–Jordania. Settlement associations from Romania, England and America, as well as the members of Agudat Achim began preparations to establish colonies. The Ekaterinoslav association convened on Chanuka 5656 [1896] and decided to name their colony Achva [Brotherhood]. 15 families intended to make Aliya before Passover or right after the holiday and settle in the Golan. Soon after that decision, news arrived about pogroms by the authorities and the neighbors. 23 members of the association, who had bought 5,916 Dunams, gave on 28 Tamuz 5656 power–of–attorney to a member of the association to go to the Golan and manage their estates. He was asked to build a home for himself and for another family. Several other families from Ekaterinoslav went as well to settle in the Golan. Their situation, however, was difficult, since in July 1896 an order was received in Damascus from Istanbul to evict all the Jewish settlers. Scheid managed to achieve in Istanbul an annulment of the decree, but new settlers were not allowed to join or new houses to be built. The settlers left the place in despair. The Ekaterinoslav people returned to their town very depressed and caused panic among the other members. The settlement in the Golan ended in a great disappointment.[17]

E.

In 5650 [1890], the Association in Odessa was founded. This opened up a possibility to act legally in favor of settlement in Eretz Israel. The Ekaterinoslav people participated in the activities of the Odessa Committee, were present at their meetings and contributed to their budget.

One of the most active and devoted was the senior member Mechl Meidanski. Dr. Shemaryahu Levin described him in his Memoirs:[18] "A wonderful type of a learned Jew of the old generation, full of Torah and all the other 'seven sciences'." The Odessa Committee elected him, for his activity for the society, a "member of honor," together with Rabbi S. Mohliver, K.Z. Visotzki and Moshe–Leib Lilienblum. In 5656-5659 [1896-1899], he was the deputy of the Association in Ekaterinoslav. At the time of the crisis in the movement, when Aliya was stopped, and purchase of land was cancelled, Mechl Meidanski was among those who did not withdraw. Although he was not a writer, he published an article in the newspaper Hamelitz, where he encouraged the people not to be afraid of obstacles: every new movement has to make some sacrifice because of lack of experience.[19] Meidanski collaborated with the young members, and when Menachem Ussishkin relocated to Ekaterinoslav he found in this man a friend and supported him all the way.

When Ussishkin came to Ekaterinoslav in 5651, the Zionist activity in town was intensified. He tried to attract the intelligentsia to the movement. During his visits in town, even before he settled there due to his marriage to Faley, the daughter of the engineer Sergei Pavlowitz (Shemarya ben Feitel), he assembled three meetings of educated people, with the aim to establish a national association for the study of the Hebrew Language, Jewish history and matters concerning the Yishuv [settlement] in Eretz Israel. More than fifty "Diploma holders" participated in these meetings. It was decided to build a synagogue named Ohel Ya'akov, where they met every Saturday night and discussed the problems concerning the Jewish people. On Chanuka 5652, one of the members spoke about Chanuka and Ussishkin spoke about Pinsker.[20] Ussishkin founded in Ekaterinoslav a small association for the settlement of Eretz Israel, by the name Hatikva [Hope]. He was a member of Benei Moshe, a secret section of the Hovevei Zion association, and was the one who introduced Avraham Harkavi and Zvi-Hirsch Maslanski to the movement. Ussishkin also founded in town a committee with the aim to publish booklets in Russian on Jewish national topics. This series of booklets published works by I.L. Levanda, Dr. L. Kantor (the life of Don Yitzhak Abarbanel) and S.I. Stanislavski from Ekaterinoslav (about Moshe Hess).

[Page 45]

The collaboration between Ussishkin and Meidanski was extended over several areas. In 5652 [1892], when they established a fund for the benefit of laborers in Eretz Israel, the two announced that they, together with four other townspeople, will donate 536 Rubles a year to the fund.[21] At the general assembly of the Odessa Association, in 5653, Ekaterinoslav was represented by Meidanski and Ussishkin. They participated in the consultation concerning the establishment of a National Library in Eretz Israel. The members signed a memorandum, in which the Hovevei Zion members were called to support "A central national library for our nation." The first signatories on the memorandum were M. Meidanski and M. Ussishkin.[22] They did not go to the convention of the Merkaz Ruhani (Mizrahi), but one of them – by their choice – was elected as the aide and consultant of Rav Mohliver, head of the Mizrahi. The younger of the two filled the position.

In 1892, beside Meidanski and Ussishkin, we find Levinski, Chaim (Vitali) Levanda, Z.H. Maslanski, Avraham Harkavi and S.I. Stanislavski. They signed a telegram to Rabbi Tzadok Cohen (Kahn) in which they expressed the condolences of Hovevei Zion in Ekaterinoslav at the passing of Michael Erlanger.[23]

In the third general assembly of the Odessa Committee the delegates from Ekaterinoslav were M. Meidanski and Engineer M. Bruck.

The number of members of the Odessa Committee in Ekaterinoslav and their contributions were: 1890 – 227; 1892 – 79, 607 Rubles; 1893 – 154, 987 R.; 1894 – 157, 1357 R.; 1895 – 149, 957 R.; 1896 – 118, 860 R.; 1897 – 139, 933R.

The publication of Herzl's book, "The Jewish State" made a strong impression on the Hovevei Zion movement in Russia. A group of Hovevei Zion, who came in the summer of 5656 to the General Assembly of the Odessa Committee and heard from prof. Z. Belkovski about the contents of the book, decided to publish a new edition of "Auto Emancipation" by Pinsker, as a "supplement to Herzl's activity." The group included M. Meidanski.[24] I. Buchmill, who was sent by Dr. Herzl to Russia, to campaign among the Jews to go to the Congress, visited Ekaterinoslav. Ussishkin, who at first was of the opinion that the Congress will not bring any advantage, later changed his opinion and supported Buchmill. Meidanski became a political Zionist and was devoted with all his heart to the activity of the Zionist Organization. Ussishkin traveled to the Zionist Congress and served as secretary for Hebrew. The First Congress heralded a new era for the Zionist Movement, as well as for Ekaterinoslav.

Footnotes

1. A letter from Leib Rubin, one of the founders of Yesud Hama'ala, 10 Elul 5644 [1884]. Yesud Hama'ala Archives, in the National Library in Jerusalem.

2. As related by Avraham–Yakov Bruck of Ekaterinoslav, in *Jüddisches Volksblatt*, Petersburg, 1887, No. 44.

3. A letter from the Association in Ekaterinoslav to SPR, no date, before the convention of the Katowice Conference, the SPR Archives, in the Central Zionist Archives in Jerusalem.

4. *Hamelitz*, 1884, No. 88. About the festivities see also my book "From Katovice to Basel" (The Movement for Zion in Russia, 1), Jerusalem 5722 (1962), pp. 396–398.

5. SPR Archives, a letter from the Association from 5.1.1885.

6. Ibid. a letter from 17 Adar 5645 (1885).

7. The list in the Droyanov Collection, Central Zionist Archives, 9/41.

8. List of Associations in "Writings on the History of *Hibat Zion* and the settlement of Eretz Israel," A. Droyanov, Odessa 5679 [1919], Vol. 1, No. 441.

9. Ibid. No. 491, in a memorandum from 19 Elul 5646 [1885].

10. The sources are mentioned in my book (see above), 2, Jerusalem 5725 [1965], pp. 142–143.

11. *Jüddisches Volksblatt*, 1887, No. 39, 44.

12. Z.H. Maslanski, in his Memoirs (his Writings, 3, New York 5689 [1929], p. 7).

13. *Hatzefira*, 1888, No. 284.

14. *Hamelitz*, 1889, No. 2, 272; 1891, No.5; 1893, No. 76.

15. My book (above) 2, p. 381; Droyanov Collection, No. 64, in a letter from M.L. Lilienblum to S.Y. Fuenn, 1 Av 5649 [1889].

16. My book (above) 2, pp. 242–244.

17. My book (above) 3, pp. 23, 28, 65–68, 123,164, 178, 183, 278–279.

18. Memories of my Life, Tel Aviv, 5699 [1939], 3, p. 185.

19. *Hamelitz*, 1892, No. 155–157.

20. Letter of M. Ussishkin to Yehoshua Eisenstadt, Moscow, 26 Marcheshvan 5651 [1890], Y. Eisenstadt–Barzilay Archives, in the CZA, file 38. Letter of M. Ussishkin to Asher Ginsburg (*Achad Ha'am*), 4th day of Chanuka, in *Benei Moshe* Archives, ibid.

21. My book (above), 3, p. 208.

22. Ibid. p. 202.

23. *Hamelitz*, 1892, No. 221.

24. My book, 3, p. 350.

[Page 46]

Ekaterinoslav Jews in the First Aliya and Second Aliya

Translated by Yocheved Klausner

Mordechai Henkin, born in 1861 in Ekaterinoslav. Made Aliya in 5641 (1881), with the last of the BILU movement. He worked as a farm laborer in Gedera and later settled in Gedera, owner of a farm.

Yitzhak Henkin, born in 1860 in Ekaterinoslav. Made Aliya in 1887 and joined his brother Mordechai. Worked as a farm laborer in Gedera, later moved to Rechovot and then settled in Hadera, owner of a farm.

Gitel Henkin, born in 1817 in Ekaterinoslav, made Aliya in 1886 and joined her son Mordechai in Gedera. She was an active community worker in that settlement.

Yitzhak Leib Toporovski, born in 1866, made Aliya in 1886, joined the founders of Rishon LeTzion and settled there.

Rostovski Yakov, born in 1860 in the small town Bolshoy-Tukmak and lived in Ekaterinoslav. A member of BILU, worked with the BILU members in Mikve Israel and later became a merchant.

Kalman Hoffman, born in 1874 in Ekaterinoslav, made Aliya in 1895, worked as a carpenter, then established in Yaffo (Jaffa) a foundry, which is functioning to this day.

Shmuel-Moshc Spcktorov (Ben-Shemesh), born in 1878 in Poltava, resident of Ekaterinoslav. He made Aliya in 1905 and settled in Petach-Tikva. During World War I he was arrested by the Turks, sent into exile to Damascus, and died there.

Yakov Kantorowitz, born in Kleck, resident of Ekaterinoslav, made Aliya in 1905, was a farm laborer, studied carpet weaving at the Bezalel School of art and became instructor in several schools.

(**From:** Encyclopedia of the Founders and Builders of Israel by Tidhar, and private sources).

The Campaign[1]

by Dr. Shemaryahu Levin

Translated by Yocheved Klausner

Everything was new for me in Ekaterinoslav. When I was offered the post in Grodna, I was warned to keep silent. However, when I was offered the post in Ekaterinoslav I was specifically told to speak up. This gave me courage, and the new place made me feel alive. My friend Menachem Ussishkin took me to

Ekaterinoslav several weeks before the elections, and the town was in turmoil. The residents of the town were divided into conflicting factions. I don't think that even the US is as agitated during election of president as was Ekaterinoslav during the election of the appointed rabbi. All were swept into the dispute – not one remained neutral. Even the Christian residents of the town showed interest in the election. The two daily Russian newspapers in town took sides as well: the more conservative one supported the old rabbi and the liberal one supported my candidacy, except for just one fault that they discovered – I was a Zionist. The attitude of the Russian press toward Zionism was, in general, either total disregard or overt hatred. The liberal newspaper in town had to take my side, for one simple reason: the other newspaper favored the other rabbi. As I was reading the Russian newspapers – many articles, Editor's Opinion etc. – about the role and function of the appointed rabbi in the community, I wondered: would we be allowed to interfere in the matters of the general population the way they meddled in our affairs... <ô> The former appointed rabbi, a graduate of the Vilna Rabbinical College, had many friends and supporters. He was a fine and honest man of good qualities.

[Page 47]

Yet, as many of his friends, students of Rabbinical College in Vilna, he was missing one little thing: the deep inner feeling for the office of rabbi, for Judaism and its problems. He was soft-hearted and guarded and was not inclined to delve deeply into any matter. He was apprehensive of social movements – theirs or ours. He was of the opinion that social movements are superfluous and that a person can easily live out his years without them. The well-to-do in town, as well as he Russian authorities, considered him an exemplary rabbi. He was, in truth, a kind man, very liked socially, and was considered one of the best players in town of the "Preference" card-game. He had one more group of supporters in town: the new "conversos" in Ekaterinoslav – the Jews who have converted to Christianity. The town was "blessed" with a great number of converts, especially in the upper layer of the social echelon: there were about twelve converts among the Jewish lawyers alone. There was no comparison, of course, between these "new Christians" in Ekaterinoslav and the conversos in Spain, whose hearts were a source of deep tragedy and a target of deep hatred: openly they were pious Catholics, but secretly they were Jews. The life of the Ekaterinoslav converts was much simpler: all they had to do was change some data in their birth certificate or passport – and this minor change led them over all the obstacles and limitations by which the Russian laws had restricted the course of life of the Jewish intelligentsia. As a matter of fact, however, these Jewish young people have not changed much after conversion: their Jewishness has not diminished, and their Christianity was not enhanced, and it was difficult to say who was more offended by this situation: the Jews or the Christians? Yet, there was one barrier that they could not break: the social barrier. The Russian high society has not accepted heartily the new converts: a change in the passport is not enough to bring about a change in relationship between people. Years later, when I became close to some of the Russian intelligentsia, I understood that it was not because of hate that the converts have not been accepted; it was due to the feeling of contempt towards these weak-minded, unfaithful, traitors.

So it happened that all these converts, being detached from the Russian high society, remained, either by choice or by pressure, within the same social milieu that they had been before conversion; unwillingly they were concerned with Jewish matters. The entire group of converted lawyers supported the former rabbi – and no wonder: as long as Jewishness, in their mind, was expressed only through religious commandments and prohibitions – which they did not observe even when they were part of the Jewish people – adopting another "religion" was easy: there was almost no change. However, when Jewishness acquired the aspect of a national vision – as it indeed happened in those days – the question arose: can a nation be the object of exchange, of conversion?? This would seem immoral or corrupt even in the eyes of a person who was not blessed with a fine and sensitive conscience.

The proud man, who was ready to reject the insult, who openly declared war on the traitors, was Menachem Ussishkin, the great Zionist. He demanded publicly that the Jewish society not allow these converts to meddle in its affairs. He argued: we cannot stop those people from adopting immoral ideas, but we can indeed stop them from casting their influence upon our community. The battle was quite easy, because the most respected families in town had been offended. Ussishkin was not a man of compromise; when the honor of his nation was at stake, he fought bitterly and energetically, without minding his manners too much. Following all this agitation, the group of converts gave up, for fear of the new national movement, its leader Menachem Ussishkin and the new rabbinic candidate, who openly declared that he was a Zionist.

* * *

My circle of friends was not very large, but all were fine people – every one of them a special personality. I shall describe some of them, as they are etched in my memory. The oldest in the group, and yet seemingly the youngest, was Mechl Maidanski, famous among all Russian Jews as one of the smartest and most active community workers. He was already eighty when I met him, his head as well as his beard white as snow. However, from this "winter-body" a pair of eyes shone, fresh and full of vigor and summer-light – eyes that would suit perfectly the youngest. These eyes in the white head made everyone wonder – was this an optical illusion, or was it the white hair that was fooling the onlooker? In any case, these eyes were a testimony of a young soul. He was alert, always active, worthy of the envy of young people; a wonderful type of an "enlightened Jew" of the old generation, full of knowledge and wisdom. He had accumulated a long experience over the years and he knew how to use it in his many-sided activity. Above all that, God has blessed him with a great sense of humor: for every situation he had a story to tell, or a joke. Everybody liked him, Jews and Christians alike. The Russians – if there was no specific law to forbid it – considered an honor to have this Jew, Michael Vladimirovitch, on their committees, and even the government would look for his advice, especially in matters concerning Jews.

[Page 48]

This man had been an enthusiastic Hassid in his youth, and at times even served as assistant to the Rebbe. What made him leave the Hassidic world and begin working for the community? He did not like to talk about this matter – but it was certain that he did not keep in his heart any animosity toward his former world. His character was such that he could not hate anybody: his constant feeling of contentment and optimism were a barrier to any feelings of hate. Since he was one of the beadles [Gabay] of the synagogue, I had a chance to meet him every day. The Synagogue Committee was considered the leading body of the community; three members were in the committee: the Gabay, who was also the chairman, the "learned one" and the treasurer. According to the Russian law, the rabbi's status was above the committee; however, the rabbi was content when the committee did not act "above" him. Mechl Maidanski was the "learned Jew" of the committee; years ago he held an important position in the Hibbat Zion movement and when Herzl founded the political Zionist Organization, the old Maidanski walked side by side with the young members and participated in the Zionist work. As time passed, we became very close friends.

The most honored and most influential in the Ekaterinoslav community was Moshe Karpas. He was an "American" type. Full of energy and initiative, he did not fear innovation; he did not consider tradition an obstacle – not even religious tradition and faith – and shaped his life by his own strength and talent. People of his nature feel that all they have earned was by their own labor and they did not owe thanks to anybody; therefore, they rise to the highest degree of self-confidence.

Moshe Karpas, who in fact was the leader of the community and had the power to restrict or enhance its activity, was one of these unique types of persons. His life had begun in poverty, and by his own efforts he managed to become one of the great figures in the flourishing metal industry. He possessed that special quality which made him suitable for community work and he devoted his talents to rebuilding the Jewish Community, from top to bottom, to serve as example for other communities. In his extended travels, in Russia and in other countries, he collected relevant material from the Jewish communities and presented his own community with plans, ideas, inventions and ways to rebuild the various communal institutions, in particular the charity institutions, in the spirit of the new times and the new needs. He generously provided from his own means, but always sought the advice of his assistants and invited the best professionals to the meetings. When the subject of discussion was education or other cultural questions, he modestly stood aside and did not intervene; his knowledge in Judaism and general education was insufficient, but he was blessed with a natural intelligence, a sharp and logical mind and an honest spirit.

Another type entirely was Ussishkin's father-in-law, Sergei Pavlovitch Paley. Shemarya had turned into Sergei and Feitel into Pavel. Feitel Paley still belonged to the old Hassidic world; his son Shemarya received in his childhood a true Jewish education, and only after his marriage and after he was a father of two children did he change his ways and went to study – first high-school and then the Aristocratic Institute for Road Engineers – and returned from Petersburg named Sergei Pavlovitch. His children were raised and educated in the Russian culture: they did not know one word of Hebrew, and not even Yiddish. Grandfather hardly understood his grandchildren, and the grandchildren did not understand grandmother at all. I am mentioning this, in order to show how fast the generations in Russia changed. There are two generations between grandfather and grandson, but culturally speaking, each generation opened a new era, a new "beginning." Yet, short periods can establish only unstable cultural structures; one cannot build a fort out of thin toothpicks.

[Page 49]

Sergei Pavlovitch managed his father's businesses – a flour mill and a modern sawmill, with advanced machinery. Since he was an only son, everybody regarded him as the head and owner of the big business enterprise. He was a completely honest man, but he stood by his opinions and was not one to give in. He was short and thin and had strong bones – not an easy task to break them! A cynic and doubter by nature and inclined to be pessimistic – his friends did not believe that he could do good and useful work for his fellows. However, influenced by Ussishkin's strong character, Sergei Pavlovitch became totally involved in the community affairs and even a little in Zionist matters. He lacked Karpas's largesse and Maidanski's optimism, but he was very helpful with his analytic mind and his sharp logic. By his quick wit and strong control he forced his fellows to weigh carefully every matter and calculate every decision. It was not an easy responsibility, but mandatory in every public or political organization.

Several worthy young people belonged to this circle as well. The most interesting among them was M. Bruk, another son-in-law of Sergei Paley, a young engineer, with a natural sense for social work. He was a Zionist as well; however, in contrast to his brother-in-law Ussishkin he did nor limit himself to Zionist work alone but was active in all social institutions and enterprises of the community. He cared in particular for the commercial assistants and status of the craftsmen: he organized them, helped them establish co-operative societies and set up study courses in Jewish matters and general knowledge. He was a committee member in many important companies and served mostly as secretary. He really enjoyed his social and public activity.

The Ekaterinoslav community was of a democratic structure. Public opinion was strong, since a great majority of the members were involved in community affairs. The activity was supported by the two Russian newspapers, which devoted space and interest to the needs and problems of the Jewish community. True, they did this out of necessity, rather than sympathy, since most of the subscribers and readers were Jews – although the Jews were only about one third of the town's population. The Christian population consisted of many simple laborers who worked in the iron industry and the advanced railroad, called "Ekaterininskaia" and of many Russian middle-class (bourgeois) families. Neither the workers nor the middle-class people have reached the stage of reading newspapers, while the Jews were educated and surpassed them culturally. This extensive preoccupation with reading newspapers may have had its roots in the Jewish heritage: "the people of the book," for centuries dedicated to the pages of the Talmud, as they were uprooted from these pages they adopted the newspaper page...

In Ekaterinoslav I was attracted, for the first time in my life, to charity work. One of the important undertakings of the community was to care for its needy and poor, forbidding them from going from house to house for hand-outs. It was not an easy task, however. Many of the well-to-do people were not ready to give-up the custom of giving charity directly to the hand of the needy, and the poor people, as well, protested against this new system. They did not accept the clear explanation and evidence that this system – joint collection of charity and just distribution after a thorough survey of their situation – will improve their state. They did not want – argued the poor people – an "allowance" set up and given to them by the community treasurers; they preferred to put their faith in God and relay on the good hearts of the good people: they preferred begging from door to door. However, the new regulation was ratified, and begging was terminated in Ekaterinoslav.

Footnote

1. Dr. S. Levin served in Ekaterinoslav as Rabbi appointed by the authorities ["appointed rabbi"] in the years 1898-1904. In his book "Memories of my life" Volume 3, published by Dvir, Tel-Aviv, he devoted a large amount of space to this period. We present here excerpts from pages 172-176 and 185-190.

[Page 50]

Impressions from a Journey[1]

by A. L. Levinski

Translated by Yocheved Klausner

... And after several hours I arrived in the big town Ekaterinoslav. The Dnieper and the iron bridge that stretches over it and leads into town, is like an introduction to a good book: a wonderful sight, joy to the eye and heart, a wide river with several islands, like a small sea. Ice covered it and gave it a multi–colored shine, like polished crystal under the rays of the sun. Raise your eyes to the East, North and South and you shall see river, and river, and river. And over it, at a terribly great height, a tri–level iron bridge: the first level for the "iron wagons" [the train], over it for carts and horses, and the top level for pedestrians. All this, from the bottom level to the top, is connected by a maze of nets and lattice–work, held together by wedges, loops, bolts and chains; a wonderful and magnificent sight. This bridge is one of the most beautiful structures in our country, as the Dnieper is very wide here, and the bridge is about two verstas. We look and are amazed by the talent of the builders. We wonder how money, made of thin paper, unable to carry any weight and issued by a weak regime, could have build such a marvel. Not only that – with their wisdom the builders determined in advance how much money to spend for every column, how much for the support piles etc. and how much for their own pockets!! They understood the secrets of money and so they have built a beautiful structure in Ekaterinoslav. And if this is really like an introduction to the town, I must tell you, that the introduction is perhaps better that the book itself... True, the town is beautiful, very beautiful; beautiful in particular is the street called Prospect, which goes from the railway station to the City Park, and from there it turns like the Greek letter Delta to the mountain until it reaches Potiomkin Park. On both sides of the street are rows of oak trees and in the middle the road for horses, like the famous street "Unter den Linden" in Berlin. That street is very beautiful, but the town in general is like a simpleton who tries to be the first in the parade, a poor tailor who got rich and does not know how to beautify his house and decorate his rooms – and is wasting his money on things he doesn't need; and things that are really necessary one will not find in his house.

So is this entire town: from behind the stove he went to become a king. From a simple county seat like any other county seat – without commerce and without energy – it became a center of the lumber trade, iron and coal. From a town whose greatest merchants traded in wheat and other grains it became a commercial center for several millions, from a town without even one factory it suddenly became "a little Sheffield" – beautiful and rich, not knowing how to get more beautiful and prouder. What it did, it did for itself, and not for the multitude of guests who began to visit. The guests knew only that since Ekaterinoslav became important, the wagon fare rose, as did the rent and the restaurant prices. And this was not enough – that it turned into a city of lumber and iron, of sawmills and foundries, with thousands of workers and employees of the main offices of the railroad company "Ekaterina," the ministers and accountants and other important employees of the County Seat....

Footnote

1. From the article "Impressions from a Journey." Works of A. L. Levinski, pp. 125–126

[Page 51]

My memories
by Hadassa Rachel Birman
Translated by Sara Mages

Hadassa Rachel Birman was born on 3 Kislev 5636 (1876) in the village of Belerfeld not far from Ekaterinoslav. She studied Hebrew since childhood, and after she moved with her family to live in Ekaterinoslav she got closer to the Zionist circles that were led at that time by Menachem Ussishkin.

She continued her Zionist activities after she got married and established a traditional home. She didn't stray from this way even during the Soviet regime, and her home served as a center for the Zionist circles who continued to exist in secret. Moral and material help came from Mrs. Birman home during those difficult years.

In 1932 she immigrated to Israel with her family and settled in Rahovot. Also here, despite her advanced age, her home serves as a center for our townspeople who respect, admire and love her. She hasa large part in the "Yekaterinoslav-Dnepropetrovsk" book.

I was born and raised in a traditional home. My father, R' Asher Yitzchak Wolfowitz, was educated in the Yeshivot of Lita. There, he befriended R' Binyamin Zakheim who was later a rabbi in Yekaterinoslav. My father z"l immigrated to this area in Southern Russia and settled in a farm near the Egran Station. At that time, my father joined "Agudat Achim," which bought land east of the Jordan River. He sent his brother-in-law to prepare all that was needed for the family's immigration, but as we know, this settlement didn't materialize.

In 1886, his father-in-law, R' Chaim-Yehusua Shapira, came to our village. He only talked about *Eretz-Yisrael*, working the land, life of austerity and the Hebrew language. He began to speak Hebrew with his family and even with the animals. He was ridiculed in the area: "Shapira is talking to the cow in the Holy Language." He influenced my father to let me study Hebrew with my brother. To my happiness, a good teacher was found for that, but there were no reading books. When I found that there is a Hebrew library in Ekaterinoslav, I traveled to the city and signed up for it, and by doing so I met interesting people. A short time later I learned that the library was about to close for lack of funds. I decided to go to Ussishkin who received me very well. I explained to him that if the library will be closed the city and its surroundings would remain without a Hebrew book. He promised me to look into the matter, and thanks to him the library wasn't closed.

Chaim-Yehusua Shapira greatly influenced me all those years. He made sure to provide me with books in Hebrew and also invited me to Zionist meetings when he was in the city. Once, he informed me about a meeting at the home of Dr. Angel, and when I entered, I found a large number of guests there. Among them was Mr. Michel Meidanski z"l, the representative of the Yekaterinoslav region. When I entered, he received me with the greeting – here's our veteran Israeli. Mrs. Paulina Yafa also participated in the meeting. She proposed to open a high school for girls – a matter that was implemented later.

B.

In 1900 I married my husband, Yosef Birman, and we moved to live in Yekaterinoslav. It was an industrial city with many large factories. Since it sat by the Dnieper River the timber trade, which was sent north by rafts, was widespread in the city. There was also a grain trade that was sent abroad. Yekaterinoslav was in the Pale of Settlement and many flocked to the city from the small towns to find a source of income. There were many institutions in the city: three "Talmud Torah" schools, a Yeshiva which had a two-story building, and a dormitory. The Yeshiva had many supporters and donors like: Karpas, Yudelson, Emanuel, Meidansky, Karczov and others. The head of the Yeshiva was R' Dov from Bobruysk and the overseer was Rabbi Halperin. Rabbi Gelman has done a lot for the development and expansion of the Yeshiva.

From the other institutions I will mention the Jewish Hospital which moved from its previous location in Bulniznaya Street to Sufskaya Street. There, a block of stone buildings, which was surrounded by a red brick wall, was built for all the departments of the hospital and also apartments for the employees. A "cheap kitchen," which was built from the donation of Mr. Karpas, was located on Banya Street. The community management offices were also located there. There were two orphanages for 80 children which were maintained by the community management. A women's committee took care of these institutions. Mr. Karpas established and maintained an orphanage for 40 children. It was a beautiful building that was surrounded with a red brick wall. In general, the social work was highly developed, and a number of women's organizations devoted themselves to it.

At that time there were several schools for Jewish children in Yekaterinosla. From them: Cohen's vocational school for girls who studied sewing and other handcraft, the two schools of the Shechter brothers, Matiletzky's school, and others. Evening classes were also held in these schools. Later, Wexler's high-school for boys was established in Kazanskaya Street, and at the beginning of this century – the high-school of P. Yafa and Yudkevitz. Classes weren't held in these schools on the Sabbat and during the Jewish holidays.

[Page 52]

H. R. Birman

There were several libraries in Yekaterinoslav. One was opened in 1895 in accordance with a license obtained by Ussishkin. The librarian was Yosef Markovsky who later immigrated to Israel with his family. This library also served as a place for meetings. There was also a small library next to the Choral Synagogue where it was possible to find a selection of new literature, and the librarian was H. Axelrod (immigrated to Israel). H. Litvak served in this position before him (his daughter Chinga – is in Israel). A large library, which was worthy of its name, belonged to the "Federation of Jewish trade assistants." At first, it contained books in Russian and Yiddish and later also in Hebrew. The librarian was Mr. Yitzchakin. Sometimes, this federation organized balls with varied programs (music, readings) for members and guests, and it was possible to find the community leaders there.

Among the first booksellers were Avraham Rogov and his son, and Y. Henkin. Their small shops were always full of shoppers because there was a great demand for reading books. The "Pakent-Regers," as they were called then, bought all types of reading books in Hebrew and Yiddish, prayer books and more, and brought them as peddlers to the Jewish homes in the towns and villages.

[Page 53]

The Zionist activity in Yekaterinoslav greatly expanded after M. Ussishkin married the daughter of S. Paleim, one of the important Jewish residents in the city, and settled there in 1890. Indeed, several members of "Hovevei Zion" were very active before his arrival, and among them: M. Meidansky, Avraham Harkabi who wrote for "Ha-Melitz" [the first Hebrew newspaper in Russia] and others. However, the activity increased only after Ussishki's arrival. Meetings were held and the famous preachers, Yevzrov and Maslianski who later settled in Yekaterinoslav, visited the city often. The synagogues, in which they've preached, were filled and many young people flocked to hear them.

"Cheder Metukan" [reformed Cheder], which was under the management of H.K. Zuta, was opened about 1898 and among the teachers was also H.Y. Shapira. A lot was done for the strengthening and existence of this Cheder (Mr. Zuta wrote about it in his book "Baresit HaDerech"). The association "Safa Chaya" ["Living Language"] was established in 1901 and its energetic and devoted members were: Z. Rabinowitch, Peitelzon, Zuta, T. Shlonsky, Y. Veksler and many others. They gathered and spoke Hebrew at the homes of M. Ussishkin, the dentist Angle and others.

C.

We were very pleased when Dr. Shmaryaho Levin came to serve as the community rabbi after a long struggle with his predecessor – Shachor. Dr. Levin captured the heart of everyone with his charming personality and fiery speeches. It's hard for me to remember and express in writhing all the respect and affection that he acquired. In Hanukkah of that year, a party, in which pictures of Israel and its landscape were presented, was organized at the municipal theater. It was filled to capacity with teachers and their students. It was rare that so many Jewish children, who felt warmth, freedom and happiness, gathered together.

Two newspapers were published in Yekaterinoslav: one was close to the right, and the second was edited by the lawyer Zeitlin and the local Russian intelligentsia participated in it. Important cultural work was conducted by the

"Association for science" which was located in a four-story building in Tzetzkebeka. There, it was possible to hear lectures on various topics from scientists and professors from the "Harari Institute" in Yekaterinoslav. In addition, various concerts and other activities were also held there, and we attended them frequently.

In 1905, on 21, 22, 23 October, pogroms, which were under the auspice of the army and the Cossacks, broke out in Yekaterinoslav. The rioters robbed, looted and killed many. The lawyer Zeitlin walked and recorded the details in all corners of the city. His newspaper published a sharp article in which the Russian intelligentsia declared that they're ashamed to be called Russian if such acts are done in the country. The yard, in which we lived, belonged to a Russian and he saved seventy people. Also, his daughter, who lived in another street, stood by the gate and didn't let the rioters to enter. Our self-defense was very active, and peace returned on the evening of the third day of the riots. We returned to our home, heated water and washed the babies. We were only able to talk after we drank tea because the speech was taken from us before that. On the same day my teacher, R' H. Y. Shapira, came to say goodbye because he decided to immigrate to Israel with his family.

In 1909, Dr. B. Z. Mossinson came to our city and greatly impressed us with his appearance and his speeches that he gave in Russian and Hebrew in a Sephardic accent. He tried to convince us to register our children to "Gymnasia Herzliya." In those years Bialik, Ansky, Pasmanik and Jabotinsky visited Yekaterinoslav. There were also several concert of Jewish music.

We spent anxious days during the Belies' trial. We lived in constant fear because we knew that the mayor and his staff, who were anti-Semite, were getting ready to destroy us with all the tools of destruction. Their men of destruction stood ready and waited for the "signal." A miracle happened to us because God saved us from their hands. The names of Rabbi Maze, [Moscow's Chief Rabbi], Gruzenberg and others were always on our lips.

D.

There were two rabbis in our city: Rabbi Binyaminka Zkhaim for the opponents, and Rabbi Bere-Wolf Kozhevinkov for the Hassidim. I've never heard a misunderstanding or unpleasantness between them or their followers. There were additional rabbis in the suburbs of the big city and also a "rabbi" (a good Jew).

After the death of the two chief rabbis the opponents appointed the genius, Rabbi Pinchas Gelman z"tl, who was friendly, pleasant, popular and active. A

"Talmud Torah" with decent dedicated teachers, who were under his supervision, was located in the yard where I lived.

[Page 54]

The "Yeshiva," that a seminar for teachers was added to it later, was also under his supervision. Rabbi Gelman hoped to immigrate to Israel and establish a faculty of law there, but he was unable to do so because to our great sorrow the rabbi passed away when he was only forty years old.

The Hassidism's rabbi was Rabbi Levi Yitzchak Schneerson z"tl. His Hassidim never denigrated the honor of Rabbi Gelman. I heard it myself. Of course, R' Schneerson worked quite a bit in his company. I knew his wife, the Rebbetzin, who knew Hebrew and spoke it to me when I met her. However, one day she told me that she doesn't speak Hebrew... Their youngest son was Leibale, and according to his mother he studied the Talmud at the age of five. We were very happy when our children were able to enter him to the Zionist movement. HaRav E. Broshtein (the previous community rabbi) educated his talented son, who studied the Talmud, in the Zionist movement, but in the end he was caught by Communism ... It was told, that when the two of them met, R' E. Broshtein complained before R' Schneerson about his sorrow and disappointment that his favorite son became a communist. R' Schneerson answered him: like me, when I learned that my son Leibale became a Zionist...

E.

And now, the First World War broke out with all its horrors and hardships. The deportees from the border settlements and the refugees arrived to our city. Many settled in our city because it was located in the Pale of Settlement. The rabbis, who were imprisoned as hostages, were also brought to our city. The townspeople welcomed them with warmth and took care of all their needs. Actually, despite all the sorrow, it was a blessing for our city because it was infused with a new Jewish blood. During those years, (1915-1916), Yekaterinoslav has been enriched by genuine Jewish power of the Jews of Lita and Poland. The Yeshivot of Lida and Slabodka moved here (later it moved to Yelisbetgrad). The voices of Torah scholars rang from all the synagogues. Also the gymnasium of P. Cohen came from Vilna with is blessed cargo – the lofty teachers: Dr. Y.L. Baruch, N. Pins, P. Shiffman (Ben-Sira), Kostrinsky, Kantorowicz, Dr. Lichtenstein, and others. Gymnasia "Tarbut" was opened and the Teachers Union was strengthened. The teachers who took part in it were: Wilenzik, Polonsky, Litvak, Shragorodsky and others. From the Yidisha'im: Kazakevich, Dworkin, Robinson, Bugoslawsky, and others. Two seminars, one on of behalf of "Tarbut" and the second under the supervision of R' Gelman, were founded. Two kindergartens were also opened, one in Hebrew under the management of Mrs., Chaya Lichtenstein-Weizmann and the second in Yiddish. The Zionist propaganda was intense and comprehensive, and the study of the Hebrew language was expanded. The Yidisha'im also didn't sit idle and opened a disrespectful propaganda. In addition, lectures were held for all the teachers. I visited several of them, and Mr. N. Pins was the living spirit in them.

The public work was extensive. We took care of the soldiers' wives, the refugees and their children. In addition to the kindergartens we also organized a "kirkara" (playground) for the children under the guidance of the kindergarten teachers Chinga Litvak and the daughter of the teacher Kantorowitch. I collected the children from my neighborhood and later returned them to their homes.

By chance, I befriended a family from Pinks who came from there together with the bank. Through this family I met Yosef Bergman, the brothers Eisenberg and others from Pinks who were active and dedicated Zionists. A welding workshop, in which the student received a small salary and lunch, was opened under Ehrlich's management. At that time, the brothers Moshe and Yehezkel Zaks, who were student in "Gymnasia Herzliya" and returned to study in Yekaterinoslav, lived at my home. Their Hebrew speech left an impression on me and they taught my children to speak Hebrew.

F.

And here is the Balfour Declaration! It's difficult to describe the joy, excitement and hope in our city! The public work hasn't weakened, and Mr. Kochanovsky's Hebrew Gymnasium was opened on Opornaya Street. Among its teachers were: the Levin brothers (today, Yehudi Leib is the Chief Rabbi of Moscow), Aresh – father of the "Habima" actor Avital, Kochanovsky's three daughters and his son-in-law. There was no lack of students and the parents committee, to which I also belonged, has done a lot to improve the Hebrew lessons and the school. Despite the danger of the civil war we organized a party for the children on Lag BaOmer. We walked in a procession through the city's streets to a forest where we organized games, sing-along and more. The Zionist activity gradually expanded and with it also the study of the Hebrew language. In Cohen's Gymnasium all the subjects were taught in Hebrew, a matter that wasn't easy to carry out.

[Page 55]

The allocation of 1000 Ruble from the philanthropist S. Barslavsky gave "Tarbut" the possibility to expand the scope of its work. Lecturers and readers gathered every week in "Tzeirei Zion" club on Opornaya Street, and the young forces – Y. Idelshon, Y. Ritov and M. Lev – took an active part in it. The brothers Gorowitz from the Pinsk group and Zalman Lubovsky were very active. Libai, who was an excellent speaker, joined later. Avraham Gutman moved to Yekaterinoslav and took an active part in the Zionist activities.

G.

Gloomy days arrived, and every day brought a curse worse than the last. A civil war, a robber leaves – a killer takes his place. Again, and again. The roads are dangerous also in the city. Everyone is only talking about food and clothes. The trade ceased, the shops were closed, and all the employees were laid off. I think that there wasn't a normal academic year, because everything was destroyed, and nothing was rebuilt. Denikin's soldiers, who came after the German troops took what they wanted, robbed and killed. Everyone traveled to the villages – to exchange items for a small quantity of grits and flour. Our work didn't stop under these conditions and from time to time we gathered at the home of Dr. Y. Dolsinsky. When it wasn't allowed to study Hebrew, we organized a school at the home of H. Shochat. Mordechai Gover and his wife Rivka taught there and one of the students stood on guard. Another group studied Hebrew in my apartment with Gover. Over time, Yona Kesse, his brother Mendel, Yeshayah Shar, N. Lev, Zalman Rabinowitch, S. Frumkin, Sprinzak and others joined the teaching staff. Despite the danger we organized parties in Hanukkah, Tu Bishvat, and other holidays. Once, we arranged a big Simchat Torah party at the home of Dr. Ginzburg and Natan Ternavsky, who was later exiled and was last seen in prison in Arkhangelsk, gave a lecture. A special committee took care of the finance and its members were: Moshe Risin. Ziama Yafit (Yufit} and others.

In 1921 the refugees started to return to their places. In 1921-1922 came the great drought and the famine related to it. In 1923-1924 came the arrests of the Zionists in our city. The first victim was the young man Moisyev, an only son to his parents who fell ill and died in exile. Among those arrested were: H. Reichman, Daniel Beresovsky, Tzvi Bokrinsky, Leah Lev, Rivka Volodarsky, Lioba Ginodman, Aharon Puzin and others. Some of them were released and some sentenced to expulsion. Later, their verdict was replaced by a departure to Israel. The arrests continued in the following years, and in 1927 Eliezer Tripolsky, my son Yehudah and others were arrested. The Zionist activity among the youth continued all these years, and those who conducted it with great energy were: Sara Milerowitz, the Orlov sisters, my daughter Miriam and others. The children were very dedicated and despite the danger they recruited new members for the movement. Our apartment was one of the places in which meetings and lectures took place.

Dr. B. Chanis was very active during the famine years. He received money from abroad to help the needy and especially for the rehabilitation of the Jewish Hospital and the clinic on Charkovskaya Street. He also helped those who turned to him, but in the end, he was exiled. There was also a group of adults who gathered from time to time. Among them: Rozinov, Avraham Gutman, Kissin, Mostovlenski and others. The previous community rabbi, E. Burstein, who was sick and lame, occasionally visited our synagogue on Novosleniai Street. He encouraged us and strengthened our hands and our spirit. Several children studied the Torah in this synagogue and Mr. Zuker took care of their needs. We printed the movement's flyers in my apartment and in the apartments of Shlonsky, Rosovsky and Kostrinsky.

On the occasion of my illness I received a treatment at the clinic on Charkovskaya Street where Dr. Cohen-Berenstein worked. Later he moved to the hospital. My daughter, who came to visit me from Poland, brought him greetings from his daughter, the actress Miriam Cohen-Berenstein. When we came to visit him, I saw the place where he lived – a large room that was divided in two by a curtain, and a kitchen which was located in a dark corner near the entrance. He was already sick, and his wife left a good impressed on me. She was always busy taking care of her home. We had several talks about Israel etc., and he was very restrained. Sometime later I learned from Mr. Toporowsky that Cohen-Berenstein passed away. There weren't any notices in the city and only a few people knew about it.

Emissaries came from the center in spite all the dangers. One day I was informed that a meeting would take place in my apartment with the representative of the center. My apartment became the meeting place for the local Zionists after my husband moved to Moscow. We prepared places to sit from wood planks, brought potatoes, watermelons, pickles and tomatoes from the cellar. We peeled and cooked and had a pleasant and cheerful meeting. The emissary was Sioma Lioberski. Once, at the request of my son Yehudah, I gave Stagier permission to hide in my apartment for a month.

[Page 56]

In 1932 I left Ekaterinoslav with my husband and immigrated to Israel. We parted from Batya Berkowski, a devoted and faithful soul who risked her life for the movement. She sewed undergarments for the market to support her elderly parents. Everyone who came from the movement, found assistance and a place to sleep in the room that she lived with her parents. She corresponded with some of the deportees and sent them everything that they asked for. Before my journey she told me: I'm keeping a "minyan" here, meaning, that she had 10 friends who were loyal to the movement. She used to send two or three young men or women to Moscow, and others came to her from there to strengthen the movement. At the end, she was arrested and sent to Northern Siberia (today she's in Israel – after years of imprisonment and hardships).

We always lived in fear and tension. We were ready, loyal and dedicated to each other. Despite all this, it was a very interesting period and I mention it with longings.

[Page 56]

Defense in October 1905
by V. Dalman[1]
Translated by Sara Mages
The pogrom

The pogrom began in Ekaterinoslav a day or two after it started in other cities. We had no idea what was happening in other cities because of the postal strike. We still didn't have a normal service and letters and newspapers didn't arrive.

On Thursday, October 19, in the evening, the first sign was given that a pogrom is approaching. On the same evening, about 9 o'clock, we learned that a group of rioters concentrated at the entrance to the community center. The rioters, who participated earlier in a march down Prospect Street, fired several shots at those who walked out of the hall, and dispersed. Most of the assembled also left the place.

After I learned that, I joined the member Pinye and we arrived to the community center together. The discussions already ended there, and a registration of members from various organizations was carried out in several rooms on the ground floor. We were getting ready for self-defense.

Both of us received a specific role from our members, and we made our way to the defense's main assembly point on behalf of our organization.

About 150 members, who answered the call of the organization's committee, already gathered in an empty yard of one of the synagogues. The member Michael conducted a members' roll-call in a loud voice, distributed weapons and sent the groups to their locations.

I, together with Pinye, were given the duty to join our members in the organization's main residence, which was located on Kazaziya Street, and we went there immediately.

The running around to find apartments for our groups, telephones, ammunition, weapons and others lasted until the late hours of the evening. The members were divided into groups, weapons were distributed, and bombs have been prepared. We finally fell asleep and woke up on Friday morning with the feeling that there is no need to worry about a pogrom. Life went on as usual in the city... but it only seemed so...

At 11 o'clock, when I thought that it wasn't necessary to do anything more for the defense, I went to the apartment of the member Pilka. Our members already gathered there, and we talked about the pogrom. Around 1 o'clock, several members came and delivered the worrisome news: processions of rioters, under the direction of plain clothes policemen, are gathering in Chechlevka and Prospect streets near the municipality building and panic is apparent everywhere. I returned to the main residence where there was a lot of activity. Information came from the observation points, instructions and orders were given, and scouts came and left. In the meantime, one of our members came running with the news that a few minutes ago one of our scouts killed a rioter on Bazarnaya Street. We were horrified, it started – each one of us though – and something cold and terrible entered the heart.

Matters have evolved in a menacing way. A "patriotic" procession took place at the edge of the city, and it was clear, the pogrom will come. We tried to locate the place and concentrate our self- defense groups there. At 1 o'clock in the afternoon, one of our groups went up Sadovaya Street under the command of the member Motele.

[Page 57]

Several members of the defense joined it on the way. On the way up the group crossed the square diagonally. Suddenly, several rows of soldiers appeared near them and opened fire without a warning, at first in the air and then directly at them. The group withdrew running back, but the gates to the houses were closed under the order of the police. In these moments the members were in mortal danger and the only victim was the member Hershel Svirsky.

Motele's group dispersed, and after it called – open the gates! it gathered in a quiet street. There, a Jew opened his gate and happily let the group enter.

After a rest the group left for the street and chased gangs of rioters who filled it from all sides.

The pogrom strengthened. I was next to the telephone, together with the member Pinye, and each report that we got was more difficult than the last. It was necessary to act, give instructions, direct people and divide the weapons. There was great confusion in the street and we had no time to look at what was happening there. An unclear noise came from a distance, and the houses on both sides of the road were robbed and destroyed. However, we weren't able to pay attention to it because we held in our hands all the strings that linked our 18 defense groups, and under the bed was the most terrible weapon of the revolutionary (bombs)...

Suddenly, we heard shots right next to us, voices and noise from people – about a hundred – under our windows. A group of rioters came running from behind the corner of the house opposite us. On their way, they roared like lions, stumbled, fell, and dropped the items that they robbed. Shots were heard behind it, about eight members of our defense stood at the street corner and fired incessantly. A few minutes later the crowd dispersed, and the fighting group concentrated in the middle of the street.

I would never forget this picture! Several dozen strong young men stood around the commander of the fighting group, who explained the next action plan, and disappeared a few minutes later. Now we heard the trampling of measured steps – soldiers walked in straight lines on the sidewalks on both sides of the road and aimed their guns at the windows of the houses facing them. They were afraid of the bombs that might be thrown from the windows and were ready to shoot at anyone who appeared in the window.

I'll not continue to give a detailed description of all the events of the pogrom, all the performances of "madness and horror," but I will write about all the acts of heroism and nobility...

In the mist of the night

I'll tell about one of the most notable incidents of our war that all our members mention with pride. It happened on Sabbath eve. At 10 o'clock we were informed from all the locations that the pogrom is easing. On this day – the first day of the pogrom – the defense performed well, and we managed to stop the riots in many locations in the city. We were satisfied despite the large number of victims. The groups were getting ready to rest and only the guards, who walked the streets and stopped passers-by, were on duty. We thought, together with Pinye, to rest. Suddenly, terrible news came to us from one of the points in the city's port. At 7 o'clock in the evening, a ship arrived in the port with many Jews who escaped from different locations up the Dnieper River for fear of the pogrom. A great number of rioters were waiting at the port to rob them.

Victims of the 1905 Pogrom

[Page 58]

The passengers pleaded with the sailors to turn the ship back, but their request was denied. The rioters broke into the ship when it reached the dock and began acts of terror. Dozens were wounded and thrown into the water. Later, about ten bodies were pulled out of the river. The next ship was supposed to arrive at 7.30 in the morning, and we had to take all the necessary measures to prevent another disaster. We immediately informed the fighting group and suggested that it should use extreme measures at a certain hour of the morning. In addition, we began negotiations with the director of the shipping company and asked him to send a boat towards the ship in the morning to warn about the danger. And here, at that moment, we heard the loud ringing of the telephone. It was from Ulyanovskaya Street at the edge of the city, from the home of a Jewish merchant. We were informed that loud voices were being heard next to the house, at the corner of Hersonskaya and Skakovaya streets. Jews are probably being attacked there and they need our help. We called the commander of the fighting group, which included 32 members, and after a discussion he returned to his group. An hour later he came to us and his eyes were burning, he fulfilled the task, the rioters paid with their blood... However, the Jewish merchant continued to call, and according to his words – the riots didn't stop after the attack of our group. Indeed, it was quiet for a while, but the noise increased, and the rioters were getting closer to Ulyanovskaya Street. It was necessary to take more vigorous measures.

We decided to concentrate four groups in two locations and to encircle Ulyanovskaya Street on both sides. Participated in the concentration: the fighting group under the command of Arkadi and Pitynzki, two regular groups from our organization which were under the command of Peretz and Pilka, and a mixed group that included our members and the people of the "Bund." These groups had to concentrate at the corner of Voskresenskaya and Bazarnaya streets, and leave, in two detachments, for their mission on Ulyanovskaya Street.

Only three groups arrived at the meeting place. The fourth, Pilka's group, didn't arrive. At the same time the soldiers, who were standing in Bazarnaya Street, opened fire at our members who didn't see them through the fog. Our members left after several attempts to evade the shots and concentrated in two private apartments. Out of a misunderstanding, Pilka's group came to the corner of Praozanovskaya and Bazarnaya streets not to the corner of Voskresenskaya and Bazarnaya streets and didn't notice the situation because of the fog. The group marched to Ulyanovskaya Street through the corresponding Starogorodnaya Street.

Victims of the 1905 Pogrom in Ekaterinoslav

On the way this group met the neighborhood watch which was composed of local people. After it added these guardsmen, who were armed with handguns, to its ranks, it went directly to Ulyanovskaya Street, from which came the sound of breaking furniture and smashing windows. The group went up the street and from there opened fire at the rioters. The rioters, who fled immediately, left about ten dead in the street. The group came running to the house of the Jewish merchant, and from there we've received the encouraging news from Pilka that the help arrived on time... A day later, on Saturday night, the rioters took revenge and burned the house of this Jewish merchant. They found the appropriate time to remunerate the victims who fell from their side...

At the hospital after the pogrom

On Saturday night the authorities disconnected the telephone. We were told by the switchboard that the telephone was out-of-order... It was clear, that the "out-of-order" telephones were those that we used to contact the defense's main residence. Later, we learned that it was done under the order of Neidhart, the district governor, to interfere with our activities. The order was given on Sunday, the day he intended to end the pogrom.

Thus, the defense, as a body that all of its parts were in constant contact, wasn't able to continue with its activities. The city turned into a military camp, soldiers and Cossacks swarmed in all directions and didn't let our groups to contact each other. Houses and apartments, which belonged to Jews, stood out in the general background. It was enough to look at the doors and windows: if white crosses weren't painted on the doors, icons with "perpetual light" weren't seen in the windows and the curtains were drawn – it was a sign that human beings, who held their breath and were abandoned to the mob, were hiding behind them ...

Now, the defense operated in a disorganized way and temporarily. The main residence, where I was, was closed because it was no longer needed. We were followed and our members, the scouts, told us that we had to leave the apartment and change the telephone number. Therefore, we left the apartment broken and exhausted, and moved to another building across the street, to the apartment of a simple Jewish family.

Our members came to visit us in the morning. They told us that the pogrom ended and notices, in which the district governor announced the end of the riots and asked the defense to hand over its weapons, were pasted in all locations.

I decided to go to the hospital because I heard that they needed help.

At about 2 o'clock in the afternoon I was called to go out to the corridor. Two well-dressed men, whose faces were red with excitement, stood there.

– Are you Mr. D.?

– Yes, that's me.

– Can you speak on behalf of the defense organization?

– No, I can't.

– In God's name! This isn't the appropriate time for conspiracy!

– I'm associated with our organization's defense committee, but it isn't active right now.

– The district governor demands that the defense will give its weapons and stop shooting in the streets. Only under this condition the procession, which is marching from the Sobor[2], wouldn't end in a new pogrom.

– I doubt that there would be a new pogrom. It's entirely up to the district governor, not us. So, what do you want from me?

– We're going to the district governor and you have to promise us that the defense will hand over its weapons.

– I can't give you such a promise. But, in order that the public wouldn't blame us later, I can assure you on behalf of our organization, and it's the most powerful organization of the defense, that we'll only

take action when a new pogrom will break out.

– How can we ensure the district governor that your promise will be fulfilled?

In my name, tell the governor that I'm so-and-so, I'm located in an unknown place, and if my promise wouldn't be fulfilled – he can arrest me.

Shortly thereafter, the steps of about ten people sounded from the stairs below. About 15 middle-aged Jews, laborers and small merchants, were brought wounded in makeshift stretchers.

Doctors and nurses rushed from all directions.

The pogrom started! It started again! Sounded from all directions.

It was the attack on the Schneider's house, the well-known attack in Ekaterinoslav's pogrom. Eighteen bodies were found there, the doors and the pavement were covered with blood. The inexplicable cruelty was "explained" in this manner – the police thought that the Schneider's house was the Revolutionaries' nest.

According to the official information, 126 Jews were killed in Ekaterinoslav's pogrom by the rioters and the soldiers' shooting, and 47 rioters were killed. According to our information – 63 rioters were killed.

Footnotes

From an article published in 1907 in Kovetz (Cepn), Moscow. It was written by Vladimir Fabrikant, an activist in the "Jewish Socialist Workers Party." Translated from Russian by Y.G,

Sobor   –   the   main   Orthodox   Church   in   the   city.

[Page 60]

Zionism in Ekaterinoslav

by Y. Ben Menachem

Translated by Yocheved Klausner

A. From the First Congress

M. Ussishkin, the head of the Ekaterinoslav Hovevei Zion movement, who was invited in 1897 by Dr. Th. Herzl personally to the first Congress in Basel, was the first to bring the idea of political Zionism to the Ekaterinoslav Zionists. Ussishkin, who accepted in Basel the new Zionist idea, convinced his friends to acknowledge it as well, and since then the Zionist movement in Ekaterinoslav began working in the new direction.

The first activity was propaganda and recruiting new members to the movement. Ussishkin and his friends invested in this activity a great deal of work and effort. Meetings were called in private homes; many members and sympathizers were invited, and the members of the movement explained to the guests the principles of political Zionism. Sometimes, with the permission of the authorities, public meetings were held in order to bring the information to the general public as well.[1] The main speaker at these meetings was in most cases M. Ussishkin. Such meetings were held mostly before the Zionist Congresses, sometimes after them, and the returning delegates reported about the debates and decisions of the Congress.[2] At the public meeting that took place on 15 November 1801, before the 5th Congress, several decisions were taken, and the delegates were asked to propose them to the Congress. The delegates that were elected were M. Ussishkin and Baruch Toporovski.[3]

In order to expand the Zionist activity in Ekaternoslav and surroundings, Ussishkin called a Zionist meeting of representatives from the Ekaterinoslav and Tavrida Districts. The meeting took place in July 1900 with 55 delegates. Several decisions were taken, their purpose being to strengthen the organizations in the various localities.[4]

Regularly and methodically, the Zionists were also active in the sale of the Zionist Shekel and, according to information, before the 5th Congress 2,000 Shekels were sold, and the money was transferred to Kiev. About 4,000 propaganda brochures, in Russian, Hebrew and Yiddish were sold, 2,000 Rubles were collected for the Worker's Fund in Eretz Israel and 773 shares of the Colonial Bank were sold as well.[5]

When the Keren Kayemet (JNF) was founded, the Ekaterinoslav Zionists began to collect donations. The town was divided into 60 regions and young boys and girls visited the homes, sold JNF stamps, collected donations and sold Zionist literature; 1,100 Rubles were collected.[6]

The activity begun by Hovevei Zion, which included Hebrew language study and promotion of Zionist education, as well as the activity of the small Hebrew library, did not stop. Mr. Ussishkin invited the famous teacher Ch. A. Zuta to open the first Cheder Metukan [improved Cheder] in Ekaterinoslav. It was founded in 1899 and the local Zionists were responsible for its maintenance and regular activity.[7] On Lag Ba'omer, festivities for the pupils of the Talmud Tora and the private Jewish schools were organized in the municipal park, including a parade in town. On Chanuka and Purim, the Zionists organized parties, which left a strong impression on the children and parents.[8] Literary banquets for the general public were organized as well, in order to strengthen the national feelings among the people, at a time when the tendency to assimilation increased more and more. The Rabbi of the town, Dr. S. Levin took part in the organization of all these activities, mainly by obtaining the required permissions from the authorities.

Dr. Herzl's call to "mobilize" the communities echoed in the hearts of the Ekaterinoslav Zionists, headed by Ussishkin. Since it was time to elect a new rabbi (the rabbi was elected once every three years) it was decided to recommend Dr. S. Levin, who was known as a Zionist and a very talented speaker. After a quite stormy campaign, he was elected and served 6 years (1898–1904). Indeed, Dr. S. Levin has not disappointed his people: the community received a rabbi who made it proud, and the Zionists – a powerful helper who reinforced the national and Zionist ideas.

The Ekaterinoslav Zionists sent delegates to all Zionist Congresses; Ussishkin was elected to every congress. Sometimes stormy meetings, where various suggestions were presented, preceded the election of the delegates. For example, Tze'irei Zion once suggested holding the elections according to lists, but their proposal was rejected.[9] The following delegates from Ekaterinoslav were elected to the Minsk Congress: M. Ussishkin, Dr. S. Levin, Eng. M. Bruk, Shimon Stanislavski, Shapira, Orlov.

[Page 61]

In general, the Zionist activity in the Ekaterinoslav District was led, very energetically, by M. Ussishkin. The town was one of the most organized in Russia and its achievements – by the conditions of that time – were impressive. In addition of the Hovevei Zion people, a group of active members gathered around Ussishkin: Mechl Maidanski, Chaim Levanda, Avraham

Harkavi, Shimon Stanislavski, Baruch Spivak, his brother–in–law Moshe Bruk, Dr. Yakov Dolzhenski, Yakov Vitalin, Yakov Berezovski, Baruch Toporovski, Shapira, Dubin, Orlov and others.

Thanks to them, the influence of the Zionists on the community increased and they improved the national education of the children in the community. We could observe the result during the election of the "appointed rabbi," when the Zionists, after a relatively easy campaign, received many more votes and Rabbi Menachem–Emanuel Brustein was elected after Dr. S. Levin left his post. Rabbi Brustein, a loyal and devoted Zionist, joined the active Zionist group and participated in its work.

The Ekaterinoslav Zionists fought assimilation – which was strong in Southern Russia – in addition to the regular work of spreading their ideas and acquiring new members, especially from among the young students. For this purpose, they organized public appearances, distributed national and Zionist literature and arranged meetings and lectures. They demanded from the Jewish and private school principals to introduce national subjects in the curriculum – and they often succeeded. They also continued to collect donations for the settlement in Eretz Israel and sent the money to the Odessa Committee.

After the Russia–Japan war, as the freedom movement in Russia prevailed, the Ekaterinoslav Zionists took an active part in consolidating the national strength. They demanded that the community, in the name of the Jews of the town, address the Central Government asking to remove all limitations and restrictions imposed on the Jews. M. Ussishkin and Dr. Bergin[10] (teacher of religion in high–school) spoke on this matter at many assemblies and meetings.

At the elections to the first Duma (Russian Parliament), the Zionists succeeded in their efforts to establish a national list and a Jewish representative was elected. In spite of the opposition of the leftist, assimilated circles, Att. M. Sheftel from Petersburg was elected delegate to the first Duma.[11]

B. Between Two Revolutions (1905–1917)

After the 1905 pogroms, the Jews experienced difficult times. The period after the abortive uprising in that year was difficult for the Russian public and more so for the Jews. In particular in the Zionist circles, despair, lack of confidence and disappointment was felt – at the public meetings as well as in the life of every individual. In addition, the Jews suffered from the anti–Semitic attitude of the authorities and the vandalism of the hooligans, who were free in the streets. In 1906 Ussishkin moved to Odessa, which was an additional factor in the decline of the Zionist activity in town.[12]

However, the Ekaterinoslav Zionists recovered, albeit slowly. They were headed by Ussishkin's brother–in–law Eng. Moshe Bruk, who managed to assemble a group of hard–working people from among the veterans, as well as mew members who had joined the Zionist movement. The organizational activity was renewed, so was the collection of money, distribution of Zionist and national literature and subscription to the Zionist weekly Рассвет [The Dawn], which appeared in Petersburg in the Russian language. The activity of the Hovevei Sfat Ever [lovers of the Hebrew Language] was renewed, as well as the active participation in the elections to the Zionist Congresses. The authorities were not consistent in their attitude toward the Jewish community – sometimes they issued permission for a Zionist meeting, sometimes not. Public Zionist meetings were organized anyway, the lecturers coming from other places, as Dr. B. Z. Mossenson, Dr. Daniel Passemnik, Zev Jabotinski, Dr. Yehoshua Buchmill, Chaim Grinberg and others. These lectures attracted a large public and left a strong impression. At times, public banquets, in the national spirit were organized very successfully.[13] A report that was read on Chol Hamoed Pesach [intermediate days of Passover] 1910 at one of the public meetings stated that from September 1908 to April 1910 the sum of 514 Rubles was collected by selling the "Zionist Shekel," 720 Rubles for the JNF [Keren Kayemet], and shares of the Agricultural Bank were sold as well.[14] The Hovevei Sfat Ever organization continued to organize courses of Hebrew language and lectures on various subjects. Among the lecturers were: M. Shlonski, M. Freiman, Z. Rabinowitz and others. Rabbi P. Gellman joined as well, when he settled in Ekaterinoslav.

[Page 62]

Much attention was given to the school children. The assimilation movement in the schools was strong, and the Zionist activity in this area bore fruit. In 1908, a circle of Zionist students, by the name of Nechdei Zion [grandchildren of Zion] was established in Jonah Wechsler's Jewish private school, headed by the principal's son Daniel Wechsler. This group included the elite of the Jewish youth in Ekaterinoslav and some of its members became Zionist leaders. The Tze'irei Zion movement had many sympathizers among the local young intelligentsia and students; its representative Daniel Wechsler was elected delegate to the first Tze'irei Zion Congress in 1912 in Lodz. The movement developed quickly during the next few years, so did its influence in Ekaterinoslav. Among its active members were: Olonetzki, Israel

Idelson (later I. Ben–Yehuda, minister in the Israeli government), Beba Idelson (in Eretz Israel), Mordechai Bekesht, Arie Gafenowitz (later Dr. Arie Ben–Gefen, in Eretz Israel), Efraim Mitlin, Eliezer Levin (Eretz Israel), M. Wolfovski (Eretz Israel), and others – most of them acting in partial–underground conditions. They fought assimilation and even conversion to Christianity, which spread at the time among young Jewish students, who were not allowed to register at the universities. In 1913, a public letter written by high–school students was published in the Russian Press, in which they express their strong protest against their friends who converted in order to be allowed to enter the Russian universities.[15]

In time, other active members joined the movement: Avrahan Berezovski, Zev Vloderski, who served also as the secretary of the District Committee, Shlomo Braslavski, Theodore Vidrin, Israel Motzkin, Mendel Pevzner, Sergei Faley, the "appointed (by the authorities) rabbi" Emanuel Menachem Burstein and others. Dr. Yakov Dolzenski was the chairman of the Local Committee.

During World War I, the Zionist activity intensified, in spite of the war conditions. The town, which was far from the battle–fields, attracted many of the Jews who lived close to the front line, as well as refugees, who escaped from the dangerous places or were evicted by the authorities. Among them were many Zionists, who joined the Ekaterinoslav Zionists and worked together. They found ways to overcome the limitations imposed by the authorities: they organized public lectures, held meetings and discussions in private homes, collected money for Zionist activity etc. We shall mention the Pinsk group with Mr. I. Bergman, the teachers of Cohen's high–school, Dr. I. L. Baruch, Chaia Weitzman–Lichtenstein, Pinchas Shiffman (later Ben Sira) and others. The number of the Tze'irei Zion members increased, and its activity extended. The local Zionists participated in providing aid for the refugees and had arguments with the "Yiddishists" concerning the language of instruction in the schools for the refugees' children.[16] They also participated in the discussions about the current questions on the Zionist agenda – activism, the Hebrew Regiment etc. A considerable Zionist power emerged within the Ekaterinoslav Jewish community.

C. The February 1917 Revolution

With the revolution of February 1917, all limitations of political activity were removed and political and personal freedom, which was absent until then in Russia, was established. For the first time, after years of working underground and partial underground, it was possible to appear in public and present the idea of Zionism, as well as to respond and react to the many adversaries in the Jewish Street itself.

The first step of the local Zionists was to call a public assembly and present the Zionist program, with the understanding that the Russian revolution cannot provide a solution to the Jewish problem, and only Zionism can and will do it. The assembly was to take place on 6 March, but the number of people who came was so great that the hall was too small to accommodate them, and it was decided to hold the meeting at another date in a larger hall. The people who came congratulated the group of Zionists that had been arrested on 26 February for collecting money for Eretz Israel and were released with the advent of the revolution. The second assembly took place on 26 March, in one of the largest halls in town. Some 3,000 people attended. The assembly was a great success and many registered as members of the Zionist movement.[17]

During the Holiday, Zionist speakers visited the synagogues. On 5 April, Dr. A. Goldstein spoke on the subject "Zionism in our time." The next day, a public discussion about Zionism was organized, with the participation of Dr. Goldstein and representatives of other parties, as the "Bund," the Socialist Zionists and others.[18] The strength of the Zionists and their influence on the Ekaterinoslav Jews increased, and the fear that the tendency to assimilate would grow due to the revolution proved to be false.

[Page 63]

One of the characteristics of the times was the great number of public assemblies, called by the various political parties, in order to advance their own ideas and recruit new members, at the same time fighting the ideas of their opponents. Yet it was the custom to give the right to speak to a member of the rival party as well. The Zionists followed the same procedure and organized meetings in various parts of the town. The lectures were in Russian and Yiddish and the lecturer was often asked to participate in a rival assembly as well and conduct a debate with members of the rival party. This system demanded talented speakers, able to defend their ideas against the arguments of the opponents. It was not easy – however we should mention that talented people were indeed found and sent to the various assemblies to defend their cause.

The Tze'irei Zion movement expanded considerably. It organized courses for the studying youth and the working youth, as well as for the Jewish intelligentsia and, under the leadership of Israel Idelson it acquired a considerable status and influence in the Jewish Street. On 8–11 June 1917, a meeting of the representatives of the districts of Ekaterinoslav, Kharson,

Poltava and Tavrida was organized, and decisions were taken concerning work in various places, elections to the communities, the municipalities and the Jewish All–Russian Congress, organization of Jewish co–operatives and collection of money for JNF and the Hechalutz.[19] Among the active members we shall mention: B. Idelson (now in Israel), Israel Ritov (now in Israel), Efraim Mitlin, Dr. Shlomo Levin, Moshe Yakobson, Yeshayahu Pevzner (now in Israel), Freidin, Olonetzki, Khitrik, Wachsner, Chodorovski, Mordechai Bakshet, A. Gottlieb and others.

The studying youth organized as well: among the active high–school students we shall mention A. Pevzner z"l, Epstein z"l and I. Polonski (now in Israel). Part of the high–school students were members of Tze'irei Zion, others were organized in the Hechaver group, headed by Dr. Chaim Kugel z"l, later the principal of the Munkacz high–school and in Israel the mayor of Holon.

The Ekaterinoslav Zionists did not have (before the revolution) regular offices. The office of the District Committee, for example, was located in the apartment of the secretary Zev Voldoderski. Now, with the new conditions, large and organized offices became a vital necessity. A solution to the problem was soon found: a group of Zionists, who bought a large building on the main street with the intention to open a bank, gave the building to the Ekaterinoslav Zionists and they transferred all their offices.

It was a three-floor building, which included the offices of the municipal and the district committees, as well as the offices and the club of the Tze'irei Zion movement. Courses in the Hebrew language, geography of Eretz Israel etc. were also given there. The building was alive all day, with students, members and visitors from out of town.

As was the custom in those days, the Zionists sent their representatives to various organizations, and often it was necessary to discuss general political problems and give the delegates proper instructions. On this background disputes and clashes between the General Zionists and Tze'irei Zion sometimes occurred.

A meeting of representatives from the Ekaterinoslav and Tavrida districts was set for 4–6 April 1917. 66 delegates from 45 places participated. The subjects they discussed were elections to the community, the Jewish national school, the national demands, organization and financial means. The decisions taken at that meeting became guides for the future.[20]

Copy of a "Zionist Shekel" 1917

The District Committee published a journal in the Russian language:

Известня Екатеринославского Районного Сионистокого Комитета

[News of the Ekaterinoslav Zionist District Committee], as well as the Еврейский Путь. These journals provided information about the Zionist activity. Several propaganda brochures appeared as well, as "Building the Community" and "The Balfour Declaration" by Pinchas Schiffman in Hebrew and Yiddish, "The Basel Program" by Toporovski, "The BILU movement" by Shalit in Yiddish, "Marksism" by A. Idelson in Yidish. Tze'irei Zion published a bi-weekly on Zionist thought, Folks Wort.[21]

[Page 64]

All this varied work – spreading the Zionist idea among the Ekaterinoslav Jews, fighting the opponent left parties, public appearances, activity for the benefit of the Hebrew language, elections to various institutions as the municipal council or the community council – required hard work of a wide circle of members, and indeed, their number increased. Financial means were also necessary, naturally, for the maintenance of the offices and for organizing the elections. The members' fees were not enough, and only the donations by well–to–do members enabled smooth work. We should mention the great help of S. Braslavski at maintaining the Po'alei Zion institutions.

In May 1917, a large delegation of Ekaterinoslav Zionists participated in the seventh All–Russian Zionist Congress, among them: M. Bruk, A. Berezovski, S. Braslavski, Z. Wlodarski, Ch. Lichtenstein–Weitzman and others. A representative of Tze'irei Zion participated as well.

At the elections to the Ekaterinoslav municipality, the Zionists established a "Jewish front" whose purpose was to keep and defend the interests of the Jewish public in town. Their effort, however, did not bear fruit, since the Jewish leftist parties worked together with the socialist parties, except Po'alei Zion. The result of that situation was that out of the 19 Jews elected to the Municipal Council the Jewish group of the Zionists, Tze'irei Zion and religious members had only 9 representatives.[22]

At the next elections, to the Russian General Assembly, the Zionists tried to present a Jewish list, with the hope to elect a delegate from Ekaterinoslav. The candidates were: Moshe Bruk, Alexander Goldstein (member of the Zionist central office), David Smorgoner (a local activist, member of the "Volkspartei" [people's party] and Eliezer Kaplan from Tze'irei Zion. In spite of the efforts, none of the candidates of that list was elected.[23]

D. Going Underground

The spring and summer months of 1917 marked a peak in the Zionist work in Ekaterinoslav. The great efforts invested in the previous years and during the months of the revolution finally bore fruit: the Zionist movement ruled the Jewish Street and the Jewish public in town accepted its ideas.

However, this period soon ended. The October 1917 revolution brought new fears, in particular as the anti–Semitic Ukrainian movement expanded. Yet, on 5 December a Zionist congress was organized and 25 delegates from 15 localities in the Ekaterinoslav District participated. The meeting authorized a list of Zionist candidates for the elections to the Ukrainian Rada [parliament]: M. Bruk, I. Bonfeld, M. Duchan, I. Tribus, I. Fischer and A. Kaplan.[24]

In November, after receiving the news about the Balfour Declaration, The Zionists organized a demonstration through the streets and held several public meetings, where they explained the importance of the declaration. A brochure on the subject was issued as well.

On 8 February 1918 elections to the community council, including Tze'irei Zion, were held and Mr. M. Bruk was elected president of the Community.

During the first few months of 1918 there were frequent changes of government – Bolsheviks, Ukrainian etc. – and the government stabilized only by the end of April 1918, when the Austrian army entered the town and the Hatman Skoropedski took power. The spring and the summer were relatively quiet, and life went on. The Austrian rule was more or less liberal, and a certain amount of public activity was permitted, by the Austrians as well as by the Ukrainians.

After a short pause, the Zionists resumed their activity. They organized again lectures and evening courses of the Hebrew language; the Tze'irei Zion club also resumed its activity and money was collected. The connection with the central offices in Petrograd was cut off, due to the civil war that broke out in Russia, but the connection with the office in Kiev was maintained. From these offices they received instructions and news about the happenings in the Zionist world, and there they sent the money collected. After the army entered Odessa and a rumor about the possibility to go to Eretz Israel spread around, a special section of the office was established, where people could register for Aliya. Several hundred people registered – craftsmen, laborers, merchants, and others.

The Ekaterinoslav Zionists achieved a great victory at the elections to the National Assembly of the Ukrainian Jews. The delegation included: I Idelson, Dr. I. L. Baruch, M. Bruk, S. Braslavski, Z. Vloderski and P. Schiffman. M. Bruk was elected chairman of the assembly.

These were the last months of systematic Zionist activity in Ekaterinoslav. During the winter of that year, the town passed several times from hand to hand, and life became harder and harder, which prevented regular work. In the summer of 1919, at the time of Denikin's rule and the rough conditions in town, the Zionist activity was very sporadic.

[Page 65]

At the end of 1919, the town came under Soviet rule, which restricted all political activity, and indeed the Zionist had to stop their work, especially as the Jewish communists were the supervisors. At the beginning of that period it was still possible to hold meetings from time to time, and Hebrew lessons were given in half–underground conditions, but not in a regular fashion. The first arrests of local Zionists also occurred at that time. They were soon released, but the general situation deteriorated. Many Zionists began leaving town for fear of persecutions – some of them made Aliya, some relocated to other places. Very few remained, and these participated in organizing help for the hungry in the years of hunger, as well as material and moral aid to those who continued, in spite of the grave situation, a restricted Zionist activity, as holding Hebrew lessons in private homes and synagogues. Among them we should mention the former "appointed rabbi" Emanuel Brustein and Israel Motzkin, brother of the chairman of the Zionist executive committee Leon Motzkin.[25] But some of the former activists distanced themselves entirely from any Zionist activity, for fear of the watching eye of the authorities. Some of them were arrested.

During the NEP [New Economic Policy] period, when it seemed that a change occurred in the regime and relative freedom was reinstated, the Zionists renewed their activity and the Zionist movements (Tze'irei Zion, Hano'ar Hatzioni) could extend somewhat their work. They acquired new members, distributed Zionist literature and periodicals as well as news about Eretz Israel (received from the Centers in Kiev and Kharkov), organized Hebrew evening courses etc. Many young people joined the Zionists, as they realized that even now, in the Soviet State, the communist doctrine did not find a solution to the Jewish problem. The activity required good speakers, knowledgeable in the communist teachings as well as in Zionism. Such people were indeed found, and they worked with the Jewish intelligentsia, craftsmen and laborers. The meetings were held in private homes – the owner of the home at risk in case the police discovered that a meeting was taking place. In spite of that, many offered their homes and the discussions about the Jewish Question and the Zionist program continued. The synagogues also served as meeting places, and Zionist newsletters and announcements were distributed. The authorities, especially the "Yevsektzia" did not approve of these public gatherings, and arrests soon followed.

In 1922, at the time of the great hunger, the Zionist movements mobilized their members and with great devotion participated in the aid activities and filled important and responsible positions in the institutions established for that purpose.

The C.S. movement, after accepting in 1920 the new program in Kharkov and after its split, continued the activity among the Ekaterinoslav Jews and even expanded it. It recruited new members, distributed literature and established a youth organization "Young C.S." Sometimes its members appeared in public assemblies against the communists. For some time a club was active, but soon the authorities closed it, and also began a series of restrictions and arrests. After Israel Idelson, Beba Idelson, Israel Ritov and Eliezer Levin left Ekaterinoslav, work was continued by P. Epstein, M.

Bakshet, A. Gottlieb, Moshe Gordon, Danowitz, Katz, Yitzhak Levin, Fima Michailovski, Koritzki, Kirzner, Kruk, Rieger and others.

After the split with C.S., Tze'irei Zion continued to recruit members, and in their activity stressed Hebrew language and culture, as the conditions allowed. They established a Members Club, which was visited by sympathizers as well and turned into a Jewish national spot in Ekaterinoslav.[26] Among the active members we shall mention Moshe Olshanski (now in Israel), Moshe Rissin z"l, Mordechai Guber (now in Israel), Azriel Zelivenski z"l, Shlomo Teslitzki (now in Israel), Zalman Yupit z"l, Chanaya Reichman (now in Israel), (in 1923 members of the Committee) and others. We should add that in those years the Hechalutz movement in Ekaterinoslav was founded and several of his members made Aliya to Eretz Israel.

[Page 66]

The Jewish national Zionist youth movements in Ekaterinoslav (the Organization of the Jewish Zionist youth, Hashomer Hale'umi, Hashomer Hama'amadi, Hatechiya,[27] Hamaccabi) wrote a brilliant chapter, full of self–sacrifice as well as loyalty and devotion to the Zionist cause. Some paid with exile and long arrests and some paid with their lives. They had to overcome huge external obstacles (the authorities, as was well–known, restricted all political–education activity) as well as internal obstacles (not all parents allowed their children to be members of an illegal movement; yet, many parents indeed helped the movements in their activity). The main obstacle, however, was the influence of communism in the Jewish Street, especially among the youth.

Young men and women around the age of twenty were those who bore the main activity on their shoulders. They organized the groups, visited the parents, found locales for the meetings, brought Zionist literature from other cities, acquired the necessary means etc. etc. If one of them was arrested, another took his place, rebuilt the contacts and continued the activity. Some of it was similar to the Scouts activity – trips, and the like – often masked by a parade in town or surroundings. These activities included several thousand of the Jewish children in Ekaterinoslav and left their mark on them.[28]

This period, however, was not long. The authorities began persecuting the members of the various groups and restricted their freedom. The arrest sentences, which at first were light, became more and more severe – many years in prison, exile to distant places etc. They began closing the few clubs that had remained, stopped the activity of the Maccabi (begun in 1917) and terminated the Hebrew evening courses.

The wave of arrests in Russia, including Ukraine, on 2 September 1924 included the Ekaterinoslav Jews and many were arrested. After that, arrests occurred often, and the Zionist groups lost many members. Some Zionists were sentenced to long terms in prison, some were exiled to distant places in Asian Russia (the first Zionist victim was Yakov Mosseyev, who was exiled and died in exile.[29] Others followed, and only few of them were later permitted to make Aliya. After the prison term ended, some returned to their town, some relocated to other places, some remained in Asia, some died during imprisonment.

In spite of all that, when a leader was arrested, another came and tried to restore the activity of the movement. It was not easy; yet the struggle between the authorities and the Zionist movements continued several years; finally, after a great deal of suffering and many victims, the authorities won. The arrests in Ukraine left the movements without leaders, the fear prevented sympathizers to join and help, and the Zionist activity dwindled. By the end of the twenties, only few people remained who were interested in Zionism and news about Eretz Israel or were concerned in helping the imprisoned and exiled.

Undoubtedly, the Zionist activity in Ekaterinoslav during the Twenties was very important: it saved many young people from communism and educated them in our national spirit.

Until World War I, few Ekaterinoslav residents made Aliya; during the Soviet regime, few managed to leave. Some families, citizens of other countries, left during the hunger years; some left legally, as their prison or exile sentence was replaced by an Aliya permit. All these constitute now the "Ekaterinoslav colony" in our country. In general, they took roots here and occupy important positions in the life of the State and in the public life in general.

[Page 67]

Tze'irei Zion in Ekaterinoslav in 1923

From right to left: **Moshe Olshanski, Azriel Zalivenski, Zalman Yupit, Chananya Reichman, Moshe Rissin, Shlomo Taslitzki**

Active members of C.S. in Ekaterinoslav in 1920

1.Kuritzki, 4.Mrs. Kruk, 6.Moshe Michailovski, 8.Rigay, 10.Eliezer Levin, 11.Rivka Idelson, 12.Israel Idelson, 13.Beba Idelson, 15.Chodorovski, 16.Pesach Epstein, 17.Mordechai Bakshet, 18.Arnold Gottlieb, 20.Katz (a man), 25. Danowitz, 27.M. Kirzner

Footnotes

1 Восход 1900 Но. 19

2 Недельная Хроника Восхода 1898 Но. 20

3 Восход 1901 Но. 73

4 Будущность 1900 Но. 79

5 Восход 1901

6 *Hamelitz* 5662 (1902) No. 181.

7 Ch. A. Zuta: The Road of a Teacher.

8 *Hamelitz* 5663 (1903) No. 73.

9 *Hamelitz* 5663 (1903) No.181.

10 Хроника Еврейской Жизни 1905 Но. 100

11 Восход 1905 Но. 40

12 Еврейская Мысль 1907 Но.6

13 Рассвет 1908 Но.17 1910 Но.8

14 *Ha'olam* 1910 No. 24.

15 Рассвет 1913 Но.31

16 Еврейская Жизнь 1916 Но 20

17 Еврейская Жизнь 1917 Но 12–13

18 Еврейская Жизнь 1917 Но 14–15

19 Рассвет 1917 Но.4–5

20 Еврейская Жизнь 1917 Но. 14–15

21 Jewish Publications in the Soviet Union.

22 Рассвет 1917 Но.8

23 Рассвет 1917 Но. 17–18

24 Рассвет 1918 Но.2

25 H. R. Birman, From my memories in this book.

26 C. I. Kostrinski, Moshe Rossin z"l, in this book.

27 A. Becker, The revival in Ekaterinoslav, in this book.

28 A Millstein, The Beginning of the Road, in this book.

29 C. I. Kostrinski, Yakov Mosseyev z'l, in this book.

[Pages 68-69]

The Community in Ekaterinoslav
By Dr. Yakov Kostrinski
Translated by Sara Mages

A Russian Jew, who before and after the changes of the revolution was out of the Jewish public life there, was struck by the sight of the drastic changes in the structure of the Jewish society when he returned to the Ukraine during the Ataman period.

After my release from the Russian Army in which I served as a "First–class volunteer" in the Czar's Army, an officer during the Kerensky period, and later, after the October Revolution, as a secretary in the Department of Organization of the Red Army in the city of Mtsensk in Oryol Oblast, I arrived, by roundabout roads (there wasn't a real border between Russia and Ukraine), to my family in Ekaterinoslav. How immense was the difference between the Jewish public life in both places!

In the Soviet regime in Russia, outside the framework of the ruling Communist Party, there was no social and political organization of any kind, and in the Jewish street the traitorous Yevsektsii[1] set the Jewish character across Russia. In contrast, I found in Ekaterinoslav a lively and vibrant Jewish community in the form of parties, newspapers, meetings, lectures and various conferences. The Jewish community served as the center of the vibrant communal life, sort of a Jewish parliament on a small scale.

All the political parties of that time participated in the community – first and foremost "HaTzionim HaKlaliym" [General Zionists], after them "Tzeirei Zion", "Folkists"[2] (the people of the "Folkspartei" along the lines of the "Voskhod" in Petrograd), the "Bundistn" and more. They were represented by the balance of power of the Jewish community in Ekaterinoslav. The community building was in Zelaznaya Street, in a low building, not big and very modest. However, it was always full to capacity during the hours of the day and in especially in the evenings. During office hours – people who needed help from the various departments of the community. In the evenings – representatives of the parties and just Jews, who came to the community building to discuss various matters and the debates, because of the difference of opinions between them, were quite turbulent...

The community management was composed of the Community Council which was elected in a proportional election on February 1918. As stated, it was represented by delegates of the main Jewish political parties, mainly the

Zionist parties, and by an Executive Committee which represented the management. The president of the community was the engineer Moshe Brok, brother–in–law of Moshe Oshiskin. The chairman of the Executive Committee was the principal of the Jewish Gymnasium. His name was Pavel Isaakovich Kagan (Cohen) and he was "privileged" during the Czarist period in Vilna. Kagan's Gymnasium moved to Ekaterinoslav from Vilna when the institutions from the western provinces of Russia – Latvia, Lita, Polesia and others – were evacuated during the First World War (among his students in Ekaterinoslav were Dan Pines from HeHalutz in Russia, the members of the Shlonsky family and others).

As chairman of the Executive Committee, P.A. Kagan, was the real director of the work of the community and its institutions. He was its driving force and left his mark on almost all of its operations. He was active, energetic and stubborn, and imposed an exemplary order and discipline. Because of his intelligence and discretion, he knew how to manage all the affairs of the community with leniency. Even though he was the representative of a small minority (he belonged to the "Folkists") he was elected chairman of the Executive Committee because of these qualities.

The secretary of the Community Council was Yisrael Lifshitz. He was modest, serious, energetic, restrained, quiet, remarkably punctual and disciplined. To his credit, so it seems to me, it's necessary to mention the exemplary way in which he managed all the community's affairs. After his immigration to Israel he served as the secretary of the committee of Hadar Hacarmel in Haifa.

Several departments managed the work of the community and its many institutions (hospital, orphanage, nursing homes, schools, welfare and others), and I'll mention those that I remember the most: The Department of Health and Social Services whose director was Dr. Boris Chanis[3] from HaTzionim HaKlaliym and its secretary, if I'm not mistaken, was Mr. Y. Ritov– one of the leaders of Tzeirei Zion in Ekaterinoslav.

[Page 69]

The Legal Department was headed by the lawyer Avraham Brozovsky from "HaTzionim HaKlaliym," and its secretary was Yisrael Idelshon – of the leaders of "Tzeirei Zion" in Russia and one of the brilliant speakers of that period (he's Yisrael Bar–Yehudah z"l who was the Minister of Transportation in Israel). Out of the rest of the workers I remember Y. Rabinovitz who, I think, worked at the Department of Welfare. He later immigrated to Israel (he's known here by the name Dr. Y. Rabinovitzbecause of his fierce war against his federation during the elections to the municipality of Tel–Aviv at the end of the 1920s.

It should be noted, that the Jewish population of Ekaterinoslav grew, many times over, during the First World War by the absorption of thousands of refugees from the western regions of Russia. There was a great need to take care of them and the matters related to the aforementioned departments. In fact, the Executive Committee constituted the "municipality of Jewish Ekaterinoslav."

The other departments of the community also opened a valuable and varied work under the difficult conditions of the exchange of regimes in those years (Petliura, "Whites," Makhno), and lack of funds for the proper management of the community's work.

The writer of these lines had the privilege of working in the community of Ekaterinoslav as the deputy of the general secretary – after his return from the interior of Russia at the end of 1918 and until its final liquidation by the Soviet regime when it conquered the Ukraine.

Translator's Footnotes

1 Yevsektsii – the Jewish sections of the Soviet Communist party. The stated mission of these sections was "destruction of traditional Jewish life, the Zionist movement, and Hebrew culture".
2 Folkists – political party that sought Jewish national autonomy in the Diaspora. http://www.yivoencyclopedia.org/article.aspx/Folkists Folkspartei – Jewish People's Party.
3 Dr. Boris Chanis – http://archives.jdc.org/exhibits/in–memoriam/boris–chanis.html

[Pages 69-71]

The Jewish Polytechnic in Ekaterinoslav

By I.G.

Translated by Sara Mages

At the beginning of 1917, Jewish Ekaterinoslav has been enriched by an institution of higher education, and it is: "The Jewish Polytechnic," or by its official name: "The Private Polytechnic Institute" – "частный Политехнический Институт."

What were the reasons for the establishment of this Jewish academic institution – the first in the Diaspora?

As is well known – Czarist Russia imposed severe restrictions on the admission of Jewish students to high–schools and universities. They were admitted by a certain "percentage" of those accepted, and it was different. So, for example: in the "Pale of Settlement"– a quota of 15% of Jewish students were admitted to high–schools and 10% to schools of higher education. Outside the "Pale" – 10% to high–schools and 5% to schools of higher education and in Moscow and St. Petersburg – the capital city – 3%–5%. Most of the schools of higher education were in St. Petersburg and Moscow. Every year the number of Jews who graduated high–schools rose, and only a limited number was able to enter schools of higher education in the country. Those left stood before the question – where can we continue our academic education? Some had a way out – to travel abroad, but it required sufficient means and not everyone was able to afford it. In addition, several schools of higher education limited the number of students who were accepted from outside the borders of their country. Also, the possibilities of earning a living in their place of study gradually diminished. The restrictions on admitting Jewish students to high–schools and universities worsened at end of the first decade and the beginning of the second decade of the twentieth century. To their shame, there were also those among the Jewish graduates who have chosen the "easy way" – to convert to Christianity and enter a school of higher education legally.

This problem, to enable the Jewish graduate to continue his academic studies in a suitable school of higher education without the use of the "easiest way," stood for several years before the Jewish public in Russia and was often discussed in the Jewish press. With no hope to wait for changes or reliefs in this matter in Russia, they started to think of establishing a school of higher education for young Jews outside its border or in Russia itself.

This idea found many supporters among the various circles except for the Zionists, who opposed the establishment of a school of higher education for young Jews from Russia[1]. Negotiations were conducted with several public bodies in Russia and abroad for the fulfillment of this idea.

[Page 70]

And here, a solution was found to the question in Russia itself. According to a law from 1914, it was possible to establish schools and courses for "other nationalities" in this country. Therefore, it was also possible to establish a school of higher education for Jews[2]. Indeed, it will not have the rights of a school of higher education, and the graduates will have to take government exams to get their college degree. But they will study according to the program of accredited school, and when they graduate – they will be able to pass the government exams.

ПЕЧАТЬ № 388

Лекціонная книжка

студента Екатеринославскаго Политехниче-скаго Института

(ЕВРЕЙСКАГО ПОЛИТЕХНИКУМА).

Инженерный .... Фак.

.... Отд.

Фамилія _Таслицкій_

Имя _Шлима_

Отчество _Іосифовичъ_

Годъ поступленія въ И-тъ ос. 19_18_

Годъ поступленія на этотъ фак. или отдѣ

леніе 19__ Дкнъ факультета ___

פנקס לימודים של הפוליטכניקום היהודי

Study register from the Jewish Polytechnic

Therefore, it was decided to use this law. The engineers A Peres and L. Rabinovitz, who represented the activists of the capital city, submitted the appropriate application to the authorities. They asked to allow them to establish a technical college with a number of professional faculties and also a faculty for economic[3] in Ekaterinoslav. The reason for the establishment of a technical collage lay in the fact that there was a great demand for engineers in Russia and many studied the profession outside its borders. Ekaterinoslav was chosen as the location for this school because of its large and rich Jewish community. There were large factories there and, the most important thing – the Mining Institute – one of the most important schools of this kind in the country was also there. It was possible to invite its teachers to lecture in the new technical college and also use its advanced laboratories. It was obvious, that it was necessary to establish this school in the "Pale of Settlement" where the students will be able to live without any limitations and prohibitions.

The required license was given in mid 1916, and the necessary preparations for the opening of this school began. They started to collect the necessary funds despite the war conditions in the country at that time, and in a short time about half a million Rubles were collected. In addition, they started to negotiate with various lecturers.

At the meeting of the polytechnic's Executive Committee from 13 January 1917[4], which took place in Petrograd under the leadership of the lawyer M. Vinaver, it was decided to open the school year on 31 January 1917 (by the Julian calendar). The grand opening was postponed to the holiday of Purim. At the same meeting, Professor Zborowski (from the Mining Institute) was approved as the principal (director) of the polytechnic. The rest of the lecturers were invited from the Mining Institute and from among the Jewish scientists. Of them, M. Bernstein, a senior lecturer at the University of Kharkov, the engineers A. Peres (one of the founders), Y. Ratonovsky in the engineering professions, Y. Grossman (in time, a professor at the technical college in Haifa), Y. Ogievetsky (from Odessa), Y. Blumstein in mathematics, and in addition, also several Jewish and non–Jewish counselors in various professions[5].

The opening of the school year was held, according to plan, in the lecture hall of the Scientific Institute building in Chechlavka Street. Because of the transportation difficulties of those days, only several members of the Executive Committee, some of the professors, lecturers and students were able to come. 122 students, including several women, were accepted to the Faculty of Electro–Mechanics, and 78 to the Faculty of Structure Engineering. It was decided to open the Faculty of Economics at the end of the year. The tuition was set at 100 Rubles for half a year.

Some of the lectures were held at the building of the Scientific Institute in Chechlavka Street and some in the Mining Institute (when the lecturer was from there). For physics, they used the laboratory of the Trade School whose director was also the lecturer in this subject.

Before long, the revolution of March 1917 broke out and the restrictions for the admission of Jewish students to high-schools and universities were removed.

[Page 71]

And then stood the question – is there any point and need to continue the existence of a Jewish school of higher education? However, in a meeting, which took place on April 11, it was decided to continue to support it, taking into consideration the needs of the Jewish culture[6]. It's interesting, that a significant number of students supported it. Later, in an additional meeting, it was decided that, for now, the polytechnic will remain in Ekaterinoslav and in 1918 – to transfer it to Petrograd[7].

Meanwhile, the life of the students continued to materialize in this school as in other schools of higher education in Russia. A consumer association of students, for the supply of books, learning instruments, stationery, etc., was established. An association for mutual aid was also established. Representatives of the students began to appear before the Executive Board with several suggestions in regard to the curriculum, lecturers and more. Of course, a few also took part in the political life. The Zionists were organized in "HaChaver" and "Tzeirei Zion", and there was no shortage of members in the various social movements, including the Bolsheviks, and in this manner, they added a special color to the Jewish communal life in Ekaterinoslav.

The first semester ended and the registration for the second year was opened. 195 new students and 13 free listeners were accepted. The number of students, which included 39 women and 12 non-Jews, has reached 400. Lessons in the Hebrew language were added to the general studies and the teacher was the author Y. Lerner. The lecturer for history and Hebrew literature was Dr. Y. L. Baruch who also held a seminar in these subjects[8]. It should be noted that only a small number of students, who treated the lecturers and the lectures with indifference, attended these lectures.

The polytechnic's curriculum was like the curriculum in schools of this type in the country, and so was the order of the exams, the work in the laboratories, etc. There was only one change – studies weren't held on the

Sabbath and Jewish holidays. Among the lecturers were good and average. A number of lecturers, who had to come from out of town, weren't able to arrive to Ekaterinoslav because of the disruption in the train service. Others filled their place, but they weren't always suited for the duty. There were also some difficulties in the use of the laboratories of the Mining Institute. All this weighed heavily on the course of study, and representatives of the students came to the management with demands to correct, add, and change. However, the management wasn't always able to do something in this respect. Despite all these, many students continued their studies, took exams and worked in the laboratories.

The school's name was changed at the end of 1917 and since then it was called: "The Jewish Scientific Institute" – "Еврейские Наýчный Институт." All the studies were transferred to the Mining Institute, and additional lecturers came from there. The studies continued, almost as usual, despite the many changes of regimes that passed over Ekaterinoslav in the fall and winter of 1918–1919. The lecturers and the students came to the lectures, took exams and worked in the laboratories. There were certain difficulties in obtaining the required budget for the existence of the institution, and it took great efforts to raise it. The handful of those responsible stood this test. The contact with Petrograd and Moscow, from which the funds came previously, was severed and it was necessary to rely more on local sources. Thanks to the runaway inflation it was possible to obtain the necessary means. To this, it's necessary to add that a number of students were cut off from their homes because of the civil war that broke out in the country, and many were left without means of support. A few, who left for a vacation in their homes, weren't able to return. At that period the lecturer, Y. Ogievetskyi, took upon himself the great concern of the upkeep of the institution.

Despite these difficulties the third school year, 1919–1920, was opened and the registration of students was announced. The tuition increased and was set at 500 Rubles a year[9]. The days were the days of Denikin's regime of in Ekaterinoslav, and Makhno's gangs prevented regular studies. To ensure the necessary budget, Mr. Y. Ogievetskyi left for several cities in the Ukraine. He raised known amounts and returned to Ekaterinoslav shortly before it fell to the hands of the Soviets.

With the consolidation of the Soviet regime, the local authorities decided to annex the Jewish Polytechnic to the Mining Institute, and together they constituted the Polytechnic Institute in Ekaterinoslav. Thus, came to an end the first Jewish school of higher education in the Diaspora.

Translator's Footnotes

1 Рассвет – 1914 (14/15)
2 [*Hashahar* – The Dawn – a Hebrew periodical published by Pretz Smolenskin]
3 Еврейская Жизнь – [Jewish Life] 1916/20
4 Еврейская Жизнь – 1917 (7/8)
5 Еврейская Жизнь – 1917 (15)
6 Еврейская Жизнь – 1917 (7/8)
7 Еврейская Жизнь – 1917 (17)
8 Еврейская Жизнь – 1917 (19)
9 Рассв ет 1917 (19)
10 Еврейская мысль – [Jewish Thought] 1919 (16/17)

[Pages 72-74]

The defense in Ekaterinoslav in the years 1917–1919
By I.G.
Translated by Sara Mages

1.

With the signs of weakening in the regime and the possibility that it will fall in the last months of 1917, and with the news of pogroms against the Jews in several locations in the Ukraine, the fear intensified in Ekaterinoslav that also this city might be harmed by pogroms, both by local residents and outside forces.

Thus, they began talking about the need to organize self–defense. They wrote about it in the newspapers and discussed it in the national parties. Ekaterinoslav already had an experience in organizing a self–defense from 1905, so, also this time they began to establish it.

For various reasons, the Community Council in Ekaterinoslav, which was led by the Zionists, didn't take on itself the initiative to establish the defense in its name. Moreover, the office of Jewish affairs, which was adjacent to Verkhovna Rada of Ukraine [Supreme Council of Ukraine), opposed the establishment of self–defense. Thereforc, this initiative was transferred to other organizations,

The first to establish a strong defense company was "The United Jewish Socialist Workers Party." The company consisted of about four hundred men and its leader was P. Mirkin, a man of great organizational talent. The company was well armed with weapons it received from the authorities and weapons that were acquired in all sorts of ways. This company was composed of members of the party, former soldiers, townspeople, students and others. The authorities gave the company a two-story building in Sadovaya Street which served as headquarters and weapons depot.

The second company was established by the "Alliance of the Jewish Soldier." It was composed mostly by soldiers who previously served in the Russian Army, and a number of Jewish officers also participated in it. The company had weapons that it received from the authorities and acquired in various ways. It was given a big building with a yard in one of the side streets that were inhabited mostly by Jews. For various reasons, this company wasn't well organized and its impact in the city wasn't substantial.

Over time, out of competition between the parties, defense companies were also established by the "Bund," "Poalei Zion," and the "Mensheviks." They received most of their weapons from the authorities, but they were very weak and had no defensive value.

Despite the concerns, there were no attacks on the Jews, except from cases of robbery, during the exchange of regimes at the end of 1917 and the beginning of 1918. The Soviet regime, which became established in the city, didn't see the need of these defense companies. In addition, the regime was also influenced by the many anarchist groups in Ekaterinoslav who demanded to disarm the "bourgeois" organizations. The truth is, these defense companies disrupted the anarchists' extortion activities, meaning, with their threatening demands from the wealthiest in the city, among them many Jews, to give them money for their needs. Those, who were attacked, turned to the defense companies with a request to save them from their attackers and unpleasant collisions occurred on this background. The local Soviet responded to the anarchists' request and ordered the defense companies to disband. They agreed and handed their weapons, some to the authorities and some they hid. "The United Jewish Socialist Workers Party" refused to disband and appealed to the authorities. Then, the building of the headquarter was surrounded by the "Red Guard" and the anarchists who fired at the building. After one of the members of the company was killed, those inside the building succumbed, they were disarmed, and the company dispersed. It happened in March 1918.

[Page 73]

2.

During the German rule in Ekaterinoslav there was no need, or possibility, to organize a self–defense. However, after the German Army started to leave the city and the danger of disorder in the regime and pogroms against the Jewish community rose again, the question of organizing a self–defense stood once again on the agenda. In light of the bitter experience of the establishment of the defense companies in 1917–1918, the national youth organizations turned to the Community Council with a suggestion that the defense organization will be under its supervision and act on its behalf. After some hesitations the management agreed to this proposal.

This defense organization was established at the end of October 1918, and its name was "The Jewish Community Company" – "Рейской Общины Дружина Ев." The company was established with the consent of the municipal administration which also gave the necessary budget for its upkeep. According to the municipality's request, the necessary weapons – guns and ammunition – were obtained from the army. The majority of the members of this company were soldiers from the Russian Army, members of "The Alliance of the Jewish Soldier." At the beginning, several men with a questionable past, who used their duty to extort money and other items from the Jewish residents, infiltrated the company. When the matter became known, they were removed from the ranks of the company.

All the members of the company received a salary which was paid from a budget that was provided by the management of Ekaterinoslav Municipality. The company received a building in the main street – "Prospect" – which served as a home for the headquarters and a weapons depot. The company was organized as an army unit and was divided into two departments, each of about 110 men. Each department appeared for a guard duty of 24 hours and afterward it had a day off. It was out of cases when the entire company was mobilized.

A certificate issued by the Municipality of Ekaterinoslav to a member of the defense company of the Community Council

תעודה מטעם עירית י"ב לחבר פלוגת ההגנה שע"י הקהילה

[Page 74]

The company's headquarters was composed of the commanding officer, A. Schreshber, who mostly handled the administrative side; the chief of staff, Reizer, a former combat soldier who took care of the military side – training, guard duty and more; Y. Goldbort who represented the Community Council and was responsible for the political side; Portnoy who was the headquarters' officer and the representative of the Municipal Security Committee, and the second Reizer was the chief storekeeper.

The company had the form of a typical military unit, which made a great impression on others, thanks to the fact that most of its members were former soldiers who received military training. The attitude of the Ukrainian Army, which camped in the city at that time, was good and the non–partisan nature of the company, in comparison with other defense units, was prominent. For that reason, this company was given the duty of guarding important places in the city such as the treasury and more. For a period of time, this company was asked to guard the Ukrainian headquarters because the Ukrainian soldiers got drunk often and abandoned their post.

The company headquarters tried to increase the amount of weapons in its hands in various ways, like acquisition and more. In order to increase the number of people, who will be able to go out with weapons against the rioters, the company organized defense groups in a number of neighborhoods in the city, taught them how to use weapons, and at times, also provided it to them.

This company existed from October 1918 to the end of March 1919. During this short period, it fulfilled guard and security duties for the Jewish community and the residents of the city.

The defense company of "The United Jewish Socialist Workers Party" was reorganized at the same time. It was led again by P. Mirkin and contained up to 250 men. Even though it had a clear partisan character and received its budget, together with other groups, from the municipality, its role in joint guarding of the city was less significant.

In addition, defense groups were organized by "Poalei Zion," "Tzeirei Zion," "Bund," the "Mensheviks" and the students. It should be noted, that one of the motives for the establishment of these groups was the possibility to enjoy from the municipality's budgets which were granted without a special distinction. These groups, except for the students and former officers and soldiers who served in them, were weak and their value in the defense was inferior.

With the occupation of the city by the Soviets at the beginning of 1919, all the defense groups disbanded themselves. Some of the weapons were given to the authorities and some were hidden. Difficult days have passed on a few members of the Jewish community defense company who were caught with weapons in their hands in places given to them, like the treasury. The Soviet soldiers wanted to execute them and only the rapid intervention of the members of "The United Jewish Socialist Workers Party," under the leadership of P. Mirkin, saved them. With that, ended the self–defense activities in Ekaterinoslav, the members scattered, some enlisted to the Soviet Army and some moved to other pursuits.

A few months later, before the Soviet Army was about to leave the city and hand it over to Denikin's Army the concern of riots against the Jews rose again. In addition, shortly before that Ataman Grigoriev tried to attack Ekaterinoslav. It is clear, that the idea of establishing a defense company and purchasing the necessary weapons for it came up again. However, for various reasons they weren't able to realize that. There was a negotiation with the socialist organizations and the Mensheviks, who promised to give a few of their weapons, but the events that followed and the evacuation of the city by the Soviet Army came so fast, that nothing came out of this idea.

It is worth noting, that the fear of pogroms by Denikin's Army intensified in the days before the evacuation of the city. A small group of activists from the Zionist youth movements, which was headed by M. Rozovski, took on the role of organizing a self–defense company, and along with it, to obtain weapons. These weapons were given later to the workers of Ekaterinoslav, most of them members of the Communist Party, who took upon themselves the protection of the city until the entrance of the Soviet Army.

[Page 75]

My meetings with Dr. Yosef Chazanowitz

by Dr. Yakov Kostrinski

Translated by Sara Mages

I remember this name since the dawn of my youth because it's associated with the National Library of Israel in Jerusalem. Dr. Chazanowitz conceived the idea of establishing the library when he was a doctor in Bialystok. He also placed the library's foundations - by collecting books from generous donors and by posting advertisements in newspapers throughout the Diaspora in which he called for the donation of books and money for the National Library. These books constituted the first layers of the National Library in Jerusalem. And thus, "Dr. Chazanowitz" became a synonym with the "National Library."

I was released from the Russian Army after the October Revolution. When I returned to my family in Ekaterinoslav I learned that this wonderful man was in Ekaterinoslav and decided to meet him in person. Therefore, I was happy when my friend Moshe Risin z"l, who was the moving spirit of the branch of "Tzeirei Zion" in Ekaterinoslav, asked me to visit Dr. Chazanowitz who was in a difficult financial and spiritual distress. I was asked to thank him, on behalf of the Jewish public in general and "Tzeirei Zion" in particular, for his eternal project and give him a monetary donation that will ease his situation during the days of shortage and famine of the 1920th. To my great sorrow, this meeting caused me bitter disappointment which remains in my heart to this day. Since then, I, and many of my colleagues, went through years of great physical and spiritual sufferings. Those were years of feverish clandestine work for the party and studies at the High Institute for Agriculture in Kharkiv. Because of my "bourgeois origin," I had to support myself and pay tuition. After many arrests in Kharkiv's prison and other prisons - I was expelled to the land of exile. It was a difficult period of great emotional stress. Between the arrests I became ill with severe typhus which sapped my strength and my memory, and thus, many events and very important facts have been forgotten from my heart. However, I will never forget the amazing impression that Dr. Chazanowitz had left on me when I visited him at the Jewish community nursing home in Ekaterinoslav. Before me stood a helpless old man, with fading eyes and a sad smile on his pale face, not the lofty energetic man that I've seen in my imagination. He lay in one of the beds in a large dim room. I introduced myself after I managed overcome my shock and confusion when I saw the visionary man in such a desperate condition. Suddenly, his face lit up, and with shaking hands and sparkling tears in his eyes he shook my outreached hand.

A few days later I "met" Dr. Yosef Chazanowitz again. I was asked by "Tzeirei Zion" to eulogize the great man in the public funeral as his coffin stood in the great square next to the Choral Synagogue. I gave a short tribute in Hebrew for the visionary man, who had built the National Library in Jerusalem, despite the fact that the people of Yevsektsii [the Jewish sections of the Communist Party] were among those present.

Many years have passed. I managed to immigrate to Israel from my place of exile in the Kostanay Province, Kyrgyzstan. There, I was able, despite the vigorous opposition of the local GPU, to grab a government job as the region's agronomist. One day, I was approached by my good friend, Baruch Shochtman z"l, who was one of the editors of the periodical "Kiryat Sefer." He asked me, on behalf of the National Library in Jerusalem, to place a tombstone on the grave of Dr. Chazanowitz in the Jewish cemetery in Ekaterinoslav as sign of appreciation from the management of the library to its founder.

I agreed to do so without hesitation despite the difficulties and the dangers that were involved with the matter in the conditions of the Soviet Union. I immediately contacted my brother-in-law, Avraham-Leib Friedman z"l, the husband of my oldest sister Chaya-Leibe z"l. Both, along with the Hebrew teacher Brohodsky z"l, were members of the Zionist movement in Ekaterinoslav during the period of Ussishkin. After many difficulties and risks, my brother-in-law Friedman, who was one of the Zionists who were arrested on 2 September 1924 - the night of the general arrest of Zionists across Russia, managed not only to place a tombstone on the grave of Dr. Chazanowitz, but also to photograph it and send the picture to the management of the National Library in Jerusalem.

[Page 76]

The JOINT in Ekaterinoslav (1921-1924)
by Shlomo Tesslitzki
Translated by Sara Mages

At the end of 1921, after the city has suffered during the revolution years and change of regime, came the great famine which included Russia, the southern part of Ukraine and the Volga regions. The hunger grew stronger over the winter, and often the bodies of those who died of starvation were scattered in the city's streets.

Also, the Jews, the residents of Ekaterinoslav, were victims of this great famine. At that time, a special committee was organized to help them. The few public activists who participated in it were: Yisrael Motzkin (brother of Leo Motzkin, chairman of the "Board of Deputies in Europe"), the former "community rabbi" M. E. Broshtein, Dr. S. Levin, the lawyer A. Brozowsky, and others. On behalf of the youth: Z. Yofit and S. Taslitsky. The committee has made every effort to enlist local resources and later worked, in full cooperation, with foreign institutions: the "JOINT" and the "Ukrainian Jewish Committee" in London.

At the end of 1921, the American organization "ARA" [American Relief Administration] started to operate in Russia. The organization distributed food parcels to those whose relatives paid for them abroad. "ARA" also distributed food to various social organizations. The food parcels included: white flour, sugar, yellow cheese, lard, olive oil, cocoa powder and more. The "JOINT" started to operate at the beginning of 1922, and its license was granted under the condition that it wouldn't discriminate between Jews and non-Jews. Dr. B. Chanis was appointed as the representative of the "JOINT" in the city and the environment.

Dr. B. Chanis opened a large warehouse in the city center. It contained various food items and also other necessities like undergarments, clothes, bedding and more. All these goods were brought from abroad by the "JOINT" which started to distribute them to various social institutions, Jewish and non-Jewish. Individuals received food and clothing by the recommendation of institutions or personalities. In addition, communal kitchens were opened in several locations and the needy received a free hot meal. The Jews received kosher food.

At the same time, the "JOINT" started to rehabilitate the Jewish community aid institutions. The first was the big Jewish Hospital on Philosophskaya Street which contained 140 beds. It was built on a large area and had 12 separate pavilions. There was also a two-story building which housed the administrative offices, a pharmacy, laboratories and more. Everything was abandoned and some of the buildings were destroyed. Windows, doors, and plumbing parts were missing, the tin roof was removed, and the wood floor was used for firewood.

The management of the "JOINT" assigned me the task to rehabilitate the hospital. We got the building materials from the local authorities for a fee, and the work was conducted without any interference on their part. After the rehabilitation work was completed, the "JOINT" brought all the necessary equipment for the hospital from America: beds, bedding, medication, laboratory equipment, and more. Doctors, nurses and the required staff were invited. The hospital, which was called at that time "The Municipal Hospital No. 2," started to operate.

The community's "soup kitchen" was rehabilitated at the same time. It turned into a center which contained: a restaurant for the poor, the offices of "Chevrah Kadisha," and part of the community council offices.

The orphanages and the Jewish kindergartens were also supported by the "JOINT." The Jewish bathhouse was also rebuilt. In addition, the cooperative "Makolet" [grocery], whose duty was to supply food to its members, was established with the help of the "JOINT." The "Makolet" store was located in the city center.

These institutions existed for a short period of time. In 1924 they were transferred to the hands of the local government and Dr. B. Chanis was removed from his activities. He was given permission to open a well-equipped private clinic for venereal diseases which were common in Russia at that time. Also, this clinic wasn't in his hands for a long period. It was transferred to the authorities and Dr. B. Chanis was arrested and expelled to Siberia.

The end of all this public activity came on the night of September 2, 1924, with the mass arrests of the Zionists across Russia. About 40 people were arrested at that time in Ekaterinoslav - rabbis, communal workers, and members of the Zionist parties. After an interrogation at the GPU, some of them were released and others were required to denounce the Zionist movement in the press. Another group was sentenced to prison and deportation to Siberia, and for some, the deportation was replaced with immigration to Israel.

[Page 77]

At the beginning of the road[1]
by Avraham Millstein
Translated by Sara Mages

"Tu B'Shevat"

The virtues of loyalty, courage and devotion to Zionism that the adults excelled in, were also the attributes of the small children, the members of the young class.

At times, they were required to do more than the adults because not all the parents allowed their children to join the movement and participate in the activities - sometimes because of the cold weather, out of concern that it would interfere with their studies, and also out of fear of the authorities. There were cases when parents were harassed by the GPU because of their children. The children had to stand a double test - to fulfill the Scout's decree of honoring their parents and obey the movement's discipline.

The parents were wrong regarding the education. Most of the scouts were good students and stood the test. Along with maintaining caution, which was imposed on them by the conditions of the underground, they knew how to fill the tasks that were imposed on them, like: arrival at the precise time to the meetings, even to distant places, active participation in the unit's activities, and the recruitment of new members.

There was a large number of scouts in the troop who knew Hebrew, most of them students of "Tarbut" school. "Plugat Nesher," which started its activities in Hebrew, was composed of them. The games, conversations and diary were conducted in Hebrew. Also, the troop's newspaper was partially written in Hebrew.

The day of 15 Shevat 5683 (1924) got closer, and it was decided to celebrate it at the bosom of nature not within the walls of a closed room.

The "kesher" [contact] was given to the scouts by "Sharsheret" [chain] close to the day of the meeting (for conspiracy reasons). The location, which was known by the name Balki, was out of town. It was an area of deep and winding ravines which were created by floods and the erosion of the clay soil. These ravines have been known as hiding places for gangs of criminals and thieves. The police visited the area even during the days of the Czar. However; there were beautiful corners in the area which excited the children's imagination, and on a good summer day it was possible to set up a scout's camp which was hidden from the eyes of the curious.

The "Tu B'Shevat" meeting was held there for lack of another place. The winter was intense and heavy snow covered everything. The frost intensified close to the day of the meeting, and schools were closed for a few days. There was a justified fear that scouts, ages 12-14, will not come to the "Tu B'Shevat" celebration because of the intensity of the cold.

The schools were also closed on that day. At an early hour of the morning, scouts appeared from different directions with their meager equipment to the meeting place. They stuck a flag, cleared the snow from the area, and started a fire. And lo and behold, everyone came. Even the little boys and girls weren't missing. The struggle with their parents wasn't easy. Some came against their parents' wishes and a few even snuck out of the house. Their guide received them with affection and admiration. He knew that he would have to accompany several of them home and calm the fathers' anger.

The activity was conducted according to the program - roll-call, gymnastics, singing, eating, reading from a newspaper, and a conversation around the campfire.

The snow glistened around, everything was white and cold. About twenty boys and girls sat around the campfire and their faces were flushed from the cold and the warmth. With an expression of joy, they listened to their guide's story about "Rosh HaShanah La'Ilanot" ["New Year for the Trees"], about the content of this nature holiday and how children celebrate this holiday in Israel. When their guide was at their age, he heard this story from the teacher, S. S. Kantorowicz, the author of grammar books.

The children were like daydreamers when they heard about a land saturated with sun, about growth and flowering during the cold days, green meadows, blooming almond trees, and about school children who leave with their seedlings to enrich the homeland with greenery.

[Page 78]

The children listened, as if they were gripped by a green dream, to the legend about "Tu B'Shevat" in a winter there, far far away.

The wind increased and raged and swirled the snow around. A scout, who was on duty, forced himself to break away from the group. He moved away from them to explore the surroundings and replace the scout who was on the lookout.

Sleighs hurried on the road leading to the villages. Behold, what is it? The scout who stood on guard noticed something green moving fast inside the white background. A fast sleigh passed and moved away. Green spots stood out on the collars and sleeves of the passengers inside it - the insignia of rank of the special unit of the GPU...

The party didn't stop

"Tarbut"

The Zionist movement expanded its ranks despite the difficulties of working underground. The ties with the movement's centers in Kharkiv and Moscow tightened. From time to time we received news of what is happening in Israel. In those days there were still possibilities to immigrate illegally and even legally.

In its extensive underground work, "Tarbut" society fulfilled an important role for deepening the awareness to Zionism and maintaining the affinity to Judaism. It organized a network of classes for the study of the language and the Hebrew literature. Children, youth and adults, beginners and advanced, engaged in the study of the Hebrew language. About one hundred students studied Hebrew in classes apart from those who studied it in private lessons. In addition, a seminar was established to train young people to teach in Hebrew.

Many showed courage and dedication in their work for the Hebrew language. Seven teachers risked themselves every day. Like them, also the students and the apartment owners who gave a place to the students. A lot of efforts were invested in the teaching of the Hebrew language by the organizers and the principals. They recruited students for the classes, gave them teachers and obtained funds to support the project.

The students of the Hebrew classes served as a valuable source from which the Zionist youth movements drew most of their members.

From time to time, talks and lectures on various topics, celebrations and memorial days were held in addition to the study of the Hebrew language. The mobile "library" provided books to read.

The loyal activists of "Tarbut" society deserve a special and more comprehensive recognition. I remember with admiration those who lent a hand and carried the burden of the activities. In addition to the teachers we should also mention Hadassah-Rachel Birman who helped with all the activities, and the family of Avraham Kostovitzky who gave their apartment for lessons and meetings even though the communists lived in their yard. In days of intense cold, when the students arrived at the apartment half frozen and shivering from the cold, Kostovitzky removed the children's shoes and rubbed their little feet to warm them up.

The Hebrew activities and the preservation of the Jewish culture were mostly done by "Tzeirei Zion." The association used all its sources for the Hebrew education of children and youth. In those years, the Komsomol expanded its conversion operation and stole masses of young Jews from Judaism. Therefore, it was very important to instill the Hebrew language to the Jewish children and save them from the Komsomol's teeth.

The blessed activity of "Tarbut" association in Ekaterinoslav came to an end with the mass arrests of the Zionists and the activists of "Tarbut" in 1920-1925.

Footnote

1. From the book "*Naftule Dor,*" published by the association of "*Tzeirei Zion.*"

[Page 79]

"Hatchiya" in Ekaterinoslav

by Aharon Becker

Translated by Sara Mages

The days were days of upheavals, revolutions and civil war in Russia. The Jews of Ukraine were bleeding and the pogroms against the Jews didn't skip a single community.

With the outbreak of the First World War in 1914, my family wandered from the city of its residence, Brisk–DeLita[1], to Verkhnedneprovsk near Ekaterinoslav, today Dnepropetrovsk.

I was a boy of eight when the war broke out, and I remember two events from those days.

A tremendous explosion in Brisk fortress which covered, on a clear summer day, the entire city with smoke and darkness. All the residents of the city fled for their lives, some on foot and some by vehicles, and the vehicles – wagons and carriages. I, of course, didn't know the reason for that.

The second event: when the front got closer to Brisk all the residents were ordered to leave the city. The deportation order was directed primarily at the local Jews. Many moved to nearby towns and villages out of the consideration – "until the storm blows over." Many took the wandering stick in their hands and turned in the direction of Ukraine which was far from the front.

The trains were occupied by the military and the roads were filled with convoys of soldiers and artillery. A huge camp was seen moving non–stop, day and night, from across Russia to the front which quickly encompassed all of Poland, Galicia and Polesia.

By a difficult route, in wagons, we arrived as refugees to the city of Mazyr and from there my family managed to board a ship in the Pripyat River which sailed along the Dnieper River.

I remember that I asked my father z"l – where are we going? He answered me: I haven't decided yet, we will look for a place that has Jews.

There were those who advised us to get off in the city of Kremenchuk, and there were those who told us that Ekaterinoslav was better. Father ruled: we will get off in the middle of the road, in a town between the two big cities, and it is Verkhnedneprovsk.

It was a place far from the front. The war, which already started, was barely felt there. Father, who was the commercial representative of the big and well-known factory "Nevsky Zavod" for candles and soap in Petrograd –Poland,

Bessarabia and Polesia, renewed his contact with the factory and continued his regular occupation.

My two older sisters entered the State Gymnasium for Girls without any difficulties, and I had to knock on the doors of the State Gymnasium for Boys.

At that time, only a certain percentage of Jewish boys were accepted to state schools, and only with the intervention of the management of the factory in Petrograd that my father was connected to, I was accepted to the gymnasium. I found myself in a department of forty local boys and two Jewish boys. Under a special agreement with the director of the gymnasium I was released from writing on the Sabbath.

Kerensky's revolution broke out on February 1917 and the city, with its residents, political parties and the youth of the gymnasium – was getting ready for the May Day demonstration.

When I studied at the gymnasium father made sure that I will continue my Hebrew studies. Every day was a double school day for me: until noon at the gymnasium and in the afternoon at "Talmud Torah." It was a modern Hebrew school where we studied Hebrew in Hebrew, the Talmud and also the Bible. Good teachers, who devoted themselves to their work, taught there and they were the ones who planted the Jewish consciousness among the students.

With the outbreak of the revolution the Zionist feeling grasped a central place in "Talmud Torah" thanks to a few teachers who were Zionists in all their souls. A couple of days before the demonstration I had serious doubts about my participation in the May Day rally.

[Page 80]

At the gymnasium all the students were required to appear at the demonstration and walk in a procession, from the gymnasium to the location of the demonstration, after the Red Flag.

One evening I learned that the students of "Talmud Torah" will also leave for the demonstration in a procession and wave a blue and white flag. My Hebrew teacher at "Talmud Torah" knew that I had to go with my school and didn't ask me to do otherwise. At home, my parents also knew that I was going to the demonstration with the students of the gymnasium. However, suddenly, as I was on my way to the gymnasium on the day of the demonstration, I thought: how can it be that the students of "Talmud Torah" will appear with a blue and white flag and I will walk among the Gentiles with another flag...?

Without asking anyone, and with anyone knowing, I turned back and walked in the direction of "Talmud Torah" which was on the other side of the city. The teachers and the students welcomed me with joy and I marched in the uniform of the Russian Gymnasium at the head of the procession as I was carrying the blue and white flag in my hands.

I knew that at that moment I became a Zionist and, in my imagination, I already saw myself in Israel.

On the next day, when I came to the gymnasium, nobody said anything to me – not the teachers and not my friends. Furthermore, a few weeks later a Student Union was established "by the order" of the Student Council and my departmental chose me as its representative. It was surprised when I was invited to attend a joint meeting of the representatives of the students and all the teachers in the staff room – the room that in the student's eyes meant respect and also awe.

The participation of "Talmud Torah" students in the May Day demonstration led to an awakening among the Jewish youth – a Zionist awakening. Together with other boys and girls we initiated the establishment of a youth association. And indeed – two association were established, boys and girls separately – "Bnai Zion" ["Sons of Zion"] and "Bnot Zion" ["Daughters of Zion"].

The management of "Talmud Torah" gave us rooms and halls and beautiful clubs, which concentrated scores of teenagers, have been established. In a short time, the gatherings on Friday evenings, the literary banquets, lectures about the history of Israel and conversations, became widely known. At the center of our activities was the preparation for immigration to Israel.

This was my first public activity – and I was a boy of 11–12.

The spring of Kerensky's revolution has passed and the autumn, which brought the October Revolution and, immediately after, the pogroms against the Jews by the White Army and the local gangs, arrived

I'll never forget the Chanukah eve in which we, our parents and the city's activists gathered at "Talmud Torah" for a wonderful party for the youth. I think that this was the first time that I spoke in an opening of a public party. The leader of the Jewish community and one of the teachers spoke after me. We scattered at a late hour and our heart didn't guess that by morning the city will be conquered by a local gang under the leadership of Zubanok. Fifteen people, among them the leader of the Jewish community who spoke at the Chanukah party about his longing to Israel, were killed.

This gang finished its work within a few hours. The Red Army returned to the city, and on the same day the city's Jews buried the victims in a mass funeral under its protection

The city's authorities changed often, day after day, and at times – twice a day.

We went to sleep with a certain confidence that the city was in the hands of the Red Army and woke up as soldiers from the White Army, or from the local gangs, were knocking on the door.

I remember an agreement that was signed between my father and our neighbor in the yard where we lived. He was the deputy director of the Sate Gymnasium and his son served as an officer in the White Army. The agreement said: If the Red Army governs the city – they would stay in our house and we'll protect them, and if the White Army enters the city, we would stay in their house and they'll protect us...

There was a case when we mistakenly thought that the Red Army entered the city and they moved immediately to our house. In the evening, there were knocks on the door and several soldiers from the White Army burst in... They placed my father against the wall and by miracle, and the addition of a ransom, he remained alive.

*

The pogroms continued, and my family decided to move to a bigger city where the regime of the Red Army was more stable, and it is Ekaterinoslav.

[Page 81]

I remember being Bar–Mitzvah in those days – the days of pogroms. We arrived at the synagogue with difficulties and I read from the Haftarah – "And My people are in suspense about returning to Me" (Parashat Vayishlach) in the presence of a minyanof Jews.

Father gave me two presents: Tefillin in a silver embroidered bag and a silver watch with Hebrew letters on the dial and Moshe Rabbeinu and the Tablets of Stone on the cover. Both fell in the hands of rioters who robbed our house shortly after.

We were in Ekaterinoslav for two years. The days were the days of the great famine and the increasing civil war in Ukraine. The White Army, under the leadership of the generals Varangal and Kolchak, stood in the front against the Red Army and also scored victories and each victory meant: rivers of Jewish blood. Petliura raged in the vicinity of Kiev and Makhno's gang captured Ekaterinoslav and held the city for several days.

A piece of bread was considered a delicious cake and a few potatoes – kings' delicacy. When the day darkened, we locked ourselves in the house and no one left on one entered.

I remember the Passover Seder of that time at our home. The table was covered with a white cloth, set with fine tableware, plates and glasses as it was customary.

Father sat at the head of the table and around him – my mother, my sister Tzila z"l, my sister Rivka and me. Father blessed the "wine" – a small bottle of sweet pink lemonade, the substitute for the four glasses. Before him – a few soot colored matzot and the main course – a few roasted potatoes.

Every day I left for the city's famous market to help my parents who sold notions in order to earn a living after the contact with the factory in Petrograd was severed. I sold notions for two to three hours and in the remaining hours of the day I was immersed in my studies at school. I also studied Hebrew in private lessons and Avraham Shlonsky was one of my teachers. The Zionist spark, which was ignited in me in Verkhnedneprovsk, didn't go out in those days.

As the Soviet regime became established and grew stronger the Zionist clubs were closed, one after the other, and all the public Zionist activities came to an end.

One club, which was run by the members of "Tzeirei Zion," survived. Its name was "Eretz V'Avodah" [country and work] and it was located at the Pebzner's house on Opornaya Street.

I arrived at this club, which was close to where we lived, and found in it a glorious group of young men. Some became important personalities in Israel like: Yisrael Bar–Yhudah (Idelson) z"l, Dan Pins z"l, Dov Shlonsky z"l, and may they live a long life – his brother Avraham Shlonsky, Beba Idelson, Avraham Lev and many others.

In comparison to my age these young men looked big in my eyes – I was about 14–15.

With their help and guidance, together with a number of boys and girls that I knew from the club, we established a youth organization named "Hatchiya."[2] Some of its members were awarded to immigrate to Israel and I met them here: the painter Aharon Avni (Kamenkovich) z"l, Shenkman z"l from the members of Kibbutz Afikim, and may they live a long life – the engineer M. Goldman who works in "Mekorot," the engineer Avraham Arlich, Liza Yofit and more.

By the way, Aharon Kamenkovich (Avni) already painted at that time and was nicknamed "Eliusha Chodoznik."

Our activities were held in closed groups, mostly in private homes. We heard lectures and each one of us had to give a lecture. I was asked to speak about Herzl on the first anniversary of his death.

I remember another Chanukah eve party – and this time it was cheerful and happy. It was held at the home of Avraham Shlonsky's parents.

It was cold outside, and the night brought snow and curfew. A group of boys and girls, members of "Hatchiya," were invited to the Shlonsky's house for latkes. We arrived early, before the beginning of the curfew, and spent time together until the early hours of the morning. We sang Hebrew songs and spoke quietly in Hebrew so that our voices wouldn't be heard outside.

We danced – and also the dance was quiet. Our host, his parents, sisters and brothers z"l – the whole home was a Hebrew home. It was saturated in Hebrew culture and the spirit of the homeland – Eretz Yisrael.

It was an evening full of light and warm atmosphere as opposed to the darkness of the night and the cold beyond the walls.

[Page 83]

In those days there was an ongoing discussion among the members of "Tzeirei Zion" prior to the general conference in Kharkiv. Two steams were formed – the stream of "Socialist Zionists" and the stream "Tzeirei Zion." In "Hatchiya" we decided to remain independent after hearing the explanations and the lectures of the representatives of each stream. The time of the split came and two parties were formed: "Socialist Zionists" – under the leadership of Yisrael Idelson (Bar–Yehudah) z"l, and "Tzeirei Zion" – with Avraham Shlonsky and others.

Both parties still used the club "Eretz V'Avodah," but only for a short time. I was a witness when on a Saturday afternoon 3 people, among them a young Jewish woman, came on behalf of the government. They closed the club, asked all of us to leave the building, and then they locked it with their own lock and a wax seal.

This was the end of the chapter of the club which served as the only warm corner for the loyalists of Zion. The older members started to go underground and some of us, the teenagers, found a place to meet at the club of the sports association "Maccabi" which continued to operate openly for a short time.

The civil war was over, the Soviet regime grew stronger, peace was achieved with Poland and the refugees were allowed to return to their homes.

We returned home – to Brisk–DeLita – by the same route – by ship along the Dnieper River, from Ekaterinoslav to Kiev.

We were forced to stay in Kiev for about half a year, until we managed to obtain the necessary permits that allowed us to return to Brisk. Finally, the day we've longed for came and we arrived by train to the border station in Rovna. A strict inspection was conducted by the representatives of the Polish government and two family members were arrested for a full day of interrogation – my eldest sister Tzila who was about 19 and me, I was about 15.

Our interrogators wanted us to admit that we were members of Komosmol [3] and tried to "prove" that they've seen us in action in Kiev. They weren't able to prove anything and let us go. We returned to Brisk at the end of 1921, I lived there for three years and at the end of December 1924 I immigrated to Israel.

*

I was 8 when we left the city and 15–16 when we returned. I was young in days but satiated with life experience, life of adversity, hardship and confidence in my heart that I'll arrive to Israel, and indeed, I immigrated.

The separation from my parents and from home was pretty tough.

Father z"l was a Hassid and a close associate of the Stolin Rabbi. He asked the Rabbi's advice on any matter. He was a religious man but not jealous, and so was also my mother z"l. Our home was a religious home. As the youngest son my parents always worried about my Jewish education. All the time, even in the most difficult times, I wasn't free of my Jewish studies and the best teachers were available to me.

When we returned to Brisk, which was part of Poland, the language of the country was Polish. The economic situation at home was difficult and I knew that I had to earn my own living in order to immigrate to Israel. I studied bookkeeping in a Polish school, excelled in my studies, and after I obtain my "diploma" as a certified bookkeeper I found a job in one of the largest stores. At the same time, I continued with my general studies in pure Russian and saved the required amount for immigration to Israel. At home, my parents, who were far from the Zionist feeling, tried to oppose my immigration because they didn't want to part from me.

One day, my father told me that he's accepting the decree, the decree of my immigration and that he'll also bless me. I didn't know then the meaning of the matter. The reason for the turn in my father's attitude only became known to me in the 1930s when he was in Israel (he came to settle in the country, stayed in our house for several years, but to our sorrow he wasn't able to adjust to life in Israel and returned to his "Shtiebel" and his environment. We didn't know that he was returning to the vale of the Holocaust. He was murdered in Brisk Ghetto by the Nazis. My mother z"l died in a traffic accident in the first year of my immigration to Israel).

Well, during my father's stay in Israel I learned that before I immigrated to Israel he went, by the request of my mother, to ask the advice of the Rabbi, and this was his answer:

"If your son wants to immigrate to the Holy Land, don't interrupt him."

Hence, the meaning of his completion with the "decree" and the blessing for the road...

Translator's footnotes

1. Brisk–DeLita – Brest Litovsk.

2. *Hatchiya* – the Revival – a Zionist youth organization whose goal was to present nationalist and cultural activities to Jewish youth.

3. *Komosmol* – a youth organization controlled by the Communist Party of the Soviet Union.

[Page 83]

My visit to Dniepropetrovsk in 1958

by Batya Riskind[1]

Translated by Sara Mages

In August 1958, on the way from Meisk to Moscow, I visited Dniepropetrovsk to learn the fate of my relatives that I haven't seen for over twenty years, since I was arrested and exiled to Siberia. From the train station I turned to the prospect [street] named after Karl Marx. In the past, the prospekt was named after Yekaterina (the second). The street was beautiful and there were many new multi–story buildings in it. Only here and there were buildings from previous years, which remained in their original form, such as the Khrennikov building. A small square emerged at the corner of Perevozva Novaskaya Street and an electric tram encircled it. In addition, I also found other innovations. I entered one of the buildings in the prospect, which looked familiar to me, and asked the neighbors if the Yodelson family lived there. I was told that I had to wait a bit and a short time later one of the sisters, Manya, came towards me (the three Yodelson sisters, daughters of the well-known philanthropist, lived in the apartment). The sisters left Dniepropetrovsk with the arrival of the Germans and didn't have any information on the fate of my relatives.

After our emotional meeting I walked to Polyceiskaya Street, now Korolenko, where we once lived, but I wasn't allowed to enter the apartment. The women, who were in the yard, didn't know me and also knew nothing about my family because they also left the city with the arrival of the Germans. On Operavaskaya Street, now Espolkomskaya, close to our apartment stood the "Soldaskaya Synagogue." I thought, maybe I'll be able to get information there on the fate of my family. Several families lived in the synagogue, which was modified for housing, but I didn't get any information there.

In Nagornaya Street, also in a synagogue that was modified for housing, a woman who lived there told me to go to the synagogue on Yordanskaya Street. I walked to this street and in a small house, next to the Dnieper River, was the synagogue (a prayer was held there during my visit). The beadle, who lived in a cellar next to the place, told to me how to get to the location of the 1941 Aktzya.

I got on the electric tram. The tram turned from the Mining Institute to a place which was once called – the city's summer camps. The entire area was well designed, the streets were wide and beautiful, and the buildings were of several stories. At the last stop I was told that I had to walk a long distance to the location of the massacre.

Finally, I arrived to the place. It was a long and deep ravine and in front of it, in a small neglected lawn, stood a simple monument with an inscription in Russian: "Here, in 1941, Soviet citizens were murdered by Hitler's henchmen." That was all, and nothing more. It's possible to imagine my mood. I shed many tears at that place, and afterwards I went back.

The next day I went to the Jewish cemetery. It turned out that it was moved to the other side of the road because the area of the old cemetery was needed for the expansion of the local airport... During my visit I witnessed the fencing around the new grave of HaRav Pinchas Gelman z"l whose bones were transferred from the old cemetery where he was buried after his death. I knew Rabbi Gelman in my childhood because my mother used to send me to him to ask "questions." I wanted to know where my stepmother, who educated me in my childhood, was buried. After I leafed through the burial book, I realized that the registration began in 1950. My stepmother died in 1941, a short time before the arrival of Hitler.

In one of the following days I went back to the apartment where we once lived. This time I was allowed to enter after I told them that I was only staying here temporarily and want to see the place where we once lived. Jews lived in the apartment and it was renovated and beautifully furnished. I learned from the neighbors that my family didn't want to leave the city. Eyewitnesses said that the Jews were collected, led to their homes, and after their valuables were stolen, they were taken to the location of the killing. One of the Yodelson sisters told me that she met a woman who remained alive in the pit after the shooting. At night, she came out from under the bodies, walked to her acquaintances in the village, and in this way she remained alive.

[Page 84]

From conversations with my acquaintances in the city I learned that anti–Semitism was very strong there. The Ukrainians, who especially excel at it, often say to the Jews: "It's a pity that the Germans didn't kill all of you." I was also told that peasants "willingly" hid Jews who came to them to be saved, but later, after they took their belongings and valuables, they handed them to the Germans.

I spent four days, days of sorrow and mourning in Dniepropetrovsk, and from there I left for Moscow.

Translator's footnote

Batya Riskind–Berkovskaya, a prisoner of Zion and an exile of Zion, was arrested in 1924. After her release continued her work in the Zionist underground and was arrested in Moscow in 1935. Then, she was exiled to Central Asia and two years later was imprisoned in a concentration camp at the edge of Northern Siberia (near Kamchatka). She was released from prison in 1946 but was only allowed to return to Moscow in 1955. She immigrated to Israel 1967 after twenty years of persecutions.

Avraham Shlonsky in a conversation with the editors of "Sefer Yekaterinoslav–Dnepropetrovsk"

by HaRav Dr. Zvi Harkavi and Yaakov Goldburt

Translated by Sara Mages

Ekaterinoslav isn't a city that I was born in. It's a city where I lived with my parents who moved from my hometown, Kriyokov, a suburb of Kremenchuk, which sits, like Ekaterinoslav, on the banks of the Dnieper River. I was five years old then. We lived in Ekaterinoslav for about 16 years, until our immigration to Israel.

Kremenchuk was the Hassidic city of "Schpitz" Chabad, a stream in the Hassidut that our family was associated with. My father was a great expert in the theory of Chabad since his youth and also a great scholar of Modern Hebrew literature. He excelled in his musical talent (he composed, among others, the melody to Chernichovsky's song "Sachki Sachki"). A man of general and Hebrew culture who had religious feelings that "attacked" him from time to time. My mother had tendencies for socialism.

We moved to Ekaterinoslav after the pogroms of 5665 [1895] because of our economic hardship. After we settled there, we received help from our relatives.

My father's house was a national–Zionist house and we didn't have an affiliation with any political party in our youth. At home we honored the tradition, observed the holidays etc., but we didn't observe matters such as kashrut. For several years, my childhood years, we lived in the same house, opposite one another, with our relative, HaRav Levi–Yitzchak Schneersohn, the rabbi of Ekaterinoslav. I studied at the same Heder with his son Mendel (then, we called him "Maka," and today he is the Lubavitch Rebbe). I spent many hours at the rabbi's house and enjoyed the world and the lifestyle of Hassidut Chabad. It was the knowledge that I acquired in my childhood, my childhood's world, and it's still within me to this day. I remember that one day in my childhood I stopped eating at my mother's house because "it wasn't quite kosher" and ate at aunt Chana, wife of HaRav Levi–Yitzchak Schneersohn.

Later, we moved to another part of the city and I immersed in my father's world. My father had a big library and in it, in addition to religious books, were many secular books in Hebrew, Russian and other languages that my father studied. I was influence by this atmosphere of books, books, books. I remember that the city's two rabbis attended the celebration of my Bar–Mitzvah – HaRav Gelman (opponent) and HaRav Schneersohn (Chabad). From the first I received the poems of Adam HaCohen as a gift and the Tanya from the second – the symbol of the tendencies in my soul which was perfumed by both worlds.

When I reached the age of Bar–Mitzvah my father wanted to enter me, for one year, to the Yeshiva in Lubawitsch so I could live in that special atmosphere and remember it in my soul. My mother opposed it. She wanted me to study in one of the gymnasiums in the city. My father didn't want me to assimilate in the atmosphere of a Gentile world, so, the compromise was, that I would travel to Israel to study at the Hebrew gymnasium in Tel–Aviv which was called at that time – "The Gymnasium of Yafo." I traveled to Israel in 5673. I only studied at "Herzliya" for one year because we, the boys who came to Tel-Aviv from Russia, Ukraine etc., were sent home for the summer vacation. But, at the end of the summer vacation we weren't able to return to Tel–Aviv. The days were the days of 1914, the days of the outbreak of the First World War. A year later I continued my studies at the gymnasium of P. Cohen which moved from Vilna to Ekaterinoslav. This gymnasium was Jewish, meaning, the language of study was Russian but all the students, and most of the teacher, were Jewish. Only the teachers for "specific" subjects: history and Russian literature – were "on behalf" of the authorities and, of course, kosher Russians... Among the Hebrew teachers were the poets: Yakov Lerner and Y. L. Baruch; and the pedagogical writers: Pinchas Schiffman, Noach Pine and others. Officially, this gymnasium was in accordance with the law and custom of Tsarist Russia, but there was a Jewish–national tendency in it and under the influence of the students and their parents it also contained a Zionist spirit. The principal tried to adapt to the authorities to ensure its existence (there were also socialist teachers and one, Brown was his name, who, as we later discovered, was a communist).

A number of students, who knew Hebrew well, spoke the language among themselves. The February Revolution aroused a national awakening among the minorities and a Hebrew–speaking association was organized in our school. Since there were also teachers who knew Hebrew, we answered their questions in Hebrew. We also established a Language Committee to prepare a list of terms in mathematics, geometry, physics and others... The Zionist activity among the youth gained power with the revolution of the beginning of 1917 (we were "Pirchai Zion"), and we immediately founded a very active Zionist club and developed many cultural activities. Over time we identified with "Tzeirei Zion" ("Tzeirei Zion" and "Socialist Zionists"). The activists in this club, together with me, were: the late Dan Pines who came with the refugees from Vilna and also Aharon Baker who, by the way, was one of my students. The days were days of anger and excitement and they were also expressed by heated debates. Young poets – Yitzchak Lamdan and Shmuel Helkin who wrote poems in Hebrew and also in Yiddish, arrived at that time to Ekaterinoslav. Peretz Markish[1] who, unlike my "attraction to Hebrew" was drawn to Yiddish, also lived in Ekaterinoslav. One day I told him: the Hebrew language has no future in this country, its future is in Israel, and you must choose: make a pioneering immigration to Israel like me and Lamdan, or settle in Yiddish that its future is also unclear... He chose Yiddish, followed Mawkish, and only by sheer luck survived the end of Markis and his friends. Later, when I was in Moscow, I met an important Yiddish poet who was Helkin's friend in exile in Vorkuta. He told me about his years in exile and his last days after rehabilitation. I have another dream – S. Helkin said – to meet Shlonsky again, to express my remorse and confess before him how right he was and how wrong I was ...

In those days we started the mitzvah of training for immigration. The "Halutz" movement was in its first stages of inception and Dan Pines was one of the primary initiators. After he left Ekaterinoslav we continued our efforts to immigrate to Israel. We, a whole group, made an adventurous journey to Minsk to "study at the Faculty of Yiddish" which was allegedly founded at the university there. Of course, we didn't study in this "Faculty." One night we crossed the border, arrived to the other side, and after many tribulations arrived to Warsaw. It was our first meeting with the ghetto, with Jews whose clothes were strange to us – the little hats, hasty movements and fast and loud speech. This meeting astonished us and it took us a long time to get close to them. Slowly slowly we were able to understand all the specific and valuable which were embodied in this Judaism of the ghetto. After all, we also didn't know the nature of the town. We were children of the city, a city in southern Russia where only a few spoke Yiddish. It was Odessa of Mendele [Mocher Sforim] and Bialik – and not only Odessa of Ahad Ha'am and Klausner – which infused our city with its warm Jewish light with all the results.

We arrived to Warsaw in 1921 during the days of "cessation of immigration" and the riot in which Brenner[2] was murdered. My first poem was published before I left the city. I immigrated to Israel after the immigration was resumed.

Ekaterinoslav was only mentioned once in one of my poems, there, I called it "The howling city" – after the wailing in which the Jews of Ekaterinoslav responded to the murder and robbery of Makhno and Denikin...

Tel–Aviv, Nisan 5730

Beit A. Shlonsky

Written by Yodan Harkavi

Translator's footnotes

1. Peretz Davidovich Markish, a poet and playwright who wrote predominantly in Yiddish, was arrested and executed in 1952 in Moscow.

2. Yosef Haim Brenner, a Hebrew author and Zionist pioneer, was murdered by Arab rioters in Jaffa in 1921.

[Page 89]

The Holocaust

The Holocaust in Dniepropetrovsk
by HaRav Dr. Tzvi Harkavi
Translated by Sara Mages

> ...though often tormented
> like a sheep being led to slaughter
> tossed in the storm of suffering...
>
> ...for the sake of martyrs tossed in the fire...
> (From Hoshanot to Hoshana-Rabba)

The Holocaust in Dniepropetrovsk, as the Holocaust in the German occupied area in the Soviet Union - have the same image. Here, too, were several causes for capturing Jews in the Germans' trap. The Molotov–Ribbentrop Pact - actually: Stalin-Hitler - caused absolute silence in the Soviet Union about the Germans' atrocities against the Jews in the territories occupied by them. Therefore, the Jews didn't know about them, or knew very little. There were those who didn't believe the news, which filtered in, when they remembered the Germans, "who brought order to the Ukraine," in 1918. In addition, there was also an ancient attitude of respect for the nation of "science, culture, order, literature and philosophy." Some of the Jews weren't eager to leave, and some saw the fall in the hands of the Germans - a way for their release from Soviet rule. Of course, the noose was hanging on the necks of those who silenced others. So it was in general before the occupation, and so it was in Dniepropetrovsk (the events are detailed in Leikina's diary).[1]

For lack of statistics it's difficult to determine how many Jews lived in Dniepropetrovsk during the Germans invasion. The Jewish population has grown steadily and Dniepropetrovsk attracted Jews from near and far to the last moment. For that reason, the estimated number of Jews in Dniepropetrovsk on the eve of the Holocaust is 150.000.

Dniepropetrovsk was far from the war front, so it seemed that it wasn't in danger. However, the defeats of the Red Army, and the penetration of the Germans to the Ukraine, changed the situation. At the end of July 1941, after the defeats near Uman, the intuitions and the factories were evacuated from the city and with them - the officials and the essential works. In addition, party members, important bureaucrats, the families of the recruits and many

Jews, were evacuated at an increasing pace. As the front drew near, and with the first bombing at the beginning of August, the non-Jewish residents, especially the Ukrainians, started to talk openly that when the Germans arrive, they - the Ukrainians - would settle their account with the Jews. The attitude changed for the worst, the matter caused fear and worry, and the desire to leave the city increased. But it was already difficult to carry it out. There were few places on the trains because many wanted to leave. Also, the nearby front prevented the normal rail traffic and the trains weren't able to leave during the day because of the bombing. Many searched for another way out - some bought or rented cart, but they weren't able to travel far. There were those who returned to Dniepropetrovsk, some fell in the hands of Ukrainian peasants who robbed and killed them, and some fell in the hands of the Germans who managed to catch up with them. Many Jews left their property with their neighbors with the hope to get it back when they return to the city. The official evacuation was largely directed to the Ural and Central Asia. A small group of evacuees was sent to the Caucasus through the ports of the Sea of Azov. Many fell in the hands of the Germans after they captured the Caucasus. A small number of those who were sent to the Caucasus managed to get out of there, some to Central Asia and some to nearby Georgia.

Some of Dnepropetrovsk's Jews were evacuated by the authorities and some left on their own despite the difficulties. Again, we don't have official figures and in the various sources the number of those who remained in the city ranges between 10.000- 60.000. We have to rely of the number that is registered in the internal-German document: "More than 55,000 killed, and they're those who remained." To those who remained in Dnepropetrovsk we should add the Jews who moved there from the nearby towns, before and even after the occupation, for fear of the Germans and the non-Jewish residents. One thing is clear: those who remained - were exterminated. Only a few, whose names we know, survived: 1) Monin the beadle; 2) Rachel, daughter of Yitzchak Leikina (maybe she's Roza Liekina or her sister who, for some reason, wasn't mentioned in the diary); 3) Sophia, daughter of Vladimir Liekina (relative of the above, or her brother's wife who perished); 4) Noah Luria. 5) Chava (Yeva) Chevernizkaya: 6) Dr. Roza Liekina (if she isn't the aforementioned Rachel).

[Page 90]

In the first days after the capture of the city by the Germans, there weren't any official acts against the Jews. Indeed, quite a few German soldiers visited the homes of the Jews, robbed, plundered, raped, and in many cases, even murdered. in the various sources we're looking for Communists, members of the Soviet regime. The Germans were assisted by the non-Jewish neighbors, mostly Ukrainians who, on this occasion, "avenged" their Jewish neighbors, stole and robbed them together with the Germans or without them. There were cases when Jews were taken to the German police with a demand to pay ransom and in this way, they were robbed. There were many acts of murder at the outskirts of the city by the non-Jewish residents. As a result, many chose to move to other locations, to their relatives in the city center, so as not to be alone among non-Jews. When they moved from their homes, they asked their neighbors to hold their property until things calm down, and in this manner a lot of property was transferred into the hands of non-Jews. With that, it should be noted that there were those among the non-Jews who helped their Jewish neighbors despite the great danger.

There was a great shortage of foodstuffs and it's clear that the Jews, who didn't have connections in the villages, suffered the most. Many of Dniepropetrovsk's Jews were severely punished when they were caught trading with the farmers. In those days, and also later on, several Jews left the city and went to hide with the peasants in the villages. This matter was easier for the women, that some of them looked like Christians, and not for the men because they were circumcised. And indeed, a small number of them survived. There were many cases when the peasants handed the Jews to the Germans, or killed them, after they took everything from them.

Shortly after the occupation the Germans issued a decree that the Jews had to wear a yellow armband with a Star of David on their sleeve. On 8 October, Dniepropetrovsk's Jews were ordered to deposit the sum of 25-30 million Rubles in the Germans' headquarters fund. Sort of a "Community Committee" was established to collect this sum from the Jews who remained in Dniepropetrovsk. The attorney Grinberg(?) was elected to head this "committee" and an office was set in Kharkovskaya Street. Each person received a note from the "committee office" with the amount he had to deposit. The payments started on 10 October, and by the day of the Aktzia, Dniepropetrovsk's Jews deposited the amount that was imposed on them as a "punishment for their crimes against the German government...

The Aktzia

On 11 October, the management of each building was ordered to submit an accurate list of all he Jews who remained there and immediately after came the order that on 13 October that the Jews should report next to the

"Univermag" in the prospekt for a "transfer to another location for their safety and security," and they should to take food and valuables with them. Many, in their innocence, believed this order. When they arrived to the gathering location their belongings stolen, they were loaded on trucks and taken to the edge of the city, to a place called the City Garden next to the "Institute of Transportation." There, they were slaughtered in one of the deep ravines. The slaughter also continued on the next day, 14 October and, according to Liekina, about 38 thousand Jews were killed in those two days.

[Page 91]

On 12 October, many of Dniepropetrovsk's Jews, who thought that they would be safer at the assembly point, started to gather next to the "Univermag" for fear of the police and their neighbors who started to attack them and rob their belongings. For that reason, 12 October is considered to be the first day of the Aktzia in several sources. Out of tens of thousands of fatalities only a few managed to save their life. It should be noted, that the Ukrainian policemen behaved with special cruelty towards those who were led to the slaughter - robbed, beat, and abused.

In her diary, Liekina describes everything in simplicity, the fears, the Germans' order to the Jews to gather, the killing and what followed. According to "Goebbels' calendar" - in which the Jewish holidays were chosen as dates for the Aktziot - the day of Shemini Atzeret 5702 was chosen as the first day of the slaughter and Simchat Torah as the second (13-14 October, 1941)[2].

According to a German source[3], an Einsatzgruppe [task force] operated in Dniepropetrovsk under the command of SS Brigadier Otto Hahs.

Noah Luria gave an oral testimony to the Anti-Fascist Committee: "In Dniepropetrovsk, near the "Transportation Institute," they (the Germans) shot and buried alive in a vast ravine 11.000 women, elderly, children (Jews) ... (Nuremberg trial report, 1947, page 47, section 1).

After the Holocaust, when the refugees returned to their city, Dniepropetrovsk, from the place of their evacuation they came across, like in many other places, with Ukrainian anti-Semitism. The Ukrainians refused to give them their apartments and property back. In 1947, for these reasons fifty families from the vicinity of Dniepropetrovsk decided to move to... Birobidzhan and arrived there together (in a freight train) ...

How many Jews were murdered in Dnepropetrovsk? As aforementioned, there were about 150.000 Jews on the eve of the Holocaust. In his article, (Eynikayt, 27.6.46, "Dniepropetrovsk") - S. Artenberg wrote that the Red Army found 10-15 Jewish survivors in the city (as mentioned, there're those who give a smaller number). All the Jews who were trapped in the city were annihilated - no one disputes that.

In regard to the first Aktzia - the decisive - most of the sources mention the date: 13.10.41, the day of Shemini Atzeret 5702. Some also mention the previous day, 12.10.41 - the day of Hoshana-Rabba, as the first day of the Aktzia. Orenburg uses the date 10.10.41 in his article (Eynikayt, 27.12.42). He entered the wrong date because he wrote the article on the other side of the front lines.

There are different reports on the number of fatalities, starting from 10.000 and up to 55.492. Additional Atkziot came after the first Aktzia, and occasional killings annihilated the survivors.

Here are the sources, from the few to the many, with their dates:

Gideon Hausner in the report he submitted at the Eichmann trial (9.5.61) - 13-10-41 - 10.000[4].

In a Nuremberg trial report, 1947, page 49 (in English) - 12.10.41 - 11.100.

S. Artenberg in his article (Eynikayt, 27.6.46) - 20.000.

Y.Z. in his testimony before the residents of Dniepropetrovsk - 13.10.41 - 20.000.

In a Nuremberg trial report, page 67: In Kiev and Dniepropetrovsk together 60.000, and if we collect 33.000 for Kiev, 27.000 will remain for Dniepropetrovsk.

S. Spector, secretary of Yad Vashem, in his letter to me from the month of Elul 5721 - 13.10.41 - 30.000.

[Page 92]

A. Arnburg, in his article (Eynikayt, 27.12.42) - 10.10.41 - 32.000.

S. Leibkovitz, in her testimony before the residents of Dniepropetrovsk: "14-18 thousand in the big new cemetery within a day or two, apart from those who were killed in the "monastery" forest. And they "shot them two days and two nights." [Most of the new Jewish cemetery was desecrated by the Nazis and their partners, and it was difficult to identify the graves after the Holocaust. (See Mark Schechter's poem - "My father's grave"].

The doctor, Dr. Leikina (Sovetish Heymland, 1965.5) - 13/14.10.41 - 37.000.

The Black Book[5], 1946, pages 366-368 and page 374, note 94 - 35.000-40.000.

Moshe Kahanovitz, The war of the Jewish partisans in eastern Europe, page 171 - 12.0.41.

And here, after I read hundreds of reports in German at Yad Vashem about the actions of the Nazi divisions in the Soviet Union, I found on page number 001721[6]: 55.432 put to death in Dniepropetrovsk at the beginning of October 1941.

In summary, in my opinion there were over 100.000 Jews in Dniepropetrovsk on the eve of the Holocaust. About half of them managed to get out - or were evacuated - from the city. About half of them, apart from about a "minyan" of Jews, who miraculously survived, were trapped and exterminated.

The main Aktzia, but not the only one, took place on Shemini Atzeret, and it's possible to rely of the Germans' statistics who "innocently" told t what they saw - their defilement.

Overall, at least 55,432 Jewish martyrs were murdered in Dniepropetrovsk. May the Lord avenge their blood.

Translator's Footnotes

1. See Molotov's words (Pravda, 1.11.39) about the ideological contrast between Communism and Hitlerism. Levi Kentor (One hundred years of struggle, Tel-Aviv, 5729, page 301), assumes, that the silencing was understood by the anti-Semitic elements in the Soviet Union for permission to exterminate Jews.

2. Only in "Behevlie kelayah," page 76, there is a surprising report about a "second slaughter" on 12.41 (21 Kislev 5702) in which 10,000 Jews were murdered. Maybe there is a mixing of the dates here for the same Aktzia.

3. Einsatzgruppe's report from 19.11.41, which states that 10,000 Jews were murdered. This number is also given in "Behevlie kelayah," page 28.

4. A. A. Goldstein, Book on Russian Jewry II, pages 89, 92, writes: 30,000(?) Jews remained in Dniepropetrovsk, 11,000(?) were killed.

5. On behalf of the World Jewish Congress, the Anti-Fascist Committee in Moscow, the National Council of the Jews of Eretz-Yisrael, the Writers Association, the Jewish artists and scientists in the United-States.

6. Microfilm in German: IM/1763
   001535- 001541
   001715-001725
   EREIGNISMELDUNG
   UD SSR N-132
   12 NOV. 1941

[Page 93]

The Days of the Holocaust in Dniepropetrovsk

by Dr. Rosa Leikina

Translated by Yocheved Klausner

The diary of the doctor from Dniepropetrovsk, during the time of the Holocaust, Dr. Rosa (daughter of Yitzhak) Leikina z"l, is a tragic Jewish–human document of primary value. She wrote it during the nights, after liberation. It was written in Russian and transcribed in the same language by Meir Polonski. The writer Shira Goreshman translated it to Yiddish (Sovietish Heimland, May 1968). It was translated to Hebrew under the sponsorship of those who have the publishing rights.

Dr. Leikina died in 1965 in Dniepropetrovsk. She lived on Tchitchrin Street 26, in a small, one–floor house. Three steps led from the street to her apartment, with a rusted iron door at the entrance.

Anya–Tzila Schwartz, her adopted daughter (she had no children of her own) and her sister Mina Yankelewitz live in Dniepropetrovsk and are guarding her tomb.

The story of Anya–Tzila bat Avraham is the story of a Jewish girl in Dniepropetrovsk. They lived in the Kaydaki suburb. She was, miraculously, the sole survivor of her entire family (see Sovietish Heimland, May 1968, pp. 93–94), since they transformed her into Maruska Ivanovna... the rest is in the diary.

To this day, Anya Tzila cherishes the memory of the Jewish doctor from Dniepropetrovsk, who "could have been still alive, had she thought about herself. But she cared for and helped others, even during the times of Hell." A Jewish soul from Dniepropetrovsk – may her memory be blessed.

Z. H.

Even if suffering and tragedy that strike a person are forgotten in time, my own tragedy will never go into oblivion, my wounds will not heal, the cries of the slaughtered will not quiet down.

I am now fifty-four, and I never wrote anything, but the things that I have experienced do not allow me to keep silent. I must tell everything, so that no person in the world would think that the fascists are in any way similar to real people.

All my life I lived in Dniepropetrovsk. Until the occupation I worked as a doctor. My husband, Lev Abramowitz Constantinovski, was older than I, and for several years he suffered from heart disease.

On 8 August 1941, the evacuation of Dniepropetrovsk began. The atmosphere of panic, excitement and noise caused a decline in the situation of my husband and he suffered daily attacks. I was certain that I would not have to move him – Dniepropetrovsk, a big industrial town, would not be handed over to the enemy. In his youth, my husband had been living in Berlin and he would say:

"The Germans are a European nation, a nation with a philosophical education."

As for myself – I had heard little about fascist cruelty. Had I realized what horrors and defilement they were capable of, maybe things would have turned out differently. But the main reason that tied my hands was my husband's illness, and I was not entirely healthy myself.

The director Dr. Yosepowitz said to me:

It is your duty to remain in your place of work. Next day, I heard that he and his family had left town.

[Page 94]

On 16 August the Germans bombed the train station. Several days later, our army left town, and the most terrible thing happened: we remained in town.

From the first day of the fascist occupation, dark figures began crawling from all corners. Anti–Semitic talk and incitement to a pogrom were heard everywhere. All that had been silent and hidden came to the surface, and violence reigned, with its tragic results: murder, rape, robbery. During the air attacks we descended with the others into the cellar. Once, the German woman Agnessa Genriks was there and she told us that the S.S. have murdered old Munin. We all knew Munin – he never harmed a soul. The same day, the S. S. forced an old Jewish tailor to dig his own grave. They shot him and threw him into the grave while still alive. Two days later, on Filosofskaya Street, they killed Jews while they prayed in the synagogue.

On 3 September, a fire bomb hit the store in the corner of Tchitcherin Street and the Pushkin Prospect. The fascists burst into our cellar and shouted:

Jews, out!

When they took my husband, I ran after him, and heard him say: "I'll go bring pails, to stop the fire." The fascists let him go, and he went to the neighbors who gave him shelter. Mentioning the pails of water saved his life and he was spared the fate of the others, who were taken to be burned.

Inhuman cries were heard from the place: the fascists threw into the fire all those who had come to help put it out.

In the morning, we decided not to return to our home; we went to our neighbor, Yaroshenko, and we stayed there two weeks. Mrs. Yaroshenko, a German woman, helped us and also watched our house, which we had left with all its content. At her request, we gave her the key to our house; facing death, we did not care who will take our property.

But Mrs. Yaroshenko did care. She took out of our house suitcases full of things, bedding, dishes and other things – not out of her great love for us...

After some time, an order was issued by the Germans, that all Jews must wear on their sleeves a Star–of–David patch. We couldn't stay with Yaroshenko and we returned to our robbed apartment. We had to live, to eat, and I asked Yaroshenko to return our things; to no avail.

In the middle of the night, somebody knocked on the door. My husband managed to hide, and I opened. Two armed fascists came in and one of them said to me:

– Your Talmud says that all people, except the Jews, are worse than dogs. Where is your husband?

I replied that I was a widow and I don't even have children, because I am a sick woman.

Later I understood that my words about being sick saved me from being raped.

Similar visits occurred often, and every time I became petrified, as if my senses stopped working: only later I understood that I was again saved from death.

On 8 October, the Germans issued the following order: "In spite of the fact that Ekaterinoslav now belongs to the Third Reich, the Zhids are robbing the town, therefore the German Command orders: The Zhids shall pay 30 million Marks; those who will not pay, will be punished by the severe Martial Law.

The Jews, panicked o death, were sitting in their robbed houses – and they were accused of robbery!

This demand for contribution forced the Jews to organize again a community, which was headed by the jurist Gernberg. On Kharkovskaia Street No. 3 they gave out notes, according to which the bank received the contributions.

The first payment, on 10 October, was the last one as well.

On 11 October the Germans issued a new order: the managements of the houses must submit exact lists of the Jews who were still living in the houses.

A rumor spread, that "bread cards" will be issued according to these lists: in truth they were prepared for those sentenced to death.

On the night of 13 October all Jews were driven to the new "Karl Marx" store on the Prospect. It was a strange procession – old and young, pregnant women, small children carrying bundles, all marching to the place the fascists told them to go.

My husband first thought that these were the persons who had not paid the "contribution," so we remained in our apartment. At noon, policemen broke into our apartment, drove us out and we also went in the direction of the new store.

After a while we met Jews returning from there, and they told us: It was postponed to the next day. What exactly was postponed we didn't know.

[Page 95]

Returning home gave me a strange feeling: I had accompanied myself to the grave and now I was returning to my robbed apartment, which looked like a dead corpse, torn to pieces by birds of prey.

Next day we went again, and again we were told by the people on their way back "postponed until new orders are given."

In the morning of 15 October, someone knocked silently on the door. I went to open and saw Moshe Kapelinko the blacksmith. He was full of mud and looked like a dead man just taken out of his grave.

– What happened to you? I asked.

– I and two other Jews who were not shot, came out of the pit. All others were shot.

He cleaned himself a little. I gave him some clothes to change, and he left. So we learned what had been "postponed" until the new orders...

The Arians did what is beyond human thought, what humanity had never known. The innocent victims fell with the last cry:

– Why?!

To this day this cry is ringing in my ears.

On 13 and 14 October, 37 thousand Jews were slaughtered in Dniepropetrovsk. Among them were my brother of 30 years old, the artist Lev Isakowitz Leikin, and aunt Bertha Yefimovna Leikina with her daughter and her grandchildren.

For us, who were sentenced to life, days of suffering began, and we envied those who have already fallen.

On 27 October, "educated" fascists officers came and said politely:

– Your apartment is needed for the army.

To my question: Where should we go? They replied:

– To other Jews.

We went to live with my husband's niece, who lived in another apartment in the same courtyard. In the evening, policemen with torches burst into our place, saying: this is the rich Jewess. They drove us out in the yard, threw us on the ground and beat us. Finally, the order came to get up. One of them caught me and said:

You are going with me to the police.

I was sure that I was going to die.

I went to the next room; 3 traitors were sitting there.

– Where is your husband?

– My husband went to look for food.

They whispered something and suddenly ordered me to go home.

I understood that I was liberated so that they would be able to find my husband.

Nights of horror. In the empty streets, terrible sounds were heard. Instead of fleeing, I approached them. A policeman caught me and began to hit me. I begged: Save me, kill me.

Another policeman approached and shouted to him:

– Take her, she is good...

For the first time in my life, I yelled the way I didn't believe that it was possible. The murderer tore my blouse and saw the money I had hidden there. He took it and for a moment forgot me, and I ran. I was saved from death, and from what was worse than death – I was saved from rape. I walked through a side–alley. Suddenly a strange creature appeared. His shirt torn, the hairs of his beard standing up, he prayed in the Holy Language, great sadness was heard in his prayer. I approached and recognized him: It was our old neighbor Feldman. Now he presented his grievances in Yiddish: "Father in Heaven, I have never stolen, I have certainly not killed anybody, God forbid. I helped my fellows as much as I could, and You punished me with the most bitter punishment. Why do I deserve this? Why did I have to see with my eyes what the murderers did to my child? 8230; I couldn't listen to that anymore and I walked in the darkness to the place where my husband was hiding. To my question – have they found him? did they take him? – I received no reply.

I wandered further, with my last strength I entered the home of a Jewish family that we knew. At first it was quiet, but suddenly terrible cries were heard: it was Feldman's daughter lamenting her fate. When she stopped for a minute and looked at the old woman near her, the silence was more terrible than her wailing. I thought: If the only guilt of the fascist were the rape of this young woman, looking through her grieving to the thin old woman near her – only for that they would deserve to be erased from the face of the earth. I could not bear to see how Feldman's daughter looked at the old woman. Her stare drove me out of the house. Suddenly I remembered that my husband had a good friend, an artist by the name of Peter Zhotchkin. I went there – my husband wasn't there. I returned to out courtyard and was told that my husband had just left. My tired brain pictured many images – one more horrible that the other. I heard terrible sounds, my husband's cries, I saw how the murderers finished him – visions that suited the reality of the day.

[Page 96]

The next day I met my husband. The entire day we wandered through side alleys, without a piece of bread, without a roof over our heads. It was turning dark – where could we go?

Tired and depressed we went to the house of Dr. Varnigora. They took us in and gave us food. We stayed there two days.

Again, we wandered like shadows through the streets. Night came; helpless and humiliated, we knocked at the door of Dr. Evgenia Papkova. They fed us, and we slept in a soft, warm bed. Early in the morning we went on.

In order to get some food, we needed our things, which had been left at the house of our neighbors. In the past we could still obtain something from them, but it became harder and harder.

But our hunger was hurting, and we forced ourselves to approach again our neighbor Prichodka. She threw at me one of our tablecloths and shouted: Don't come anymore! I gave your things to the police, I don't know you and I don't recognize you!

For several days we hid at the house of the nurse Danyetz. She went with me to another neighbor to help me receive something from her. She gave my husband some new underwear and said quietly:

You see, I am giving you new underwear, not old. But do you really need it? You will be killed anyway, like all other Jews. Not one will remain alive, I am sure of that.

I could go on and on with these stories. But I will not. I always thought that one savior outweighs many hangmen.

*

Much suffering is caused by hunger, but so much greater is the suffering of the person who is sentenced to see how the one who is closest to him fades away and becomes extinguished like a candle and there is no way to help. Thousands have perished, I and my husband are still alive.

I am disgusted with my life.

I decided to obtain morphine, but I did not succeed. When my husband heard that I had been looking for morphine, he became a believer and would tell me often:

Rosa, Divine Providence is stronger than we are, we shall survive, we shall stay alive.

And we did. We continued living. I decided to go to the Health Section. When I entered the office, and saw the manager, my eyes lit up: it was Alexander Stankowitz, a Soviet German. I had worked with him in the past, many years. I did not have to explain, he understood my situation very well.

He said: I am going to the Secretary General, you stay here!

And to the guard at the door he said: Don't let anyone in here!

An hour later Dr. Stankowitz returned, happy, showed me a paper and said smiling:

This is a license for you. You will work as a nose, ear and throat doctor, together with your friends the Jewish doctors, who hold similar licenses.

All five of us, the Jewish doctors, knew that our work was temporary. They were: the surgeons Motzan and Tzertok, Karsonski (venereal diseases) the dentist Schulman and Genboim (general practitioner). Dr Motzan became ill and died (a natural death - happily!). His wife did not look as a Jewish woman, so she ran away, but was caught by the Gestapo and murdered. The other doctors were also murdered. I sought a way to go to Amur (this was the name of a large suburb of Dniepropetrovsk), where I was sent by Dr. Stankowitz to work. I decided that I should first go there alone, then bring my husband. I asked Dr. Popovka to hospitalize my husband in the hospital for contagious diseases as sick with scarlet fever, and she did so. My heart was torn to pieces – how long would my husband be able to remain in the hospital? In spite of all our troubles, my husband looked quite good for his over 60 years. He was handsome, full of life and in a good mood, and he said to me with confidence:

– Go in peace and don't worry – we will survive, just be smart and careful.

*

It was raining heavily. I walked through the mud, since the Germans had forbidden the use of the bridge to Amur and the temporary bridge was destroyed. Only after several hours I reached the boat that was supposed to take me to the other side. A long line was waiting. The workers on the Dnieper were war prisoners, wearing rags, dirty, skinny to the bones. The fascists would beat them all the time with their whips. I looked and was silent. I only wished that a flood would come from heaven and wipe everything off this earth.

[Page 97]

About two in the afternoon it was my turn to get into the boat. They took seven people, I was the eighth and was not allowed on the boat. The cold rain was like a whip on my skin, not even one dry thread remained on me.

Finally, the next boat came, and I got in, thank God. Suddenly loud cries were heard "Help, we are drowning!" The boat that I was not allowed on turned over. The owner of our boat did not approach to help, just said to us: I am waiting here, you swim to the shore, it is not far!

It was true that the shore was not far and the water not deep – about to the shoulders – but it was cold. I was trembling, my woolen coat like lead, pulling me down. Only a while ago I wanted to be covered with water – and now I am struggling with the last of my strength to get out of the muddy, icy water. I was already near the shore; my teeth were shaking, and my heart stopped. I looked – do I still have my shoes on my feet? – Yes. I remained standing for a second, water pouring from my body. The other people who crossed with me were wet as well, but they kept walking, a warm corner was waiting for them. I stood, confused – where should I go? I fell to the ground, and for the first time in my life I prayed:

– My God, take me, put an end to my life!

Suddenly I heard a voice:

– Lady, what happened? Why are you crying?

A human voice has been speaking to me? Was I still alive? I lifted my eyes and saw a young man.

– Son, you see what is happening to me. I need to go to the hospital and I do not know how.

The young man took me by the hand and led me straight to the door of the hospital. I was so overwhelmed and happy, realizing that there were still good people in the world, that I forgot to thank him.

I showed the director, Dr. Ponomarski, the letter given to me by Dr. Stankowitz, that I was sent to work there; he read the letter and ordered to bring bread and dry clothing for me. There are still some good people in the world! I decided to keep half of the bread for my husband.

In the evening, I asked the director:

– Where can I sleep?

He replied: In the waiting room; tomorrow I'll find a place for you.

In the waiting room was so cold, that even wolves wouldn't be able to stay. But I had on me dry clothes. I lay down on the bench and tried to figure out a way to take the piece of bread to my husband, who was in the department of contagious diseases, at Dr. Popovka. After I finished working the next day, I asked Dr. Ponomarski again – where will be my corner? And he said, "the laundry room, for the time being."

The laundry room was a large room, its floor made of cement, the windows broken and fixed with wood panels. The wind was like outside. In the room there was a cooking stove, but it was not enough to keep the room warm. I put my bed close to the stove, but I didn't sleep all night. I hid the bread under my pillow, but the mice smelled it and I had to keep an eye on it all night.

After I got used to the place a little, I met the surgeon Dr. Korsonski, who also had a permit to work there. He knew, as well as I, that our work was temporary.

To tell the truth, I didn't feel good in the hospital. In particular, it was difficult to keep a good relationship with Dr. Zivatova. In bad weather, she would stay during the night in the hospital, would move my bed away from the stove and place hers there, and would tell me about her lyrical memories. Although she was a young doctor and received her education in the Soviet University, it did not help her much.

– When I worked at the hospital in Igran, I had everything, I didn't have to buy a thing, since the hospital was managed like a household. I often told my husband to find work with the police, but he continues working in his awful factory and earns "water for the porridge."

I decided to be careful and keep a distance. Once, when we were alone, she approached me and said quietly:

Just now one of the workers told me, that the fascists burst into the hospital at Igran and killed the Jewish doctors, the hospitalized patients and the pharmacist Frank. My advice is that you leave here.

Her advice was good, but where could I go?

On 27 November Dr. Korsonski and I were called to the police. The investigator, a Russian German said:

A military plant is going to be built here. I could order you to leave immediately, but I have good manners and I give you ten days.

[Page 98]

We returned to the hospital and told Dr. Ponomarenco. He calmed us, and we continued working. Every day I received 900-gram bread and two plates of soup. I would save some of the bread for my husband, but I didn't know how to take it to him.

On February they stopped giving us bread. But worse than the hunger and the cold laundry room was the fact that I knew nothing about my husband. But again, I met some good people – this time it was the pediatrician Frimak. Her life was not easy, still she would give me sometimes a piece of bread. I could also visit her home, sometimes, and my heart would warm up from her heartfelt words. She told me that her husband was a soldier in the Red Army and I told her my secret as well. Sometimes I would give her a piece of bread and she would take it to my husband.

Dr. Popovka was so good – she gave him a short note from me. Now I knew that Lev Abramowitz was alive, that he was still in the department of the scarlet fever, and I well understood that this situation could not continue for long. But it was also out of the question to transfer him to my place.

By the end of December, again they called me and Dr. Korsonski to the police. Dr. Korsonski told me:

– This is the end. I am going in the direction of Pavlograd–Lozovaya. Perhaps I will make it to the front. I am not staying with the fascists anymore.

He went, wearing a light coat; I don't know whether he reached our army, or he froze on the way, I never saw him again.

I went to the police, alone. The "good–mannered" policeman looked at me and my blood froze.

– Have you forgotten what I have told you? Now – in three days I don't want to see you here.

Later I received the explanation: in one of the darkened streets I met the hospital accountant. He told me, that exactly three days after my encounter with the policeman, the fascists assembled all Jewish doctors and the other Jews who were still alive and took them all to be slaughtered. Then I understood that the severe order of the policeman had saved my life.

On 31 December I left Dr. Ponomarenco. He gave me a permit to work in Dniepropetrovsk. With tears in his eyes, he expressed his hope that I would not fall again in the hands of the fascists. On 2 January, a cold and foggy day, I began walking toward town. Nobody besides me was on the bridge, only he guards at their posts. I was crawling, and the bridge had no end. And lo, I reached the town where all my life passed, the town that was so close and now it became a total stranger! My first aim was to see my husband, but this was dangerous, because everyone knew me in the hospital where I had worked for years. Should I go to Dr. Popovka? – No, since it was a Holiday and she could have guests. I went to my house, but I could not get in. I went to my former neighbor, Wilkov. He was alarmed when he saw me. I calmed him, rested a bit and got warm. From there I went to my husband's niece, who still lived in the apartment in our courtyard. She told me, that my husband had not appeared at the registration to the fascists by the end of December. He went again to Dr. Popovka, who gave him a bed in the hospital, but in another section. I went to her. She gave me regards from mu husband, but I couldn't spend the night there. I finally went to the hospital on Filosofskaya Street, where Dr. Warnigora directed the Women's ward. I asked her to accept me as a patient: in agreement with the chief doctor Zhokova I was interned as a cancer patient. He also changed my name and the name of my father – and from then on I was named Rayssa Ivanovna Leikina. The warm bed and the silence around me had their effect and I fell asleep immediately.

There was not much food – 200 gr. bread and two plates of watery soup. Other patients received their food from their homes. But I saved bread from the rations I received.

The patient in my next bed, a sick woman, asked me once: For whom are you saving the bread you receive?

I told her about my misfortune and I did not regret it: Her daughter would take the bread and give it to my husband.

One evening, Dr. Zhokov told me, whispering: Dr. Stankowitz asked me to tell you not to worry, he will arrange work for your husband.

I didn't understand and asked to be sent to Dr. Zhokov; I asked him:

– In the ward it is not easy to talk to you; please tell me, what kind of work can Dr. Stankowitz find for my husband?

– They are about to establish a ghetto in Dniepropetrovsk. Dr. Stankowitz thinks, that he will be able to find work for your husband there.

I did not understand; for whom were the fascists preparing a ghetto? For the Jews who were murdered?

Later I heard that the ghetto will be for Jews from other towns, who were still alive.

Several days later Dr. Zhokov called me again.

– I received a telegram from Dr. Stankowitz, telling me to take you out of the hospital immediately, since the fascists are planning to kill all the hospitalized Jews; go get your things.

[Page 99]

After the forty days that I had been in the hospital, I was still very weak; but the fear that maybe Dr. Popovka wouldn't take my husband out in time, drove my actions. I slipped and fell, got up with difficulty, but I couldn't reach Tchetchlovka, where Dr. Popovka was. I reached only Anton Dienka, who lived in the courtyard on Tchitcherin Street. They received me warmly and didn't let me go. I stayed with them two days, and although my leg was still swollen and aching, I went to Dr. Vernigora. As I came in, the doorbell rang, the door opened – and there on the threshold was my husband. It was difficult to recognize him.

This was on 12 February. We stayed for the night at Dr. Vernigora. Early in the morning we left. The dirty kerchief was tightening around our throats.

Again, we were wandering and trembling at every step. Every moment it seemed to us that they will come and take us to be slaughtered. And so, wandering from street to street, we suddenly met Moshe Kapilenko, the same person who had saved us from death on 13 October. He told us that he was working as a blacksmith at Alimov's workshop, and he took us to him. Every day I had to go out and look for food. I worked as a beggar, and if the day was successful, I could stay home for a few days. Once, in the middle of the night, there were knocks at the door. My husband and Kapilenko went to the hiding place. Two fascists came in, flashlights in their hands. They checked the house and asked if there were deserters hiding there. Then they left. Next day, Kapilenko asked us to go register our passports at the Gestapo, as required by a recent order.

I had no choice. I said farewell to my friends who had helped me, gave me bread and let me sleep in their homes. Dr. Stankowitz and Dr. Wernigora advised me not to go, but they, too, understood that there was no other way. Wernigora said to me:

If they impose a fine on you, agree and tell them that you will pay the next day. We will obtain the money for you.

At the end of February, two months late, I went, scared to death, to the Gestapo on Korolenko Street.

At the entrance, I lifted my coat so that the Star–of–David on my sleeve could be seen. The porter, an elderly man, looked at me and said in a whisper:

Are you sane? Go away immediately!

At that moment the Gestapo man inside called me:

Come here!

He took me to the second floor, where another Gestapo man was sitting. When I came closer, he yelled:

Go away! You don't look like a human being!

Scared, I said that I came to register our passports.

– Why so late?

I am working in the hospital in Amur, and except for the sick people I didn't see anyone, so I didn't know until now.

– Why did you bring your husband's passport? Where is he now?

– My husband is sick.

The officer took the passports and asked the other, who had brought me in:

– What fine shall I set?

– No fine!

When I returned downstairs to the waiting room, the old porter started to cross himself and said:

Thank God, you were saved, now you will stay alive. Go home and may God protect you.

*

I returned to Dr. Stankowitz. He was glad to see me and said:

Now everything will be OK. At the first chance I will arrange work for you.

My husband didn't realize where I had been, and when I returned home, he said:

– I knew that you would come back, they will not touch those who have survived.

We remained with Kapilenko. His mother was also there, and also, I young woman by the name of Mania, whose husband had been killed by the fascists and she was alone. A Russia woman she met told her:

– An old Jewish woman is living on Pushkin Street, why don't you live together, it will be easier for both of you.

Mania told me, that not far from us lived a Jewish girl aged about ten, her father was on the front and the rest of her family were killed by the fascists. I asked to call her, and she came shortly, very thin, her eyes looking at me, full of fear.

[Page 100]

– What is your name?

– Yulotchka.

– Why do you live in this ruined house?

– Father will come back from the war and I am keeping the house for him.

The girl was so gentle, full of longing, she rested her head on my shoulder. But by no means did she agree to remain with us. After she left, I said:

– If we survive, Yulotchka will be our daughter.

– Of course – my husband agreed.

The girl visited us every day and the bread I had I divided into three parts. When we left Kapilenko (because he simply drove us out) I kept asking about her. I suffered a great deal not having a place to stay, until a woman with a good heart said:

– Come and live with me. What God will decide – so be it!

The name of the woman was Nina Fiodorovna Boyko. Once I asked her to go to Lyastchenko and bring some of my things. This was not easy, since the Lyastchenko woman was seldom at home, and when she was, she "welcomed" Nina in such a way, that she told me angrily, when she came back: Rozalia Isakovna, you are an educated woman, but you certainly don't know people. Lyastchenko is not a friend, she hates you with all her heart.

On 15 July, Dr. Stankowitz arranged for me work in the Fourth Polyclinic in Kaidaki.

The chief doctor in the Polyclinic was Yarilo Dimitri Ievgenewitz and his wife was also a doctor. They were really good people. Every morning, as he came to the Polyclinic, he came to see me. It was clear, that he had doubts whether he would find me alive. Many times he warned me:

– Be careful with the eye–doctor in our Polyclinic, she is not a Soviet woman.

On 25 June, Boyko's a neighbor informed on us and we were taken to the Gestapo. Dr. Yarilo did not desert us and took care of our release. Again, someone informed, and we were arrested and again we were released thanks to Dr. Yarilo. But it was difficult to obtain a card for bread, and when Dr. Yarilo sought the help of Dr. Stankowitz's aide, he was told:

– Why are you so concerned about the Jewess Leikina?

Yarilo told me: With the Gestapo it was easier to work.

Still, Dr. Yarilo obtained for me a bread card for one month. After that, as I didn't obtain a card, he would bring me now and then a piece of bread, but I refused to take his ration away:

Dear Dimitri Ievgenewitz, I know that it is your ration, and I doubt whether tomorrow I will need food...

As part of my work in the Polyclinic, I would sometimes visit the sick at their house. It happened several times that a relative would wait outside and put a piece of bread in my pocket. I refused to apply for a Russian passport, as Dr. Zhokov and Dr. Wernigora advised me, because I didn't want to leave my sick husband. They gave the passport to the surgeon Tamara Tchertok, but on 4 March they took her and her husband and child, and they perished. I was the only Jewish doctor left. Every day I waited for Death to come. Once, as I walked from the clinic through Kaidaki I saw two young men on bicycles approaching. When they came close, they stopped and called my name. I froze. One of them asked:

– Are you Dr. Leikina? Are you working at Kaidaki?

– Yes.

– You live on Martinovskaia Street?

– Yes.

In my head I felt: "They know everything, this is the end..."

– Show us your passport.

– My passport is at the Police.

– Go, they said; quietly they mounted their bicycles and left.

When they were gone, an idea came to my mind: The partisans – how didn't I realize that immediately?

Later, when Dniepropetrovsk was liberated, I met one of my acquaintances, the head of a group of partisans. When I told him, that I was in town the entire time during the occupation, he said, sadly:

– Who could have known? All the time I was looking for a doctor for my unit.

I was sorry, too.

On 19 November Dr. Yarilo said:

– They are taking the last Jews left. Yesterday they killed a Jewish teacher. I am locking you in the laboratory, and I will consult with my wife how to hide you.

But I couldn't agree. My husband was at Shlyachovka and how could I remain in a locked laboratory?

At night, I went to Shlyachovka to Nina Boyko, where we had lived before, I and my husband. I approached the bridge, and saw Vasya, who was also staying with Boyko, together with his mother.

[Page 101]

– Why are you standing here? I asked him.

Nina Fiodorovka sent me to meet you. After you went to work this morning, policemen came and took your husband. Now they are back and waiting for you.

– You will not tell that you saw me? I asked.

– I will keep silent, I told the policemen that I was going to the toilet.

Now I couldn't go there anymore. I remembered our good acquaintance, Vera Kotliar. I went to her and both of us mourned and eulogized my husband. I shall never forget that night! It snowed all night and it seemed that all was covered with a white shroud.

I hurried to Dr. Stankowitz, hoping to find him home, before he goes to work. He was very worried.

– My wife and I didn't sleep all night, seeking a way to tell you that the Gestapo was here and asked that in the morning Dr. Leikina would come, dead or alive, and if not, they will come again and together we shall look for you.

– Dr. save my husband from the hands of these humanity–haters and we shall not bother you anymore, I promise you.

– I am afraid we cannot help your husband.

– Have pity on me, my only friend, give me morphine.

– It is true that I am German, but I don't kill people. And in this case, you will not get any help from me. Yes, don't go to work, and, by no means, don't go to Shlyachovka, because I will go with the Gestapo people to look for you there. Hide until troubles are over, beg in the streets...

He offered me money, I didn't accept and went to Dr. Zhukow at the hospital on Filosofskaya Street, where I had been hospitalized 40 days, and said to him:

– My husband is lost, my people are lost, I am begging you to do a last kindness – give me morphine.

He answered:

– Morphine I will not give you, but I will give you drops for your heart.

Nurse Kolik gave me drops to strengthen my heart – with much anger she put the glass to my lips, she almost broke my teeth.

She yelled at me: In 1937 my sister's husband was executed, she remained alone with her children, and she didn't behave like you!

The enormous wish to live, and the wish to die – both were beating in my heart together.

From 20 November 1942 to 27 October 1943, eleven months, I wandered from one family to another, simple working families who agreed to hide me, in spite of the fascists' orders, that hiding Jews is punished by death. I taught them how to say "We don't know this old woman, she asked us to let her spend the night...

Once I came to the nurse Soloviova, who lived on Tchitcherin Street. She welcomed me, like in the old days.

– Come in, Dr. Leikina, stay with me as long as you wish.

I remained there, hoping that there it will be easier to end my life. Later I realized that her place was a brothel, visited by Germans, sometimes 20 men at one time. They were eating and drinking, and she would join them. One day a Czech man saw me and asked her:

Who is she?

I had no time to hide, but Soloviova was not scared:

She is my helper, she replied, and to me she said:

Maria, prepare an omelet for this man and me.

I understood. They ate and drank. Later, after liberation, I found out that Soloviova was Jewish.

But I still couldn't sit in the dark warehouse and hear how she enjoys herself with the Germans.

Once, at night, as I was seeking a new place to hide, somebody stopped me and asked:

Dr. Leikina?

My hands and my legs froze, but he said:

Are you afraid? It's me, Chuliavko, a patient of yours. I am pursued just like you. After my surgery, I couldn't go out. Now I am coming from the village, where I got food for my family.

I remembered, before the war I had a patient named Chuliavko. He said:

– I am a member of the Party and I live not far from here. Come in for a minute.

I went, and he gave me a loaf of bread and a bottle of oil. Before I left he said:

– When you have a hard time come to us, we will always welcome you.

And so, when I couldn't stay with Soloviova anymore, I went to him and I stayed with them two weeks and felt good. But once, early in the morning we heard knocks on the door. I got up from my bed and approached Chuliavko's wife. She began complaining:

– My God, we are all lost, and it is because of you. And to me she said:

– Stand in back of the door, and as it opens, run to the garden and hide.

So, I did. I stood behind the door, and as it opened, I ran fast, went to the storeroom and hid behind a pile of coals.

[Page 102]

I heard the policemen come in and ask:

– Who is living here?

– Only our family, no one else.

I heard the policemen ask for the book of tenants and I heard their heavy steps near the storeroom where I was hiding. When the humanity haters left the place, I left my hiding place, and heard Chuliavko's wife complain:

– Why did he bring her? They will catch her and kill her. May God forgive us our sins – I advised her myself to run to the garden.

This was how they eulogized me.

After they saw me dirty and black from the heating room, they were happy, embraced me and kissed me and Chuliavko's wife didn't stop shouting:

You are smart, my dear, luckily you didn't listen to me and didn't run to the garden.

They heated water, I cleaned myself and, in the morning, I said:

I'll go, you had enough of me.

But they didn't let me go and I stayed with them some more time.

I asked Chuliavko's wife to try and go to Liastchenko and give him a short note from me. When he read the note, he began yelling:

I will take you to the police, if you come to ask for the things of that Zhidovka [Jewess]. What parasite, they killed all of them and she is still alive. We can never get rid of them.

Afterward he calmed down a little – Chuliavko's wife related – gave half a loaf of bread and said:

This is for you, don't give the Zhidovka even one crumb. Let her die.

Nadezhda Chuliavko returned and asked me angrily: How did you send me to such an enemy!

One other time, when I visited Chuliavko, it was in the spring of 1943, he said:

One of the partisans visited me. He is from Kharkov. When he comes again, meet him, maybe he will take you to our people.

I was glad, I waited, but in vain. He didn't come again.

*

As it seemed, the fascists were close to their end. Before the town was liberated, the Germans announced that they are beginning the evacuation of the town, and that those who refuse to leave will be considered enemies of the Third Reich and be executed.

They organized the evacuation very orderly: the town was divided into six districts and every district had exact orders when to leave and where to go. Every resident received a "leaving document." I received one as well. I decided to go to Dr. Vornigora, I thought maybe he would hire me as a housemaid? But no one was home. I went to Maria Kotolskaya, where I had slept sometimes. I met her niece, who told me that her aunt had just left.

I went to Matriona Petrovna Gratzkova – there, too, I had spent several nights. As she saw me, she burst into tears, and later I heard that her husband has been taken to Buchenwald. She cried, for herself and for me. Suddenly there were knocks on the door. I managed to hide. A neighbor came in and said that the police have surrounded the house. Matriona Petrovna whispered:

Rozalia Isakova, when they see you, we are all lost.

I left my hiding place, put a large scarf around my body and walked toward the door, like an old weak woman. A policeman stood there.

– Son, can I pass?

He touched my shoulder and said:

– Go on, grandma.

I didn't go far, because I wanted to know why the police surrounded the house.

And I saw, that they were catching young men and young women and put them in cars. They didn't touch older people. People took out things from the houses – a slaughtered goat, a dish with dough and so on. Suddenly a man approached me, his leg was bandaged.

– What happened to your leg? I asked.

I bandaged it so that the Germans wouldn't take me to work. I ran away from Amur. The Germans almost shot me and killed me. And where do you go, grandma? So old and weak? Listen to me, come with me, I am a cobbler, I will always earn enough to buy a piece of bread, and you will also have work cooking and sawing. It is not for long – our people will be back soon...

When he found out that I was Jewish, he paled and asked:

– How did you stay alive?

I told him all the details.

[Page 103]

What an unfortunate nation you are! I saw what the murderers did. But I won't harm you. My son is at the front, and I will help you; maybe thanks to that, my son will be spared and stay alive?

He crossed himself and whispered a prayer, and I went with him. But I didn't stay long with him. One day, I heard the women shouting:

– They are ours! Ours are coming!

I saw a soldier of the Red Army. Many years have passed, and I see him alive. I rushed to him:

– My dear son, take me to the commander's room.

I came in, and saw at the table several officers, one of them with three stars. I approached, tears were choking me, but I managed to say:

– I am a Soviet doctor, Jewish by nation; take me to the front, I cannot stay with the fascists anymore.

– Grandma, where can we take you, in your condition? You will not see fascists anymore. Go to the Department of Health, there is plenty of work there.

After this conversation, I returned to Dniepropetrovsk and started working. Valia, who worked with me, told me that a Jewish girl had come to the hospital. I asked to send her to me, if she comes again.

The girl came the next day. She was about 14, very skinny. She told me what she had experienced and how she survived. She hid when the Germans took all the young people, then she worked as a nanny at the home of a teacher, then two old people saved her.

– Stay with me – I said.

– When Valia told me, that you wanted to see me, I thought that you had news about my family.

– No, my child. What is there to know. Stay with me, I'll be your mother and I'll see that you get a good education and become a learned woman. But you have to promise me, that you will be an honest and trustworthy woman. Can you promise me that?

– Yes...

Since then, I had no problems with Ania. She completed 11 grades and graduated, then she went to the village and was a schoolteacher in the low grades, and at the same time studied and graduated from the Department of Pedagogy at the University of Dniepropetrovsk. She was a good and devoted teacher and was a daughter to me. She told me that she had a brother named Abrasha, who was a somewhat wild boy, and that she thought that he had survived. Indeed, one evening a young man came to our home and asked:

– Is Tzila Schwarz living here?

– Yes, and who are you?

– I am her brother.

I asked him how he was saved, where was he all that time? What is his name now?

– I ran away from the pit of death. I went to a village, not far from Alexandrovka, and I stayed with an old woman where Tzila worked.

– How did you find out where Tzila worked?

– The old woman, where I was hiding, would visit there. She told me, that in the home of the teacher a girl was living, who took care of young children. Once I asked the old woman to take me there, and I saw Tzila carrying two pails of water.

– Did you approach her?

– The old woman didn't let me. She said: Now you are Vovka Novikov. And I don't know who this girl is. Quickly, let's go home.

I said to Abrasha: Stay with me, I shall write to Tzila and she will come. We will take care of you, you will study and work.

– No need for that. I will go back to the old woman, she will know what to do.

Later, we learned that he went to Kriboy–Rog and married a Russian woman. Tzila wrote to him but he didn't reply to her letters. We understood, that he was worried that his wife would find out that he was Jewish. Tzila told me:

– It happens sometimes, that a person, who almost drowned and was saved, is afraid of water all his life. My brother, who experienced the great tragedy of our people, suffers from "nation–fear."

*

I return with my story to the black days of the occupation. Once, in the days of my work in Kaidaki in the 4th Polyclinic, I visited Boyovka. Her son was sick. I passed through the kitchen and I saw a woman sitting there and bent over a dish full of wheat grains, cleaning them. Boykova told me:

– Don't be afraid, she is one of yours. She is an artist, goes through the villages and paints portraits, and for her work she receives honey, eggs, chickens. When we finish eating what she had brought, she again goes to the village. Only yesterday she returned and brought food, and she also helps me with work around the house.

After I examined the sick person, I passed again through the kitchen, and the woman was still there, working. In those cursed days, when one saw a Jewish man or woman, one would look away. When I left, I noted in my mind the number of the house. When I came to Dniepropetrovsk after liberation, I visited Boyovka and asked:

[Page 104]

If the artist will visit you, ask her to visit me too, at Tchitcherin Street 26.

Several days later I heard a woman's voice:

– Is Dr. Leikina living here?

I opened, and the woman stood there:

– Are you Roza Leikina?

– Yes, and who are you?

– I am Sonia Leikina, uncle Wolodia's daughter.

How could I have recognized her the first time? Frightened, thin, wearing a torn dress? It was her – the artist, who sat with Boyovka's wheat grains.

Words cannot describe our joy, our tears, the many questions that we asked one another. When we calmed down a bit, Sonia told me about the horrible day of 13 October. Only now I found out how my family perished, how my brother, Lev Isakowitz Leikin, took Sonia's child from her arms and gave him a piece of bread, and how they drove all of them to the pit in back of the Transport Institute... and how she, Sonia, seeing a small opening in the fence, managed to go through, and in that moment a wagon driver saw her and shouted:

– Why are you crawling like a cockroach? Don't you see what is going on there? Quick, come on the wagon! He covered her and so she was saved. Later she hid at Baykov in Kaidaki.

Of course, I offered Sonia to stay with me. But she rented an empty apartment in our courtyard, recovered, worked and made a good living. Sometime later, her husband returned from the front. Their meeting was cold. He did not even have the patience to listen to the story how their child perished. He left and sent her a short note: "All is over between us."

Sonia came to me with the note and cried. I was angered and said aloud:

– After all that we have gone through, this is not a big misfortune; he does not deserve your weeping and pain.

But it was a long time before Sonia calmed down and her pain subsided. She came to stay with me. Tzila Ania would come often from the village. My sister and her family returned from the place they had been evacuated and we were again a large family. We comforted and strengthened one another. I held two jobs – days at the Polyclinic and nights I did duty service. Once, a soldier entered my room and asked:

– Do you remember the child Yulutchka?

– Yes, I remember her well.

He began to cry, and he asked me to tell him about Yulutchka. "I am her father." I remembered what Yulutchka used to say:

– "I cannot come to live with you, my father will come back from the war and I have to keep the apartment for him..."

I worked hard, I lectured, I had very little free time and I was weak. During the nights I wrote my diary, until... I received a book about Auschwitz. Then I realized that my suffering and my fears were nothing compared with what was going on in that camp. What historic value did all that I went through have? What did I actually do? Whom did I save? Was I part of the Partisans? Did I kill even one German fascist?

I stopped writing, and my diary remains unfinished...

[Page 107 - Hebrew] [Page 105 - Yiddish]

Dniepropetrovsk

by David Bergelson hy"d

Translated by Sara Mages

Free again! On October 25, the Red Army extracted, with mighty force and astounding balance, this important industrial and cultural city from the murderous hands of the fascists and brought it back to life.

Another stone was lifted from the heart of the Soviet country, the Ukrainian nation and all the Jews of the Soviet Union - a heavy stone.

Dniepropetrovsk wasn't just a city for us, but a metropolis among other cities.

The city grew before our eyes and became an industrial and cultural center. It's nourished to satiety by the wealth of the Donbas [Donets Basin], the quarries of the Krivoy Rog region, and the rich black soil around it.

It bloomed especially during the days of the Soviets. In the first three years of Stalin's "First Five-Year Plan," the number of its workers has increased, all at once, from 37 thousand to over 94 thousand. Newspapers and three periodicals appeared in Dniepropetrovsk. About 11 thousand students visited the universities there. About 50 thousand students studied in Dniepropetrovsk's technical colleges and in schools of seven and ten years. About 2000 loudspeakers transferred the news, in the country and in the world, in the beautiful wide streets. Every evening, the five theaters, clubs, and the magnificent cultural center were filled to capacity. The city of laborers breathed a youthful Soviet air, and the entire Soviet Union drew satisfaction from it.

What's new in Dniepropetrovsk?

In this manner they asked those, who came from the young Dnieper-city, out of confidence to hear something good.

The city is growing! - was the answer, and therefore they sensed that they deal here with a live and young matter.

And we don't have a nation in the Soviet Union, who wasn't happy to send its sons to build, not far from this city, the country's genius factory - Dnieper G.A.S. And there isn't a Soviet person, who, on the day of the activation of this mighty plant, didn't feel in his heart that it was a good day of labor for the victorious country. We'll never forget the joyous smile which appeared on every face in the country. It was like the joy of a father on the day of his offspring's wedding: - well, Dniepropetrovsk, Donbas, Krivoy Rog, Zaporizhia, you've won!

And since then, the city grew more rapidly, and its value was more important for the Ukraine and the Soviet Union.

The city also had an important role in the life of the Jews. Around it is the largest and oldest agricultural areas. Even before, when the Jews were pushed into the "Pale ofSettlement," the city was a refuge for Jewish youth who wanted to save itself from the wilderness of provincialism. Already in 1897 there were 1613 Jewish metal workers, 109 Jewish miners, 109 Jews in the chemical industry, and additional 806 Jews in other industrial jobs. The Jews of "Katerynoslav" even managed to penetrate, as laborers, the industry that was "absolutely forbidden" to the Jews at that time - the train.

[Page 108]

In Ekaterinoslav, the Jews of the south-west tasted, for the first time, the flavor of using muscle power. Nice young men, aged 16, abandoned without mercy the "sitting" professions - tailoring, furrier, cobbling, watchmaking, etc. - came from the towns to Ekaterinoslav, and stayed there until they were recruited. Aligned, healthy, with muscular hands, they "darkened" the High Holidays for their mothers, who cried unceasingly in the synagogue: "My son was a nebach [weakling], totally weak - now he comes to enlist, he's so healthy, an oak, oy vey to his mother."

Dniepropetrovsk has become more important after October Days. In 1932, there were thousands of Jews, young and old, among the 34 thousand workers in the metrology factories named after Lenin, Molotov and Petrovsky. The children, of the thousands of members of the Jewish kolkhozy in the environs, weren't absent from the schools near the factories, and from the technological institutes of Dniepropetrovsk. This youth was full of energy and joy of life. After every performance (in Yiddish) at the Jewish institute in Dniepropetrovsk, every Jewish writer felt as if the healthy youth, who was in need of his creation, filled him with new flesh and blood.

Now the city is in ruins, the city which was full of the joy of young workforce - the German ruled it for over two years (August 25, 1941 - October 25, 1943). He lay on it with all the force of his murderous loathing, robbed it, persecuted, raped, and murdered.

The buildings in the streets are still smoldering, and the smoke penetrates the eyes of the soldier - the man of the Red Army, who liberated the city not long ago. He grits his teeth and gathers his strength so he could leap to the next battle.

The Jewish soldier is grinding his teeth not less than him. He knows very well the special "methods" that the Germans use to spill the blood of the Jews.

They arrive to all their settlements, big and small, and don't leave a single Jew alive there. And all this command the Jewish soldier: don't leave a single German fascist alive on the land of the Soviet Union.

His duty, to his country and his nation, requires him:

– Remember what the Germans did to you, to your country and your nation!

– Each shot that our soldiers are firing at the German fascists is sacred and their work, for the benefit of the battlefront, should be appreciated by every Jew in the rear. Please remember, that when our soldier increases his work quota, he kills another German fascist.

And every Jew should take comfort in the fact, that the fascist murderers didn't have the time to kill all the Jews of Dniepropetrovsk. An important part of Dniepropetrovsk's Jews were taken at that time from the city, together with the rest of the population and the industrial plants. Those who were saved are located in the battlefront and in the rear, and they fulfill their obligation to their country and their people with honor. Alive and working is Haim Rivkin, the respected metal worker who for decades didn't separate from his metallurgical factory. When he was forced to move his factory to the foot of the Ural, he turned it there into a giant industrial plant. Alive is Miriam (Mary) Sheydwasser, the Jewish woman who worked since 1930 in one of the sewing workshops in Dniepropetrovsk. Far in the rear, she carried bricks and materials to rebuild the workshop, and excclled in her work quota. And now, she has the joy of life and a creative spirit to write poems in the spirit of the nation:

One   child   holds   her   dress,   the   other   in   her   arms, the woman fled from her burning home.

Thousands of "Haimim" and "Miriamot" from Dniepropetrovsk are still alive. Many of them will return to their hometown, and they'll build it anew.

They left Dniepropetrovsk in tears, and they'll build it with exultation...

So, wrote the author David Bergelson, member of the Anti-Fascist Committee, who, a short time later, was one of the people who were executed by order of the authorities. The flattery to Stalin and all the display of Soviet patriotism - didn't help. The article was translated in its entirety, as is.- Z.H.

From Yiddish - Z.H.

[Page 109]

The City on the Dnieper

by S. Ortenberg

Translated by Sara Mages

Life of tension, wealth and creativity is the lot of Dniepropetrovsk. The smoky chimneys of the steamboats, which sail back and forth, are reflected in the broad waters of the Dnieper River. They are loaded with iron products and other metals, anthracite and building materials. The broad building of first car plant in the Ukraine is located at the outskirts of the city. From a distance, in addition to the lines of the buildings, you can also see the beautiful new housing project that is being built.

On the left bank of the Dnieper River stand the metallurgy factories named after Karl Liebknecht and the "Comintern" [Communist International]. 12 furnaces and 19 rolling machines (waltzy) are already operating at full power. There are two dikes in the factory for chemical products with purification (coxes). The factory for work tools, named after Kahanowitch, is already operating. One wing, in the metallurgical forging factory, is operating again at full force.

"We would beautify our city, and it will be more glorious than before! With this slogan the residents of Dniepropetrovsk approached the rehabilitation work. This is the second year of the socialist competition between the two industrial centers in the Ukraine - Dniepropetrovsk and Kharkov - to rehabilitate the two cities better and faster. Here are several summaries. In a short period of time about a quarter of a million square meters of residential space was built and renovated. Seventy kilometers of tram tracks were paved (11 lines, approximately 100 cars). Many trees were planted in the streets, etc.

And here is a short list of restoration projects that were set for this year: open the movement of trolleybuses and buses, establish a bathhouse for 1,000 bathers per day, build a 250 room hotel, finish the project of supplying gas in pipes to the buildings in the city, establish a physiotherapy institute, open a convalescent home for children, and build a new clinic in the area of the car plant.

Today, there are over 100 medical institutes and healing centers in Dniepropetrovsk. There are almost 10,000 students in the 12 universities and scientific research institutes. There are 22 secondary technical schools (9,000 students) and over 60 high schools.

Two dramatic theatres - Ukrainian and Russian, 8 cinemas, 13 clubs and culture halls, serve the needs of the growing population.

In the city center - a park for culture and rest named after Chkalov. In the middle of the park, bright and clean rail cars (the smallest in the world) are moving swiftly on tracks. This is a train for toddlers named after Stalin - how much joy and satisfaction this train provides to its little passengers!

*

Wide perspectives are opened before Dniepropetrovsk in Stalin's "Five-Year Plan." In 1950, the industry in the city will produce twice as much of its output before the war. The construction of the large factory for cars (one of the largest of its kind in Europe), will be completed. The plant will produce 60,000 cars per year. Auxiliary factories will be built around it, and each one of them will be an independent industrial factory. The new factory for radios will produce 20,000 radios per year. Two tremendous power stations and a large glass factory will be built.

The city will be restored thoroughly under the "New Five-Year Plan." In 1950, the living space will reach 3 million square meters. The number of electric trams will reach 300. 60 trolleybuses and 200 taxis will sway in the streets. The construction of the monumental train station in Dniepropetrovsk already started (the plan was designed by architect Duskin, the recipient of Stalin's prize).

[Page 110]

We'll reveal the full details and the perspective lines of the rehabilitation program which was designed by talented architects.

...From both banks of the Dnieper extend streets and avenues, clean, wide, that greenery and flowers adorn them. In the center - a prospectus of Karl Marks - a magnificent theatre for opera and ballet for 1,500 spectators, a theater, operetta and a youth theater, the philharmonic building, a cinema with three halls, the regional library, a grand "Intourist" hotel, and a "club for Soviet civil servants."

In the city center stands erect the tall "Soviet House" - an architectural pearl.

Around the car plant - a well planned new town for 30,000-40,000 residents. The planners and the manufacturers of the cars live there. A park, named after Shevchenko, is adorned with magnificent pillars, pavilions for various attractions, stages, etc.

*

Up to the war (the Second World War), Dniepropetrovsk was a distinguished Jewish center. About 150 thousand Jews lived there.

Thousands of Jewish laborers worked in the heavy industry factories (metals and machinery).

At the beginning of the "Patriotic War", a large part of the Jewish community in the city went to the rear or to the front. More than 20,000 Jews, who didn't manage to get out, were brutally murdered by the fascist murderers.

On the day that city of Dniepropetrovsk was liberated by the heroes of the Red Army, there were 10-15 Jewish inhabitants in the city. They were saved by chance, mostly with the help of their neighbors.

However, the Jewish community began to grow from day to day, especially after the war.

A large number of Jews, who were released from their service in the Red Army, returned to their homes in Dniepropetrovsk. Also, a substantial number of those, who left the city, returned to it. Today, there are 50,000 Jews in the Jewish community of Dniepropetrovsk.

The Jews occupy a significant place in the metal industry as laborers, managers, engineers and technicians. Lipshitz, who is "certified for technical sciences," is the director of the technical department of the factory named after Petrovskyn, and he greatly contributed to the renovation of the factory. The member Basel serves as a deputy in the same factory. The chief engineer in the factory named after the "Comintern" [Communist International] is the member Magidson, of the factory named after Liebknecht is the member Stopel. The chief engineer in the factory named after Lenin is the member Scheck, and so on.

There are quite a few Jews among the scientists in the universities and the technical institutes of Dniepropetrovsk. The scientific achievements of the professors and researchers - Gottlieb, Zeitlin, Taiz, Brock, Slutsky, and dozens of others in various sectors, especially in metallurgy - are well known in the scientific world.

The Jewish community contributes its share to the reconstruction and the development of the city of Dniepropetrovsk, in the economy, industry and culture.

(Aynikayt [Unity - a Yiddish periodical] 77 (327) - 27 June 1946)

Due to the subject matter the article is given in its entirety, as is, with its exaggerations and the enthusiasm for Stalin's "Five-Year Plan." Why a slaughtered nation should be happy with the Gentiles' rehabilitation program since many of them have collaborated in the slaughter?

From Yiddish - Z.H.

[Page 113]

Life of Torah

The Rabbis of Ekaterinoslav
by Rav Yehuda Leib Levin [z"l]
The Rabbi of Moscow
Translated by Yocheved Klausner

R'Ber Wolf Kozhvenikov z"l

I was only five years old, when my parents moved, in 5659 (1899), from Nikopol to Ekaterinoslav. My paternal grandfather, the Gaon [great scholar] and Tzadik [righteous man] R'Nathan Levy* z"l, offspring of the Gaon R'Refael of Hamburg z"l, pupil of the Gaon R'Eliyahu of Kalish z"l[1] lived, at the end of his life, in Nikopol. In his youth he was a judge in the religious court of the Gaon, the author of Pitkhei Teshuvah [2], and at the end of his life he was a judge in the court of the Gaon the MALBIM z"l.[3] In 5640 (1880), the MALBIM traveled to Krementchog to accept the post of rabbi there, but on the way he became ill – an illness of which he finally died. As he arrived in Kiev, he was not able to continue his trip, and my grandfather R'Nathan, who traveled with him, remained in Nikopol, which was not far from Ekaterinoslav. They needed a rabbi and had heard about the MALBIM's judge and had decided to invite him, but they didn't know where he lived. Chance had it, that my grandfather was at that time in Aleksandrovsk, not far from Ekaterinoslav. Rav Ragolin z"l met him, and immediately informed the Nikopol people about him. The leaders of the community came to Aleksandrovsk and invited him to serve as their rabbi. They presented him the formal documents and he accepted.

Rabbi Nathan lived in Nikopol and passed away in 5657 (1897) and my father and teacher, the Gaon R'Eliyahu Shmuel took his place. In Nikopol there was a Hassidic community as well, they had their own Hassidic rabbi, and this caused disagreement in town. My father was from Lithuania, a graduate of the Lithuanian Yeshiva and he hated disputes. Therefore, although he officiated as rabbi and judge, he relocated to Ekaterinoslav and was given the post of rabbi and judge in one of the suburbs.

The head of the religious court was the famous Gaon Rav Binyamin Zakheim z"l, offspring of the holy R'Israel of Rozhinoy. In his youth he was the head of the Yeshiva in Rozhinoy and in 5620 (1860) he was accepted as Rav and head of the religious court in Ekaterinoslav, following the Gaon and Tzadik R'Chone'le z"l. In this post he served 52 years. He was famous in the entire region of Ukraine and all difficult matters were brought before him. He was compassionate and lenient, and moderate in his verdicts. He lived in the center of town.

In another section of the town, near the river, the Rabbi was the Gaon and Hassid R'Dober-Zev-Wolf Kozhvenikov z"l. He was always wearing his prayer-shawl and phylacteries and was immersed in study and prayer until four in the afternoon every day. A dear man and a "doer of good deeds" – no needy person was turned away from his door. His wife the Rebbetzin would complain that the rabbi used up his salary for charity and there was nothing left for the needs of the household. Following that, a regulation was issued, that the Rebbetzin would receive the rabbi's salary from the community. The river brought many merchants to Ekaterinoslav, since the boats and barges had to stop there because of the many rocks down the river, and the merchants would always bring charity money to the rabbi's house. But all this was not sufficient to cover all the expenses. When the rabbi passed away, he was in debt of about four thousand Rubles. Part of the story of this great man's life was known: he was born in Dubrianka in the Tchernigov district. Many great men of Torah and study lived in that town. He was educated by one of the great men of Torah and piety, who implanted in him knowledge and feelings of kindness toward his fellows. At the age of twelve he was already knowledgeable in many legends and teachings of Our Sages. In that town, many Jews lived who did not know even the meaning of the words of our teachings. Rabbi Dov-Zev, out of pity for these simple souls, set up times to study with them and teach them "Sidur" [prayer book] and tell them about the Midrash and the legends of Our Sages. He did this several years, but it was not easy, since he had a speaking impairment and sometimes could not even talk to them. Later, when he lost his father, he began to stutter constantly, however he continued to study with them. At the age of 17 the Rav R'Dov-Zev went to Lubavitch to the Hassidic ADMOR, the author of Tzemach-Tzedek. He told the ADMOR how he was studying with the simple people, and how difficult it was to talk to them. The ADMOR told him to continue working with them as before and blessed him with the gift of teaching and clear speech.

[Page 114]

As he left the ADMOR's house – Rabbi Dov Zev related – he did not recognize himself: he felt like another person. He began speaking clearly, not understanding where this ability had come from. When he arrived home, he repeated the Hassidic sayings that he had learned from the ADMOR, and his listeners were truly amazed. Rabbi Dov-Zev proudly told them that he was the Golem of the ADMOR; moreover, The MAHARAL of Prague had made a Golem out of dust and the ADMOR Tzemach Tzedek made a golem of flesh... He became a SHADAR [shelucha derabanan = messenger of the Sages] and instructor at the ADMOR z"l; was also knowledgeable in the language of the Zohar.

My father z"l obtained the office of Rabbi in the new section of the town, which included about ten synagogues, the Jewish hospital, a Home for the Aged and a Talmud Torah. The Jewish institutions in town were in bad state, the rabbis were elderly men. My father was the youngest and it was natural that all the community activity fell on his shoulders. Every day he would go to the house of the rabbi, the Gaon R Ber Zev, and almost all matters of divorce and Dinei-Torah [religious trials according to Halacha] and all questions that arose would be handled by him. He was also supervisor in the Yeshiva, in matters of kosher meat and Matzah baking before the Passover Holiday.

In those days there was peace among the rabbis of the town. In Ekaterinoslav there was a suburb called Thetchlovka, where factories and large stores had been erected. The Gaon rabbi Baruch Zaslavski lived in that region, and he was also a member of the religious Court.

In the month of Tevet 5668 (1908) the Rav R'Dober Zev-Wolf Kozhvenikov became ill and on 27 Tevet he passed into a better world, aged 88 years. In the month if Nissan in the same year R'Baruch Zaslavski became ill and passed away two days before Passover. After Passover, on the day of Lag Ba'omer, when my father and teacher z"l was at the Talmud Torah examining pupils, he caught a cold and became ill, and on 26 Iyar he passed away; he was 42 years old. The most famous doctors in town treated the three rabbis and after they died the doctors said that they will never again try to treat rabbis because they have weak hearts... So, it happened that three of the Ekaterinoslav rabbis died in the course of five months.

After the death of the rabbis the peace in town was disrupted. The town was in turmoil; it became divided into Hassidim, Mitnagdim and Maskilim ["enlightened"]. The Hassidim preferred the Gaon rabbi Levy-Yitzhak Shneursohn z"l and the Mitnagdim and the wealthy preferred the Gaon rabbi Pinchas Gellman z"l, who was, at the time, rabbi in Tarashcha. The dispute went on and on, and it came to beatings and sacrilege in the synagogues; it continued for several months. Finally the parties came to an understanding, that Rabbi Pinchas Gellman z"l will serve as rabbi in the section of town near the river, taking the place of the Hassid rabbi Dov-Zev z"l and Rabbi Levy-Yitzhak z"l will serve as rabbi in the part of town where my father and teacher z"l had officiated.

A man from Vilna lived in Ekaterinoslav, his name was Moshe-Yehuda Yudelsohn z"l. He was a merchant, a great Torah scholar and God-fearing. By the influence and persuasion of rabbi Gellman he agreed to construct a building for the Yeshiva. Work began in 1910 and by the end of that year a three-story building was completed. This building contained apartments and stores, the rent serving as income for the Yeshiva. Soon a second, two-and-a-half-story building was completed, comprising housing for the students, a restaurant, a Bet Midrash [synagogue and house of learning] and study rooms. The Yeshiva existed and operated until 5679 (1919).

In 1913, on the eve of Passover, Rabbi Binyamin Zev Zakheim died, after officiating 52 years. After his death it was decided that Rabbi Pinchas Gellman would take his place and Rabbi Levy-Yitzhak would take the place of Rabbi Dov-Zev Kozhvenikov. Rabbi Nachum Gurewitz z"l, who was in his youth a lumber merchant, was appointed in the place of Rabbi Levy-Yitzhak. Another new appointment was that of the Gaon Rabbi Yakov-Gershon Akoshki the Kohen, who had been a Maggid Meisharim [preacher] in the Kazatchi synagogue: he was appointed Rabbi in that synagogue and the neighborhood.

In 1917, a Teachers College for religious teachers was founded, by the bequest of R'Chaim Cohen z"l from Petrograd.

[Page 115]

All studies were conducted in Hebrew, under the leadership of the Gaon our teacher R'Pinchas Gellman z"l. About 50 students were enrolled, most of them coming from Lithuania's great Yeshivot, which did not function during the war. On 22 Tamuz 5681 (1921) R'Pinchas Gellman died of cancer, after an operation. May his soul be bound in the bond of the living. After the death of Rabbi Gellman, Rabbi Shneursohn relocated to the center of town, and there he officiated until 1937, when he was arrested and sent in exile to Kazakhstan. He died there and was buried in Alma-Ata (Almaty).

After the Second World War, when the remnants of the Jews began to return from the places they had fled, the authorities issued an order to build a new synagogue in Ekaterinoslav, or, by its new name Dnepropetrovsk. Every synagogue was required to have a rabbi.

I and my family returned to Krasnoarmieskoia (formerly Grishino, Duntzk region) not far from Andizhan (Uzbekistan), and in 1946 I was summoned to fill the post of rabbi in Dnepropetrovsk and I accepted. With my own hands I opened the doors of the synagogue, and I served there until 1947. For family reasons, I had to return to Krasnoarmieskoia. In 1948 I was called again to serve in Dnepropetrovsk and I remained there until 1953. Due to informers who acted against me, I was forced to leave the town and never returned. They did not hire another rabbi, to this day.

Rosin was a simple man, a tailor. He supervised the building of the synagogue and later was the head of the synagogue committee. He was the one who signed "the famous Manifesto"[4].

Today the local synagogue is functioning well, and there are two minyanim of Shacharit (the morning prayer). They have a cemetery, but not a mikve [ritual bathhouse]. The number of Jews is approximately fifty thousand.

*

My grandfather was not a Levy (Levite). In his youth his surname was Schullman. When the decree was issued, that every young man must enlist in the army, only those who possessed a "Kvitantzia" were exempt.

And this was the history of the Kvitantzia: During the 1854-1855 Russian war against the "Alliance Nations" (England, France and Turkey) the government mobilized, among Christians and Jews alike, soldiers in a greater number that was allowed by law. As compensation, the government granted a "Kvitantzia" to the heirs of those who have fallen in the war, stating that the person who holds it is exempt from serving in the army. My grandfather bought such a document, in the name of Levy.

The author

Editor's notes

Known as "R'Eliyahu Ragoler" after the second town where he served as rabbi; he became famous through all of Lithuania.

In Otyan, Lithuania, the rabbi R'Zvi Hirsch Eisenstadt.

In Koenigsberg.

Against Israel during the 1956 war (the Sinai War), issued by Jewish representatives in the USSR, rabbis and heads of the Synagogue Committees. The manifesto was published in the Soviet press (for example Izvestia 29 Nov. 1956). Interestingly, Rabbi Levin in his article condemned the signers of the "Manifesto", but now he publicly condemns Israel, Zionism and "Jewish Fascism"!

[Page 116]

Houses of Prayer in Ekaterinoslav
(Synagogues, Batei Midrash, Minyanim)
Translated by Yocheved Klausner

According to the newspaper Hamelitz (1887), in that year there were in Ekaterinoslav 17 synagogues and Batei Midrash, and additional 19 regular Minyanim (private gathering of a quorum of men), as follows:

The Great Synagogue on Ebreiskaia Street

The Great Synagogue on Kazatzia Street

The Great Synagogue on Fabrik Street

The Small Synagogue on Fabrik Street

The Synagogue Orach Tefilah

The Synagogue Ohel Moshe

The Upper Bet Midrash

The Bet Midrash of Igren (?)

The Bet Midrash Tefilat Yeshurun

The Bet Midrash Hachnasat Orhim

The Bet Midrash according to the Ashkenazi ritual[*]

The Lower Bet Midrash

The Bet Midrash Achva on Fabrik

The Bet Midrash Hevrat Tehilim on Fabrik

The Bet Midrash Naye Planes

The Bet Midrash of the Ironsmiths

The Bet Midrash Nidvat Lev

Regular Minyan Chochlovkin

Regular Minyan R'Yakov Lifschitz

Regular Minyan R'Zvi

Regular Minyan Anshei Chayil (soldiers)

Regular Minyan R'Zalman Menuhin

Regular Minyan of the fair

Regular Minyan Zalitzki

Regular Minyan Valoshin

Regular Minyan Gronim

Regular Minyan of the Hekdesh [poorhouse]

At the end of the 1920s, the following synagogues and Batei Midrash existed:

The Great Synagogue (Choral) on Ebreiskaia Street

The Great Synagogue on Kazatchiya Street

The Great Synagogue on Troytzkaia Street

The Great Synagogue on Novoselnaia Street

The Great Synagogue on Bazolovskaia Street

The Great Synagogue on Filosofskaia Street

The Great Synagogue on Aleksandrovskaia Street

The Great Synagogue on Jordanskaia Street

The Great Synagogue on Starodvorianskaia Street

The Great Synagogue on Gimnasticeskaia Street

The Great Synagogue on Balkovaia Street

The Great Synagogue on Korashevskaia Street

The New Piorovi Synagogue

The Old Piorovi Synagogue

The Synagogue on Kaidaki

The Ironsmiths' Synagogue

The Synagogue on Tchetchelevka

Paley's Synagogue

The Upper Beit Hamidrash near the Great Synagogue

The Lower Beit Hamidrash near the Great Synagogue

The Beit Hamidrash in the Karpass Orphanage on Filosofskaia Street

The Beit Hamidrash on Prospect near the Main Post Office

The Beit Hamidrash in the Home for the Aged

The Beit Hamidrash on Kazatchiya Street not far from the Synagogue on that street

Today the local synagogue is functioning well, and there are two minyanim of Shacharit (the morning prayer). They have a cemetery, but not a mikve [ritual bathhouse]. The number of Jews is approximately fifty thousand.

---

*As in all of Ukraine, the prayer ritual was that of Hassidic-Sefarad [Nusach Sefarad]. In the Great Synagogue – the Choral Synagogue – it was Nusach Ashkenaz.

[Page 117]

Rabbi Pinchas Gellman z"l
by Rav Dr. Zvi Harkavy
Translated by Yocheved Klausner

The years after the 1905 revolution were difficult years for the Russian Jews: they went through psychological crisis, frustration and disappointment, pogroms and persecutions, and for many it was true misery and despair. A direct consequence was a tendency to retreat to private life, a feeling of isolation, keeping distance from community matters, and on the other hand pursuit of entertainment and amusement. There were many cases of conversion to Christianity, in particular among young people. In addition to all that, the Ekaterinoslav Jews suffered from harassment and provocation by street hooligans and from vulgar Anti–Semitism by the local authorities.

The Jewish community in Ekaterinoslav was in great need of a spiritual leader and guide. Rabbi Binyamin–Zev Zakheim z"l was old and sick; Rabbi Dov–Zev Kozhvenikov z"l had died; another two rabbis, R'Baruch Zaslavski z"l and R'Eliyahu–Shmuel Levin z"l died as well. The national circles in the city decided that it was necessary to invite to Ekaterinoslav a younger rabbi, a Torah scholar, an educated man and an articulate speaker, who would, after some time, become the chief rabbi. The name of the young rabbi from Tarastcha, R'Pinchas Gellman, was already well–known. After a short campaign, he was elected in 5668 (1908) as rabbi of the central area of Ekaterinoslav, and in fact he was the chief rabbi of the city until his death on 21 Tamuz 5681 (1921) [this was related by Gottlieb in Oholei Shem 5672 (1912). In 1914 the newspaper Modi'a, No. 23, announced the arrangement of the Rabbinate in Ekaterinoslav: two chief rabbis – Rabbi Levi–Yitzhak Schneurson the rabbi of the Hassidim and Rabbi Pinchas Gellman the rabbi of the mitnagdim. In addition, there were 3 other rabbis who served as Morei Tzedek (deciders of Halachic questions)].

Rabbi Gellman was born in 1889 in the town Tarastcha, Kiev district in Ukraine, his father was R'Israel Efraim Gellman. He graduated from Lithuanian Yeshivas, was a student of R'Chaim Oyzer Grodzhinski z"l in Vilna. At the beginning of his career he served as rabbi in his town. He was a follower of Zionism and loved the Hebrew language, was also a Hebrew writer: in 1911 his articles were published in "Ha'ivri" – a publication of Rav Meir Berlin (Berlin, No. 31–34): "Letters to a young Jew" – on the appalling spiritual emptiness in the secular life of a person "free" from mitzvot [commandments].

His first publications he signed by the pseudonym Ben–Ya'ir. He was a great Torah scholar, wise and smart, of great personal charm, good looking, red hair, elegantly dressed. Yet he was modest and friendly. He was a great orator, and as member of the City Council (Duma) he delivered fiery speeches. He was courageous, knew no fear and defended his national–religious views in the time of the Czar as in the time of the Bolsheviks. His students and acquaintances mentioned him with awe and admiration. His home in Mstavaya Street has become a meeting center.

He intended to make Aliya, dreamed of a position as lecturer of Hebrew Law in Jerusalem. He studied Roman law, in particular comparative study between Roman and Hebrew law.

Rabbi Gellman turned the small Yeshiva into a big and superb Yeshiva, which attracted from the Lithuanian Yeshivas students and teachers, headed by the great scholar Rabbi Grodzhinski z"l, and students from the surrounding villages as well. One of the students was Zalman Aranne z"l, former minister of education in Israel. Rabbi Gellman often conducted his lessons in the Yeshiva in clear and perfect Hebrew, as he was a member of the Safa Chaya [living language] Society. He established a Hebrew–national–religious Teachers College – among the students were Rabbi I. L. Levin, the Moscow Chief Rabbi and Mordechai Gover from Kfar Achim in Israel. At the Zionist Rabbis Conventions, he was one of the chief speakers.

At the Achdut convention in Kiev, in the summer of 1917, he was elected member of the presidency together with his teacher, the great scholar rabbi Chaim Oyzer Grodzhinski [Achdut was the unified party of the religious organizations in Ukraine]. The convention was opened by Rabbi Shlomo Ahronson z"l. Rabbi Gellman, in co–operation with his Zionist–religious friends, passed the Eretz–Israel resolution: "The settlement of our Holy Land according to the Torah and Commandments if one of our holiest duties. The Achdut organization is very active in the area of education in the old and new settlements." This included supporting the Talmud Torah and Yeshiva institutions as well as laborers and craftsmen in Eretz Israel.

[Page 118]

Rabbi Gellman gave two lectures at the convention: 1. On the religious education, which needed changes and improvements, and the establishment of new Torah institutions; 2. On the ultra–orthodox literature and press, suggesting establishing a special fund to aid this literature, support publishers, establish a modern printing shop, and publish educational literature and newspapers.

His suggestions were approved by the convention, and as a direct result, the newspaper Achdut began to appear in Kiev, with Rabbi S. I. Zevin as editor. Unfortunately, only two copies were published, and in each of them Rabbi Gellman had an article. He wrote also in the newspaper Hazman.

Rabbi Gellman died at the age of 40. He had no children.

About Rabbi Gellman see also: The entry in the Religious Zionism Encyclopedia; Struggle for Salvation by Arie Refaeli, p. 73; The Struggle of a generation, B. West; Att. Aharon Friedenthal, (letter to the editor, Ma'ariv); Research of Families, Zvi Harkavi, p. 52; The Ekaterinoslav community, *He'avar* 1957, from p. 128; Ekaterinoslav, a big Jewish city, Year after Year to 1969, from p. 288.

Rabbi Levi–Yitzhak Schneurson,
may he rest in peace

by Rav Dr. Zvi Harkavy

Translated by Yocheved Klausner

On Thursday, 28 Av 5704 (1944), Rabbi Menachem–Mender Schneurson received a telegram with the sad news of the passing of his father, the great scholar and famous *Hassid* Rabbi Levi–Yitzhak Schneurson may he rest in peace. He died on Shabat 20 Av 1944, in the city Alma–Ata, Kazakhstan. The death of the great rabbi shocked the entire Chabad Hassidism.

The Rav R'Levi–Yitzhak, born on 18 Nissan 5638 (1878) was a grandson of the great scholar Rabbi Baruch–Shalom, the author of the book Tzemach–Tzedek. His father was the great scholar R'Baruch Schneur, son–in–law of the respected Chasid R'Zalman Chaykin of Padabrianka [Russia].

Already as an adolescent, R'Levi–Yitzhak was recognized as an extremely talented person. He was a student of the Padabrianka rabbi R'Yoel Chankin, who was the student of the famous scholar R'Pesach Malastovker, one of the Chasids who served the "Old Admor." R'Levi–Yitzhak was the son–in–law of the great scholar Rabbi Meir–Shlomo Yanovski z"l, the rabbi of Nikolayev.

He was ordained by the great rabbis of his generation: R'Chaim of Brisk, R'Eli–Chaim Meizlish of Lodz and others. In 1909 he received the position of rabbi of Ekaterinoslav.

In addition to his scholarship in Torah, he was very knowledgeable in Kabala and Chabad Hassidism He was pious and God–fearing and of good qualities. He was one of the famous Hassidim of the Lubavitch ADMOR [the RASHAB], who befriended and treasured him very much.

Since 1912, R'Levi–Yitzhak participated in every meeting concerned with community matters, headed by the Lubavitch ADMOR. He played an important part in the "matza–operation" – baking matzot for the Jewish soldiers in the war between Russia and Japan (1914–1915); he also helped collecting material in preparation of the defense in the Beilis blood–libel trial.

He assisted in the absorption and support of the many refugees who came to Ekaterinoslav from Poland and Lithuania and was devoted to the support of the Lubavitcher's learning and economic institutions. In general, during the time he served as Rabbi of Ekaterinoslav Torah study and Community life flourished in town and surroundings.

For all these activities, he was arrested in 1940 by the Soviet authorities and deported, with his family, to a desolate place in Kazakhstan. This had a damaging effect on his health and probably caused his death.

He left many written works on Torah and Kabala.

Woe for those who are gone and cannot be replaced. May his soul be bound in the bond of the living.

[Page 119]

[The above was written by his in–law, the Admor, and I translated it from Yiddish to Hebrew, from the "Lubavitch Collection", New–York 1944 – Z. H.]

As a matter of fact, he was destined to be Admor. He understood the Chabad teachings in a special way, but he did not put his ideas in writing during his lifetime. Part of his works, which he wrote in Alma Ata, did reach his son the Admor of Brooklyn, and they are printed as "The Collections of Levi–Yitzhak": Notes on the "Tanya" (Brooklyn 1970, photocopied the same year in Kfar Chabad, Israel); Notes on the Zohar in 2 parts (as above), which includes his photograph taken in Alma Ata, his own history in the framework of Chabad, a facsimile of his handwriting and now a new volume – on the Talmud.

I remember him standing on the Bimah in the Kazatchia synagogue on the Shavuot Holiday, passionately speaking about the Mashiach. I saw him also in his own synagogue – Pyorovka.

His heroism and his shining and charismatic personality are described by his wife the Rebbetzin in "The Memories of the Rebbetzin Chana Schneurson, may she rest in peace" (I have 135 photocopied pages). She wrote in Yiddish, after the Holocaust, when she came from the Soviet Union to the United States to live with her relatives. [I intend to publish it, as it deserves, and I gave a copy to the Institute of Contemporary Jewry, the Hebrew University of Jerusalem]. A review by Rav Chanoch Glitzenstein "Rabbi Levi–Yitzhak Schneurson, may he rest in peace," published on his Yahrzeit 20 Av in Kfar Chabad, also contributes to the description of his wonderful personality and his life–history. See also about him: The Struggle of a Generation, B, p. 301; an article by Att. Freudenthal in "Heint" (year?); In a letter to the Korostin Convention in 1927 ("Chabad Publication" Elul 1970, p. 129) the Admor [the "Reitz"] writes:

On 26 to 28 Av 5677 [1917], at a meeting of Rabbis in Moscow, the following participated: Rabbi Shmuel from Moscow, Rabbi Yitzhak–Yakov from Ponywezh, Rabbi Eliezer Rabinowitz from Minsk, Rabbi Menachem–Mendel Chen from Nezhin, Rabbi Israel Meir HaKohen Chafetz Chayim from Radin, Rabbi Chaim Oyzer Grodzhenski from Vilna, **Rabbi Levi Yitzhak Schneurson from Ekaterinoslav**, Rabbi Shemaryahu Leib from Vitebsk, Rabbi Menachem Mendel from Paritch and others.

He had three sons: Dober, never married, died in Kazakhstan, apparently from depression. May God avenge his blood.

The youngest was Israel–Arie–Leib, an illuy [prodigy, genius], was caught by the "enlightenment" movement, followed Marxism and Trotzkism, and wrote for the Marxist publications in the Soviet Union. He made Aliya to Eretz Israel, distanced from Torah and Chabad. He worked as librarian in a private library in Tel Aviv, was married and a father of two. He was an autodidact and mathematician and was invited to teach mathematics at the University of Leeds in England. After several months he died a tragic death, in the prime of his life, and was brought to be buried in Tzefat [Safed], by the instructions of his older brother R'Menachem–Mendel.

The third son – was the pride of the family, the pride of the town, the pride of the generation, today's Admor of Lubavitch, may he live long and good years, who is still living, for some reason, in Brooklyn.

He left the Soviet Union with his father–in–law the REITZ z"l. Torah and Chabad he learned with his father. While still at home he studied secular studies, his first teacher in Ekaterinoslav was Israel Idelson (the late minister Israel Bar–Yehuda). He studied philosophy at the Berlin University and Engineering at the University of Paris. He is a certified Engineer.

He is the head of Chabad, one of the great men of his generation, influential in the entire Jewish world, including Israel. A great deal has been written about him. Eliezer Steinman z"l, writes an entry about him and his teachings in Beer Hachasidut [The Well of Hassidism] ("The Teachings of Chabad", Volume 2, section 3). Ch. Glitzenstein notes at the end of that volume that until 1957 many articles and biographical details by R'Menachem Schneurson were published – some years up to 74 items – in Hebrew, Yiddish and English. He mastered the Russian, French and German.

About the Rebbetzin Chana, may she rest in peace, see my article in the newspaper Davar: "The mother of the Chabad kingdom."

Rabbi Yehuda Leib Levin z"l
by Rav Dr. Zvi Harkavy
Translated by Yocheved Klausner

He was born on 13 Adar 5654 [1894] in Nikopol, 12th District. His family originated in Lithuania, descendants of the famous Rabbi Refael of Hamburg, author of The Teachings of Yekutiel and other works. His in–law was the Gaon R'Arie-Leib son of the Gaon R'Shmuel, head of the religious court and Rabbi of the Grodna District, author of Shmuel's Responsa, grandson of the Gaon author of Beit Shmuel; his family lineage led to Rashi and from there to King David.

As mentioned before – in the article by Rabbi Levin about the Ekaterinoslav Rabbinate – his grandfather was Rabbi Nathan son of Rabbi Moshe Schullman, nicknamed Levi–Levin (he was **not** of the Levi Tribe), this being the origin of his surname Levin. He was a great rabbi and served as dayan [judge in the religious court] at the MALBIM's court. He was also rabbi in Nikopol, and after him, from 1897, officiated his son, R'Eliyahu Shmuel z"l, father of R'Yehuda Leib. In 1899, when another Chabad rabbi was brought there, he left Nikopol (in order to avoid machloket [dispute]) and accepted the office of Rav in Ekaterinoslav. R'Yehuda Leib was 5 years old when he moved to Ekaterinoslav.

[Page 120]

On 28 Iyar 5668 (1908) his father R'Eliyahu Shmuel passed away and left 9 orphans, boys and girls. Yehuda–Leib was 14 years old; while during his father's lifetime he studied at the Ekaterinoslav Yeshiva, after his father's death he left and went to study at other Yeshivot.

At first, he wanted to go to Radin, to study with the Chafetz Chaim, and Rabbi Binyamin'ka wrote to the Chafetz Chaim, but enrollment at the Yeshiva was full at the time. By the advice of the rabbis Zackheim and Gellman he went to Nezhin, near Tchernikov, to the Yeshiva headed by the chief rabbi of the town, Rabbi Menachem–Mendel Chen, may God avenge his blood, brother of Rabbi Avraham Chen z"l.

The last photograph of Rabbi Yehuda Leib Levin z"l, sent to the Editorial Board of this book

When Rabbi Menachem–Mendel came to Nezhin in 1907, to replace Rabbi Shlomo Aharonson (who relocated to Kiev and then to Tel Aviv) he revived the Yeshiva, which had been founded 50 years earlier by R'Levi–Yitzhak Schneurson, grandson of the author of the Tania. It had about 50 students, who learned with the Lithuanian teacher Rabbi Yakobson. The Yeshiva was supported by the Balebatim [respected well–to–do people] in town and was not well–known [but see **Nezhin** in Oholei Shem by Gottlieb, 1912]. R'Yehuda Leib studied there diligently.

In 1909 he came to Slobodka, near Kovno, to the Yeshiva Kneset Beit Yitzhak, named after R'Yitzhak–Elchanan Spector z"l, the rabbi of Kovno and recognized by all the Jews in the country. Contrary to the Kneset Israel Yeshiva in Slobodka (Rabbi Salanter z"l) headed by R'Baruch–Ber Leibowitz, in this Yeshiva the study was not directed by the Musar [ethics] method. Until the outbreak of World War I, R'Yehuda Leib was supported by his relative in Ekaterinoslav, my grandfather R'Moshe Karpas z"l, a descendant of the author of Torat Yekutiel.

[Page 121]

R' Yehuda Leib was first ordained by Rabbi Gellman in Ekaterinoslav and was authorized to teach [Yore–Yore] and in 1916 he was certified to sit in Judgment [Yadin–Yadin] by the Gaon R'Yehuda–Leib Burstein z"l, head of the religious court in Nizhni–Novgorod. Rabbi Burstein was the son–in–law of R'Mordche'le Ushminer – the Gaon R'Mordechai Rosenblatt head of the religious court in Ushmina and Slonim, to whom many went to receive advice and blessing.

He returned to Ekaterinoslav and studied 3 years at the Teachers College – a Hebrew–religious–Zionist institution – founded in 1917 in Ekaterinoslav by Rabbi Pinchas Gellman z"l from the inheritance of R'Chaim Cohen from Petrograd. In 1919 he completed his studies [Mordechai Gover, his friend from Slonim, also completed his study at that time] and for some time worked as a high–school teacher in Ekaterinoslav.

All that time and later as well he was member of the Zionist Movement.

On Lag Ba'omer 5681 (1921) he married Frieda, daughter of Aharon Feldman, from Lunitz near Pinsk.

By the end of 1923 he was summoned to officiate as rabbi in Grishino, in the region of Ekaterinoslav–Dunetzk [From 1924 the region was called the Stalinski district, today the Dunetzki district, named after the main city Stalino–Dunetzk, Yozovka when it was founded, in 1869. Since 1938 the name of the city was Crasnoarmyeskoya]. He replaced Rabbi Avraham–Yoscf Guttman, author of Israel Ba'adam (Warsaw 1913; and see an article about him in Shomrei Hagachelet, which I published together with Rabbi A. Shauli in 1966). He served there until the Nazi invasion, and in the month of Tishrei 1941 he was deported, together with all the other Jews, to the East. Two months later he arrived with his family in Uzbekistan to the Gronetz–Mazar Station, near Idizhan and lived there until the end of 1943, when he returned to Crasnoarmyeskoya. In Uzbekistan he earned his livelihood by working as a religious scribe [sofer stam] and as a watchmaker (?).

In 1946 he was called to serve as rabbi in Dunetzk. He opened a synagogue and remained there – with a short pause in 1947 – until 1953. Following the slander of an informant he was forced – as he testified in his article in the book – to leave Dunetzk and return to Crasnoarmyeskoya, where his three married daughters lived: Rivka, a dentist, Hadassa, an engineer and Tamar, a doctor–therapist. He had 13 grandsons and granddaughters, as the gimatria [numerical value of the Hebrew letters] of the word Echad [one]. The children were circumcised and were influenced by their grandfather the rabbi. Once, on the day before Yom–Kippur, his daughter the doctor asked him what she should do: The next day (Yom–Kippur) she was on duty and one of her tasks was to taste the food cooked for the hospitalized patients...

In 1957 he was invited by the Moscow Rabbi, R'Shlomo ben R'Yechiel–Mechl Shliffer z"l to head the Yeshiva Kol Yaakov, about to be opened. The Yeshiva was named after Rabbi Yitzhak–Yakov Reines z"l, the founder of Mizrachi and of a Yeshiva combined with a high–school in Lidda; he was also Rabbi Shliffer's in–law. The Yeshiva was opened on 5 Shevat 1957. On 38 Adar II 1957 Rabbi Shliffer died suddenly of a heart attack – it was said that it was due to the fact that he was forced to sign, along with other rabbis and heads of synagogues, a declaration denouncing the Sinai War of 1956. Rabbi Y. L. Levin (who was not among the signatories of the declaration [1]) was elected by the Council of the Great Synagogue in Moscow as the head and rabbi of the Synagogue and head of the Yeshiva. The appointment was confirmed by the Soviet authority. The Yeshiva consisted of 20 students, all over 18 years of age as required by law, but the number diminished and today not one was left.

When Rabbi Levin began his triple job, he wrote a detailed reply to the questions he was asked about himself and about the Yeshiva, in the Jewish periodical in English "Zionist Record" published in Johannesburg, South–Africa. His notes were published by the Jewish press in Hebrew, Yiddish etc. [I also published an article on the subject in the Hatzofeh newspaper]. In the meantime, Rabbi Levin resigned (or was forced to resign) from his job as chairman of the Synagogue council. For years he kept his title as head of the Yeshiva, hoping that the Yeshiva will reopen. Every Jew who visits the Soviet Union and Moscow goes to the synagogue and meets with Rabbi Levin, and sometimes he is invited to the Sabbath meal to his house. This is how he treated me as well during my visit in the USSR in the spring of 1962, and upon returning home I wrote about this visit and in particular about Rabbi Levin [for example a series of articles in Ma'ariv: "11 Days in Moscow and Leningrad" published by the Jewish press over the world; "Rabbi Yehuda Leib Levin – his life and work," Kol Sinai, 54 1966].

His visit in the United States in 1968 brought him world fame. Not always was his opinion accepted, and he was often criticized. It must be remembered that he never said a word against the State of Israel or its Jews, but the criticism was sometimes cruel, and it probably led to his death... In 1968 he published in Moscow a second edition of the prayerbook Sidur Hashalom [The Peace Sidur], in which it is stated that at the end of the Yom–Kippur prayers the congregation must proclaim three times (!) "Next year in Jerusalem". For several years he printed a yearly calendar, published by the Great Synagogue in Moscow. He participated in the Collection of Halacha Studies Shomrei Hagachelet mentioned earlier.

[Page 122]

The celebration of his 75th birthday was a Jewish world event. In spite of the absence of diplomatic relations between the USSR and Israel, two invitations were sent to Israel: one was sent to me (due to my health situation my trip was delayed, but I was informed that my visa will not be cancelled) and the other to the chief Rabbi Yitzhak Nissim (his request for 4 visas was denied).

Rabbi Levin was attentive to the affairs of his town Ekaterinoslav – Dunetzk; he sent a telegram (in Hebrew) to Mount Zion when a memorial plaque was erected; he mentioned in particular the Dunetzk martyrs at the Yizkor ceremony in Moscow in memory of the two million victims murdered by the Nazis in the USSR; and he participated in the book.

At the beginning of 1970 Rabbi Levin visited Budapest as a guest of the Jewish communities and was welcomed with great honor. It must be mentioned that in the Hebrew Encyclopedia (volume 21 1969) the 26 lines entry about him is incorrect and is not signed [on the cover of the volume: Soviet Union Jewry – Mordechai Chenzin]. This should be corrected. His loyalty and devotion to Israel was demonstrated as he wrote on the envelope of a letter he sent to me "Jerusalem the Capital" in Hebrew.

A note to this article: My article about Rabbi Levin was still in print when the sad news arrived that he passed away on the eve of Rosh–Chodesh Kislev 5732 (17 November 1971) and was buried on 3 Kislev, 25 kilometers from Moscow – May his memory be for a blessing! A great luminary died, who preserved and guarded the glowing embers of the Torah, a figure of a rabbi of the old days – and he was from our own town. May his soul be bound in the bond of the living.

He has relatives living in Israel. One of his daughters, with her husband and children, intended for some time to make Aliya, and now all his daughters as well as his wife the Rebbetzin, are coming to Israel.

When I visited him in Moscow, he suggested that I take the post of Chief Rabbi of the Jews of USSR. Now it is possible to reveal this matter, but it is not the place to go into details.

This is what I said about him on the Israeli radio Kol Israel on the day he died:

In New York in his hotel he met General Arik Sharon. He invited him to his room, and they talked for about an hour. As they parted, Sharon gave Rabbi

Levin an IDF Siddur [prayer book]. In tears the rabbi accepted the gift and heartily embraced the general...

This was Rabbi Levin z"l.

Editor's notes

Rosin's signature is representing the Committee of the Synagogue. See about him in the article by Rabbi Levin in the book.

The Yeshiva in Ekaterinoslav

by Nechemia Lev

Translated by Yocheved Klausner

"And as you walk alone through one of those blessed towns..." (Ch. N. Bialik)

The great poet, using these words at the beginning of his poem Hamatmid [the studious, the diligent] did not think that a town like Ekaterinoslav would be counted among those blessed towns. But I, being one of the Yeshiva students in Ekaterinoslav, and adding my voice to the voices of the "studious" at midnight – my ears echo, to this day, the words of Bialik's poem, which I had learned by heart while studying at the Yeshiva.

Who would have thought that Rav Pinchas Gellman's modern Yeshiva, situated in a three-story building, would find its place in the well-planned City of Ekaterinoslav, on a four-lane wide street, with two electric trolley-car railways and two rows of trees – known as the "Pushkin Prospect." On the right side of the boulevard were cultural institutions – secondary schools, the city-park, elementary schools with large sports fields, and even a prison.

The Yeshiva was built several years before the First World War and was active until the final establishment of the Soviet Rule in Ekaterinoslav in 1919 – less than a decade. The founder was Rabbi Pinchas Gellman, helped by several members of the community: Mechl Meidanski, Emmanuel, S. Braslavski and most of all M. Yudelson; this man was very devoted to the Yeshiva but died while the project was still in its first stages. For years a memorial was held at the Yeshiva on the date of his death, and Rabbi Gellman and others would speak about his devotion and loyalty to the enterprise.

[Page 123]

It began with a simple synagogue on the Yelisovetgradaskaya Street, at the corner of the Pushkin Prospect. In the courtyard of the synagogue a small house stood, containing several shops. The Community bought the courtyard and the shops and erected a three-floor building above the synagogue, so that it included the synagogue. This was the building of the Yeshiva. On the upper floor there were 4 rooms – classes and a teachers' room. The middle floor contained the synagogue with a separate entrance, and a dormitory for the students from out-of-town. The ground floor comprised the kitchen, the students' dining room and an apartment for the workers and attendants. In the basement there was the central heating room and an apartment for the caretaker and his family, who was not Jewish. Several years later another wing was added, for a Talmud Torah school, preparatory for the Yeshiva. Yeshayahu Scher studied there and after graduation he went to study at the Yeshiva. During World War I another three-story building was erected on the grounds, with several apartments for rent, the income to be used by the Yeshiva.

The Teachers and the Curriculum

The Head of the Yeshiva was the great scholar rabbi Pinchas Gellman z"l who, together with some very hard-working members of the community, was the living spirit of the enterprise. The executive director was Yehoshua Halperin z"l, who by profession was a shochet [ritual slaughterer]. At the beginning he would still work as a slaughterer several hours a day, in his own house near the railway station. Later he left his house and devoted himself entirely to the Yeshiva. He relocated with his family to an apartment at the Yeshiva and managed all administrative affairs. He would also teach Hebrew and TANACH [the Bible] several hours a day. He was the brother of Zarchi from Nahalal and his wife was the sister of Yakov Uri Zaslavski.

The backbone of the curriculum was, of course, the Talmud, taught by two rabbis, called by the names of their towns of origin: "the Semyaticher" and "the Bobroysker." The first taught the two upper classes and was considered "a sharp mind" in Talmud study. He was short, thin, agile and quick, his intelligence shining from his eyes, his mouth and his entire body. The Bobroysker taught the lower classes. He was a heavy man, had a long beard, was always quiet and calm and was considered very erudite. Later, when the Yeshiva expanded, and the Southern towns absorbed the refugees of World War I, Rabbi Eliyahu Meir Feivelson from Kopishuk joined us. He was a member of the Aguda, author of the book Netzach Israel, a great scholar and a philosopher of ethics. I was in his class, and since there was not enough room on the upper floor, we studied on the ground floor, in the "women's section" of the synagogue. During lunch hour, the Rabbi from Kopishuk did not go to the teacher's room but remained instead in the "women's section" and continued the study. I took upon myself to perform a duty, which I did with love: I would bring him from the teachers room a cup of tea and cake. He would object: "Why should I cause you inconveniency and interrupt your lunch?" When I came again to remove the dishes, he would thank me for doing my "job" so conscientiously.

A student was accepted to the Yeshiva following a "talk" with the teachers. The candidate was asked about his town of origin, whether he came from a religious and observant home (this was an obligatory requisite) and was given a short examination on several issues in the Talmud. The number of candidates was great, from the town as well as from the surroundings. Only a small number was accepted to the Yeshiva. Students from out of town were given a place in the dormitories, for a fee. The Talmud was indeed the main topic of study, but there were also teachers of Hebrew, grammar, the Bible [TANACH] and some general studies. It was true, however, that these studies were considered of secondary importance, and as a matter of fact they were not compulsory, but optional.

We had a wonderful teacher of Hebrew and Grammar, S. Kantorowitz, who arrived in town with the Warsaw refugees. He had written several elementary grammar books. In 1919 he was teacher at the Hebrew Teachers College. General studies were taught by teachers graduated from the Government Teachers College in Vilna; they taught us in the afternoon (the mornings were dedicated to the study of Talmud), after they had finished their work in other schools. Although these studies were optional, as mentioned, we managed to absorb knowledge, especially in Hebrew Literature. The love for Bialik I acquired from the teacher Kantorowitz.

The Students

Most of the students were from Ekaterinoslav, but the real quality students came from out-of-town. This was understandable, since a boy from town was sent to study at the Yeshiva for one reason or another, went home after school, met his friends and was constantly under contrasting influence – unlike an out-of-town boy who was sent by his parents from a distant town or village, was mostly a son of a rabbinic family, of a shochet [slaughterer] or another Torah-oriented family, and remained day-and-night at the Yeshiva among his friends, in an atmosphere of study. It was safe to say that study at the Yeshiva, for a local boy, was not too demanding for his family or for himself. It was easy to go in and easy to leave. The contrary was true for the out-of-town boys. They were about 20% of the students, but they studied in the upper classes and constituted the backbone of the institution.

[Page 124]

There was no fanaticism in the Jewish life of the students. The fact that the synagogue was in the same building was a mere coincidence, as was explained above. Indeed, formally the synagogue was situated outside the Yeshiva and the students were not required to pray there. There was no "prayer supervisor" – the students were free to choose their place of prayer. During holidays they would organize a special Minyan. They had cantors with pleasant voices and good Torah reciters, and often the townspeople would come to pray with them, and also donate for the Free-of-Interest Loan Fund [GEMACH] or for the students' library. Sometimes they would take the Torah Scroll from the synagogue to the Yeshiva building and conduct the prayers there.

The language spoken in the Yeshiva was mainly Yiddish, whether at study or in private with the teachers, but Hebrew was spoken as well. During the festivities held on Chanuka, Tu Bishvat [the 15th day of the month of Shevat: the "Holiday of the Trees"] and Purim the dominant language was Hebrew. The students wrote compositions in Hebrew. Rav Gellman's speech – I remember fragments to this day – was in Hebrew mixed with Aramaic. From his speeches we understood that the Rabbi had an argument with those who thought that in the Yeshiva it was not necessary to study Hochma Yevanit [lit. "Greek Wisdom," that is, secular studies]. I remember that with the director of the Yeshiva (in Yeshiva terms: the mashgiach [supervisor]) we spoke Hebrew – whether it was on a religious or a secular subject. By the way, we had the chance to hear Rabbi Gelman's Hebrew-Aramaic mixture later, when we participated in his lectures on Agada [legends of the Midrash] at the Teachers College founded by him, where he brought with him Yeshiva students from Slobodka: Mordechai Guber, Arie Levavi, Yosef Tziftan the poet and the two Levin brothers; one of them, Yehuda-Leib, became later the Moscow Rav.

Only two of the Yeshiva students had the privilege to be accepted at the teacher's college: myself and Kopilov, from Krementchug. I do not know where he is now, but I heard from Zalman Aranne that he was active in the Zionist Movement.

The Yeshiva students organized a GEMACH fund, which served as a source for loans to the students, and sometimes we used it to buy presents for the teachers, for example we bought a present for the Rav from Kopishuk. The sources of the Fund were the fees of the Yeshiva students and various donations, "Calling to the Torah" donations and others. We had also a library for the students.

The students were not required to pass examinations. Every student, before he went on vacation or home for the Holy Days, received a "paper of evaluation." I remember that on one occasion I received a letter from Rav Gellman: "He has good understanding, when he will so desire, he will become wise." The director Halperin wrote to my father: "Your son is one of the good and important students, and we are looking forward to his brilliant future."

The Yeshiva students did not abstain from playing various tricks. For example, trading with unused bus tickets that had been thrown away by the passengers, or "taking" from the bakery several pieces of cake or muffins and paying for one. Only after a reprimand by the Rabbi from Kopishuk did they stop, but probably not entirely.

The first years of the Revolution brought about a decrease of the number of Yeshiva students. A "helping" factor was the establishment of the Cohen High-School, which attracted many of the students.

The difficulties of communication and of obtaining supplies, the frequent revolutions, the pogroms – all this was an important reason for the decrease in the number of students. The consolidation of the Soviet regime in Ekaterinoslav in 1919, with its many decrees and restrictions, brought about the final closing of the Yeshiva, after few, but intense and interesting years of activity.

Several of the Yeshiva students came to Eretz Israel. Among them I shall mention the minister Zalman Aranne z"l, and the Hagana commander David Rothenfeld z"l. Some became teachers, others held important positions in other areas.

[Page 125]

My Grandfather – R'Moshe Karpas z"l
by Zvi Harkavi
Translated by Yocheved Klausner

He was a leader of the Community in Ekaterinoslav; a well-known philanthropist in Russia; a great donor to Zionism and Eretz Israel; a rich man and a great economist – mines, heavy industry and international commerce. He erected many Jewish educational institutions, including academic institutions, in the Diaspora and in our Land. Dr. Shemaryahu Levine describes him in "Memories of my life" (Volume 3, from p. 87).

Her was born in 5612 (1852) to his father Yehuda (a Lithuanian God-fearing small businessman) in Vilna. His parents relocated to Vassilyevka in the Ukraine and he spent his childhood years there. Later he moved with his family to Ekaterinoslav, learned in the Cheder and already as a young boy excelled in wisdom, knowledge, talents and music. He built a violin with his own two hands, but his father broke it since he did not want his son to become a "klezmer" ... When he grew up, he played the violin quite well, by ear only.

After his Bar-Mitzva his father sent him to study at one of the Vilna Yeshivas, but at 16 he was forced to enter the life of work, to help with the livelihood of the family, since his father was sick. After his father died (he was then 20 years old), he managed to marry off his 3 brothers (one of them, David, I met in Tel Aviv as I made Aliya in 1926) and his sisters and took care of his mother with great respect in his own home until her death at a ripe old age.

He began by working as a simple clerk. At 26 he married, in Simperopol, Pearl (Paulina) Nezhinski, a graduate of the Russian High-School and later the Principal of her own Private School. She taught him Russian and general studies and was his faithful aide in his business and charity matters, in particular in the education of poor children and helping the needy.

In 1881 he returned to Ekaterinoslav. He worked as manager at the railroad construction, at first on a small scale, but he raised fast. His business grew, as he invested in it money, initiative, energy and wisdom – all loyally and honestly, as fit for a God-fearing Jew. He became rich in money and property, owner of iron and coal mines in Dunbas, manager of heavy industry as well as inland and foreign commerce, owner of houses and a hotel (Francia, on Prospect 105/107). His wealth was estimated at 18 million Rubles, with one million yearly profits.

As was his wealth, so was his generosity. He was one of the leaders of the community for many years, until his death. He was the head of the Hevra Kadisha [the burial society], and founder, active, head or supporter of almost all the religious, aid and educational Jewish institutions in town (about 24 institutions). He gave to charity a tenth [ma'aser = tithe] of all his earnings and employed a special person (in later years it was Mr. Frenkel) to distribute the charity money regularly and respectfully, to institutions and individuals, as if it were a tax or a regular salary. The authorities respected him, and he succeeded in helping the public and individual persons, in a polite and considerate way. He was for many years' member of the Town Council. During his many travels through Russia and Europe he learned the rules of community management and applied them in his community. He was a democratic leader. Many years he was the Gabay [chief attendant, manager] of the Great Synagogue and his opinion was always respected. He was one of the few who really directed and regulated the activity of the community. He contributed to the budget of all community institutions and was one of the main supporters of the Yiddish newspaper "Freind." Among the institutions that he financed was the orphanage named for him and his wife. The orphanage included a synagogue, and he prayed there (I joined him since I was five years old).

His house served as a meeting place for rabbis, community leaders and Jewish artists. He had in his home a remarkable Yiddish-Hebrew library. He donated large sums to general Jewish causes, and in particular for Eretz Israel. His home was a Torah-observant home. A Hebrew teacher came regularly to the house to teach his sons and daughters [when Mr. Zuta was in Ekaterinoslav he held this position – see his Memoirs "The Way of a Teacher." As he told me – I was his student at the Teachers College in Bet Hakerem, Jerusalem – he received a salary of 60 Rubles monthly.

[Page 126]

His house served also as a shelter at the time of a pogrom. He was in favor of self-defense, knew how to use weapons and had a revolver, to be ready to tackle any trouble. He was one of the founders and a strong supporter of the Commercial High-School, where Jews were accepted freely, without the "percentage norm" – 50% – as was the rule in other schools. I went to that school for several years. The teacher of Jewish religion was Bragin; his books on the subject were published in Ekaterinoslav.

Among his friends were: Ahad-Ha'am, Dr. Shemeryahu Levine, M. Usishkin, Dr. Tchlenov. He participated in the Zionist Congresses and corresponded with Herzl personally. He was inscribed in the first Sefer Hazahav [the Golden Book of JNF], reg. No. 275. He was one of the first to buy shares of the "Colonial Bank" and his house served as the bank's office of the Ekaterinoslav Branch. He also bought shares of the Hashka'a Company and donated to the fund raised for the settlement of Yemenite Jews in Eretz Israel. He was also active in campaigns for the benefit of the Torat Chaim Yeshiva in Jerusalem.

When Tel Aviv was founded, he bought, following the advice of his friend S. Levine, a plot of land (now Rothschild Blvd. 2, near the empty plot where Levine's house once stood).

R'Moshe Karpas z"l

[Page 127]

He was one of the three donors-founders, with Jack Wissotzki in Moscow and Yakov Schieff, of the Technion in Haifa. Karpas donated 110,000 Marks. He supported Levine and his friends in the "Language War" at the Technion.

Before World War I he planned to go to Eretz Israel and build a house for himself on the plot he had bought in Tel Aviv (see Levine's letters to Karpas in "His Letters" pp. 275 and 283). In 1916 he helped the Zionist Organization, during the preparations to receive the Balfour declaration, with a loan-donation [90% loan with indefinite date of payment and 10% donation] of one million Rubles, which he transferred secretly, in Kisloborsk, to Dr. Yechiel Tchlenov, to take to London.

Karpas did not ignore the improving situation of the Jews in Russia. At the time of the February Revolution – actually some time before it – he helped establish a "Jewish Polytechnic School," together with his son Eng. Gregory (David Hirsh Karpas) and his son-in-law my father Eng. Lev (Yehuda-Leib Harkavi (see an article about this institution in the book). Several months before he died (Saturday 27 Iyar 5677 - 1917) The Jewish Politechnicum in Ekaterinoslav opened its doors and study started.

Out of respect, his funeral was postponed until Monday (instead of Sunday) and he was put to rest with the participation of tens of thousands of Jews from Ekaterinoslav and foreigners as well, and delegations from all over

Russia. The funeral lasted seven hours, passing near more than 20 institutions that he founded-managed-supported. Businesses closed for the time of the funeral. Many rabbis headed by Rabbi Shneurson and other public figures eulogized at the funeral. Rabbi Gellman, a personal friend of Karpas was out of town – at the Herut convention in Kiev – and could not attend the funeral. The entire Jewish press echoed his passing, as well as the Russian press.

His offspring: his oldest son Gregory z"l, mentioned above; his son Lev (Leib) z"l, an attorney, died at 83 years of age in Moscow, had two daughters; The artist Ludmila (Liva) in Moscow and Chana (Ana-Nusia) in Teheran; his son Alexander, professor (Emeritus) of biology aged about 82, lives in Leningrad, in 1972 was editor of a Literature and Arts Magazine in Russian in Ekaterinoslav; his daughter Rasha (Rayssa-Ra'ya, my mother may she rest in peace, wife of Eng. Harkavi z"l mentioned above; his daughter Rosa may she rest in peace, wife of professor Dr. Chananya Schechter z"l [their daughter Vera is a pianist and professor at the Moscow conservatoire and their son Mark Schechter z"l was a poet].

[Page 131]

Public Personalities and Zionist Activists

Translated by Yocheved Klausner

Eliyahu Orshanski

Eliyahu Orshanski, the great journalist, and one of the first researchers of the Russian Jews, was born in Ekaterinoslav in 1846. As all Jewish children, he learned in Cheder and since he was very talented, he began to study Talmud at a very early age. At the same time, he studied general studies and science. At the age of 18 he passed the Matriculation exams, was accepted at the University and studied Law, at first in Charkov and later in Odessa. He excelled in his studies and was offered a post at the University as teacher and researcher, on the condition that he convert to Christianity – which he declined immediately!

Eliyahu Orshanski

In Odessa, he began writing for the Jewish press in Russia, which just then began its first steps: "Dan" and "Yebreiska Biblioteka." His articles dealt with the problems of the Russian Jews, their difficult situation and the various restrictions imposed on them. The Jewish press, even before Orshanski, indeed asked the government to change its anti-Semitic policies that were harming the Jews; however, the articles published used mostly a tone of supplication. Orshanski used a different method: He did not beg but requested equal rights for the Jews. As a human being – he argued – the Jew is fully entitled to enjoy all the civil rights he deserves, and no person or system can limit them or deny them; it is, therefore, the duty of the government to cancel all restrictions and limitations.

[Page 132]

His many articles were based on material that he continuously collected, concerning the life of the Jews in the country. He proved, relying on a great deal of data, that the economic situation of the Russian Jews, their constant wandering from place to place, their lack of capital, their poverty etc. – all these were a direct result of the anti-Jewish legislation of the government and were not characteristic national traits. Orshanski proved that the Jewish merchant has introduced new methods of practicing commerce, (as free competition, short and fast turnover) and developed new lines of work in the agricultural industry and more – all that in contrast to the frozen monopoly and inactivity of the Russian merchant. Orshanski proved that the many government laws against the Jews were based on blind hatred toward the Jews, on the desire to limit their economic activity and exploit it for the benefit of the government and the defense of the primitive Russian merchant. These laws seemed to have come directly from the dark Middle-Ages and not from our modern times...

The Orshanski articles had a powerful effect: for the first time the voice of the Russian Jewry was heard – a strong self-conscious voice, a voice that dared criticize the many anti-Jewish laws and requested their annulment. The articles were based on the truth, were interesting and proud. This way of writing influenced the readers, who joined the struggle for the rights of the Russian Jews.

The articles were collected in: The Jews in Russia and Russian legislation concerning the Jews. These two collections provided for a long time valuable and important material on the economic and judicial situation of the Russian Jews, and a source of many essays, memoranda etc.

Orshanski lived a short life; he died at the age of 29. However, during the few years that he was busy writing he worked for the benefit of his people. His name will be remembered among the first to defend and fight for the rights of the Jewish people in Russia.

Orshanski excelled in the research of the Russian Civil Law as well.

Yitzhak Orshanski

Yitzhak, the brother of the well-known Eliyahu Orshanski, was born in 1851, studied medicine and specialized in mental health, and in this profession, he reached fame in the medical world.

He participated in the Jewish press in the Russian language and was part of the community work in Ekaterinoslav. He represented the community vis-à-vis the authorities and was a delegate of the Ekaterinoslav Jewish Community at the Conference of the Jewish Communities held in 1882 in Petersburg. There he met with the Minister of the Interior Ignatyev, who clearly informed him that the Russian government does not oppose Jewish emigration from Russia, saying: "The Russian Western borders are open for the Jews."

He was appointed Professor at the University of Charkov – and soon after that he converted to Christianity.

Mechl [Michael] Maidanski

He was one of the famous and devoted community workers in Ekaterinoslav during many years. Was born in 1825 in Zaskavel (Wolhyn Region) and in 1875 moved to Ekaterinoslav. Soon he occupied an honored place in the life of the local Jewish Community. Always willing to help others, of an open heart and life wisdom – he reached an important position among the community workers in Ekaterinoslav and became a popular personality among the local Jews. For many years he was member of the management of the Great Synagogue (which actually served as the management of the community), as well as the representative of the Jewish Community in the City Council. He was also member of the management of the local Talmud Torah, the Jewish hospital and other Jewish institutions in town. He collected charity for various institutions in town and for needy people in neighboring localities and often represented the community vis à vis the authorities in the Ekaterinoslav District and at various conventions and meetings.

Maidanski was among the first active members of the Hovevei-Zion movement in Ekaterinoslav. He participated in the Founding Convention of the "Odessa Committee" and traveled to Eretz Israel as a member of their delegation, which was headed by Rabbi S. Mohliver.

[Page 133]

He continued his activity in the Zionist Movement and participated in all its institutions. He was a devoted supporter of the revival of the Hebrew Language and his family was one of the first to use Hebrew in daily life. In all his activities he was devoted and energetic, until old age. He was loved by all Ekaterinoslav Jews, many of whom were indebted to him for his assistance in time of need. He was the type of a Jewish intellectual of the "old generation," with years of life experience, who knew how to manage and act during the New Times as well.

In 1910 he died at the ripe old age of 85, after a full life of activity and deeds.

Mechl Maidanski

Chaim (Vitali) Levanda

He was the brother of the known writer Arie Levanda, born in 1840 in Minsk. He wrote articles about the Jewish society in the Jewish press in the Russian language and became famous after publishing his essay "The collection of laws and regulations concerning the Jews of Russia from 1649 to 1873" which was very helpful for the people who dealt with judicial matters concerning the Jews.

He relocated to Ekaterinoslav and starting in the eighties of the 19th century he was an active member of the Hovevei-Zion movement. He was one of the important spokesmen of the movement and represented it at various opportunities. He took part in the regular local community work as well, was a member of several of its institutions, represented it before the authorities, and was elected as its delegate to various conventions (for example the Convention of Rabbis in 1893). His public activity lasted over thirty years.

[Page 134]

Menachem Ussishkin

He was one of the world leaders of the Zionist movement. He was born in 1863 in Dubrovna, Mohilev District, his full name was Avraham Menachem Mendel. He went to live in Ekaterinoslav, after receiving in Moscow the title of Engineer and marrying Esther, the daughter of Sergei Faley, one of the pillars of the Jewish community in Ekaterinoslav. This marriage enabled Ussishkin to join the influential society in Ekaterinoslav and reach an honored place there.

As soon as he came to Ekaterinoslav he joined the Hovevei Zion association, which had been established there in the early eighties (of the 19th century) and was elected its head. Together with others – Mechl Maidanski, Avraham Harkavi, Chaim Levanda, Levinski, Baruch Spiewak etc. – he intensified the activity of the association and its influence in town increased. At Ussishkin's initiative, a Hebrew library was opened in Ekaterinoslav and the study of the Hebrew language was reinforced, by giving lectures and by establishing "Hebrew speaking circles." He invited the famous Hebrew teacher Ch. A. Zuta to teach in Hebrew in the first modern cheder that he established – all this in addition to collecting funds for the Jewish settlement in Eretz Israel and other activities of Hovevei Zion (see on this subject the detailed article by Dr. Y. Klausner in this book).

By these activities he earned fame in the Zionist movement and Dr. Th. Herzl invited him in 1897 to the first Zionist Congress. He returned as a great supporter of Political Zionism and this influenced Hovevei Zion in Ekaterinoslav: since then, organized and systematic Zionist activity began in town. New members joined, Zionist Shekalim were sold, funds were collected for Zionist work, for JNF and for the Colonial Bank, Zionist and national literature was published etc. Ussishkin received from the government a permit to assemble a regional convention of Zionist leaders; there the foundation was laid of regular organizational work in the Ekaterinoslav and neighboring districts. In addition to introducing national content into the Jewish educational system, Ussishkin helped organize public events such as a children's parade on Lag Ba'omer, Chanuka festivities and others. These activities had a great effect on the Jewish population at the time. Lectures were given as well, on national and Zionist topics. His strong, leading spirit was felt in all these activities – he had a clear vision of the program he intended to carry out and was not afraid of difficulties. No wonder that the Ekaterinoslav District was one of the most organized and its leader Ussishkin was known and respected by so many.

He also succeeded in assembling a group of good and talented helpers, among them: Dr. Yakov Dolzanski, his brother-in-law Eng. Moshe Bruck, Baruch Toporovski, Shimon Stanislavski, Shlomo Breslavski, Yakov Berezovski and others. Loyal to Herzl's motto to conquer the communities, he suggested inviting Dr. Shemaryahu Levin, the well-known Zionist and great speaker, to be "crown-rabbi" in Ekaterinoslav. After an election campaign, Dr. Levin was invited in 1898 to occupy the position, and he immediately joined the active Zionist circles and acted to strengthen the Jewish national spirit in town.

Ussishkin played an important role in the elections of the first Duma (the Russian parliament) as well. He was one of the first to request a Jewish

National Block in order to ensure a Jewish delegate from the Ekaterinoslav District. In spite of the opposition of the assimilated Jews, the Zionists succeeded, a Jewish block was organized and the attorney M. Sheftel was elected delegate to the first Duma.

[Page 135]

After 15 years of fruitful work, in 1906 Ussishkin relocated to Odessa, to serve there as chairman of the Hovevei Zion "Odessa Committee". In 1919 he made Aliya to Eretz Israel and served as the head of JNF [Jewish National Fund = Keren Kayemet LeIsrael], in addition to his other activities. During that time many important land acquisitions were made. He died on 12 Tishrei 5702 [3 October 1941].

(On his work and his importance for the Zionist movement – see The History of Zionism and general literature about him).

Menachem Ussishkin

[Page 136]

Baruch Spiewak

Baruch ben Shmuel Spiewak, one of the most devoted community workers in Ekaterinoslav, was born in 1866, in the small town Samila, Kiew District.

When he relocated to Ekaterinoslav, he became involved in commerce and at the same time he took an active part in the Zionist work in town with the Hovevei Zion movement, as one of Ussishkin's loyal assistants. He devoted himself in particular to extending the use of the Hebrew language, and to organize and support the first "Modern Cheder" [lit. "improved Cheder"] and other local cultural activities. Spiewak's Zionist activity increased with the advent of Political Zionism. As a reward for his constant work for the movement he was sent by the local Zionists as their delegate, to various conventions and to the 7th Congress.

Spiewak took part in the committee for the aid of the victims of the 1905 pogrom and ten years later in the committee for the aid of the refugees who arrived to Ekaterinoslav during World War I. He devoted himself to cultural activity and sought to introduce the study of the Hebrew language to the schools for refugees, which were opened by the Aid Committee. His Zionist work was intensified again during the February 1917 revolution, when new opportunities arose for legal activity. Spiewak was one of the leaders in the struggle for broadening and strengthening the Zionist ideas among the Ekaterinoslav Jews.

In 1922 he made Aliya to Eretz Israel, where he continued his public and Zionist activity. He was one of the founders and supporters of "Ohel Shem".

He died in 1932.

Moshe Bruk
(1868– 1920)

was born in 1868 in Ekaterinoslav to a wealthy and respected family. As all children he went at an early age to the Cheder, and at the age of 13 he enrolled in the local school. At home he continued to study Hebrew language and literature and was fluent in Hebrew. After graduating from High–School he began the study of chemistry at the "Politechnicum" [technical college] in Riga. He was a member of the Jewish student's association "Anatolica," whose chief aim was to enable close contact between the Jewish students. The Association organized lectures on Jewish topics, parties etc. Bruk took an active part in the activity of the Association, gave lectures and for several years was its chairman. He was a talented speaker and excelled in his warm relationship with his friends.

After completing his studies in 1892, he relocated to Ekaterinoslav, where he married the daughter of S. Paley and so became the brother–in–law of M. Ussishkin and A. Yakobson. Bruk was at first not attached to the Zionist movement; however, influenced by Achad–Ha'am, who visited Ekaterinoslav several times, and Ussishkin, he joined the movement. His preference, however, was general Jewish public activity; he was a devoted follower of the method of "gegenwarts Arbeit" [working directly, face–to–face], and the idea of "conquering" the communities was close to his heart. Accordingly, he dedicated all his energy to working within the many institutions supported by the community and was soon recognized for his talents and devotion. He was one of the initiators and founders of new public institutions, as: a society for the aid of the poor, which enlarged yearly its area of work; a society of mutual credit, which he headed for many years; institutions for the aid and support of the craftsmen and others. Thanks to his personal qualities and his managing ability, his peers elected him as chairman of the institutions that he had founded. He was known as one of the important community workers in town - one that could be asked for help at any time.

Several years later, Bruk joined the Zionist activity and soon rose to a leading position. He participated in the Zionist Congresses and in several conventions, as well as in the yearly meetings of the "Odessa Committee." In 1905, at the seventh Congress he was elected representative of the Ekaterinoslav District and member of the Great Zionist Executive Committee. Since then he headed the Zionist activity in the District, after Ussishkin's relocation to Odessa. His area of influence included several districts in Southern Russia, where there was quite a large Jewish population. Bruk attracted new people to the Zionist movement, among them young and energetic men and women, and the District became one of the most organized and most active of the Zionist Movement in Russia. Bruk combined his Zionist activity with his activity in other public institutions: he always appeared as a Zionist and thus his influence on his friends was strong. Soon he was recognized as a national and Zionist leader not only in Ekaterinoslav but in the near and far neighborhood, and people would address him asking advice and guidance. People admired him for being a proud and warmhearted Jew,

[Page 137]

a mixture of Hebrew culture and European education, who considers above all the interest of his people and strives for the Return to Zion. No wonder that he headed the Jewish election lists to the Russian parliament and to other Russian national institutions.

Moshe Bruk

During and after the 1917 revolution, with the revival of public life in the country, Bruk's public and Zionist activity broadened. He participated in all meetings and conventions, heading many of them (in 1917 he was member of the presidential board of the Zionist convention in Petrograd and in 1918 of the convention of the Ukrainian Jews in Kiev). He supported in particular the Zionist activity in Ekaterinoslav and surroundings, at the same time acting against the Jewish leftist parties that insulted the Zionists and their activity. At the democratic elections in the Ekaterinoslav community the Zionists won and M. Bruk was elected president of the community. In that function he was in 1919 member of the delegation to General Denikin, commander of the White Army that conquered Southern Ukraine and carried out pogroms. The delegation requested to stop the pogrom, but the response was negative.

His public activity was terminated suddenly, with his death of typhoid fever on 8 January 1920 on his way to Kavkaz, in the town Kerch where he was buried, far from his family and friends. The Russian Jews lost a great man, devoted to his people; the Zionists lost one of their important and loyal leaders.

[Page 138]

Shimon Stanislavski

He was a member of one of the old, intellectual families in Ekaterinoslav, and very popular in town.

He was born in 1848 in Nikopol, Ekaterinoslav District. In his youth he relocated with his family to Ekaterinoslav and, following the advice of Eliyahu Orshanski he enrolled in the local high school, at the quite "advanced" age of 23. He rose to the first ranks of the local community workers and excelled in his literary work as well. He was active in several community institutions and a constant contributor to the Jewish press, in Hebrew and in Russian. In his articles he described the Jewish community life and requested to strengthen it and conduct it according to democratic rules. He gained an important position among the Jewish public and his opinions were respected.

He was very knowledgeable in Jewish history and was one of the first to request to collect material on the Russian Jews. He published articles on this topic, as well as on Jewish writers in Russia.

He was active in the Zionist movement in Ekaterinoslav, from the establishment of Hovevei Zion, and worked many years with M. Ussishkin and M. Bruk. He helped spread the Zionist idea among the local Jewish population, by his personality and activity as well as by his articles in the local Jewish press. He was respected and loved by the Ekaterinoslav Jews.

With the consolidation of the Soviet rule, his voice became silenced and his public activity as well as his participation in the local press were stopped. He died in 1921, after years of financial distress and suffering.

Dr. Shmaryahu Levin

Dr. Shmaryahu Levin was the third rabbi in Ekaterinoslav appointed by the authorities [rav mita'am] and the most outstanding of them.

He was born in 1867 in Swisslotz (Minsk District). After graduating from universities in Germany and acting as a talented speaker in the Zionist movement, he served as rav mita'am in Grodno. At the request of the Ekaterinoslav Zionists, who wanted a rabbi who was educated, Zionist and involved in public life, he was invited to serve in Ekaterinoslav.

Dr. S. Levin occupied this position for 6 years (1898–1904). He did not disappoint the people who elected him. He was always in the center of the Jewish public life in Ekaterinoslav. The number of his sympathizers increased, as well as his influence. His speeches, in which he reacted to the Jewish daily life, promoted patriotism, explained Jewish values etc., attracted many members of the community.

He regarded his function in the community not simply as an employee appointed by the authorities, but as educator and guide. He was very active in the field of education of the children, establishing schools and other educational institutions in the Jewish national spirit, and he welcomed and helped any initiative in this area.

As an active Zionist, he supported the local Zionist activity, helped registering new members etc. It is important to mention his collaboration with M. Ussishkin, who was one of the people who suggested to offer him the position of official rabbi in Ekaterinoslav.

Dr. Shmaryahu Levin

The Russian authorities respected and valued him, and often honored his requests concerning the Community. In his Memoirs, parts of which appear in this book, he relates about his life and activity in Ekaterinoslav.

In 1904 he left Ekaterinoslav and relocated to Vilna, working as a preacher in the Great Synagogue. He was elected to the first Duma [Russian parliament]. He was member of the Zionist Directorship, made Aliya in 1924, died 8 Sivan 5695 (1935).

[Page 139]

Sergei Paley

Sergei (Shmaryahu) Paley belonged to one of the most respected families in Ekaterinoslav. He was one of the first Jewish engineers in Ekaterinoslav and managed his father's large business enterprises in town. Influenced by his son–in–law M. Ussishkin he became involved in local Jewish community matters, and thanks to his sharp intellect, his logic and his sense of criticism he rose in importance and his advice was sought by many.

Sergei Paley

His other son–in–law, M. Bruk, one of the leaders of the Zionist organization in Ekaterinoslav, attracted him to the Movement. His house became a Zionist house and he became active in Zionist work. His daughters were married to well–known Zionists: Esther to M. Ussishkin, Ziniada to M. Bruk and Rosa to Dr. Avigdor Yakobson, representative of the Zionist organization in Istanbul and later in Geneva. He died in 1918.

Menachem–Emanuel Broshtein

Menachem–Emanuel Broshtein was the last rav mita'am [rabbi appointed by the authorities] in Ekaterinoslav. He was given this position in 1904, after Dr. Shmaryahu Levin relocated to Vilna.

During his term of office, the Ekaterinoslav Community went through one of its stormiest events - from the 1905 pogroms to the 1917 Russian

Revolution, the establishment of the Soviet regime and the end of the community and its institutions.

As his predecessor, in addition to his official functions (registering births, marriages and deaths, as well as issuing documents and speaking at the synagogue on holidays), M.E. Broshtein loyally represented the community, and participated actively in its life and its institutions, helping as much as he could, especially with the educational institutions. His home was open to all, and people would come constantly, either to seek advice, to "pour out the heart" when in trouble or to look for aid. All found a listening ear, a word of comfort and often material help when needed. He was always concerned about the education of the young, especially since the increase of assimilation in Ekaterinoslav. As a teacher of the Hebrew Religion in the Commercial High-School in town (which had many Jewish students) he enriched his curriculum with chapters of Jewish history and literature and was very loved by the local Jewish youth. He was active in the Zionist Organization in town and appeared publicly as a Zionist, in particular after the 1917 revolution as all the limitations and restrictions were removed.

He was elected Rabbi again and again, always by a great majority, and was sent as delegate to many conventions and councils. Before the authorities he always appeared as a proud Jew, not begging but insisting on his rights.

The 1917 revolution limited even more the functions of the rav mita'am. Yet he continued his activity in several areas and his experience was of great help in the difficult conditions of those days. He was one of the few community workers who remained in Ekaterinoslav and cared for the community and its few institutions that were still active. In 1922, he helped organize a committee for the aid of the hungry, which later received help from Canada. Old and ill, he continued to support the few Zionists that were still active in town, visited the synagogues and had always words of comfort and hope. He died in the mid-twenties.

[Page 140]

Dr. Yakov Dolzhanski

He was one of the well-known and important activists in Ekaterinoslav. He was born in 1866 in Kriboy-Rug, not far from Ekaterinoslav. His parents have given him a traditional education, and on his own he passed the matriculation examinations and went to the University to study medicine. After graduation he went to Germany and specialized in surgery. Returning to Russia, he worked as a doctor in a village in the Tula district, and in the 1890s he relocated to Ekaterinoslav, working at first in the local hospital and later in a clinic of his own, where he performed private surgery.

Dr. Yakov Dolzhanski

He soon became famous as a great specialist in his profession; but he took part in the local public and Zionist activity as well. He was active in the Hibat Zion movement and later in the Political Zionist movement. He helped M. Ussishkin, the Zionist leader in Ekaterinoslav and his followers. He was member of Zionist institutions in the region, and his home was the meeting place. He supported other public institutions in town as well, helping especially the refugees who reached Ekaterinoslav during the First World War.

As a doctor and a public worker, he earned an important name and position among the Jewish and non–Jewish population. He helped and supported many, in particular during the Makhno occupation of the town. Thanks to him, many were saved from death or heavy punishment, since his hospital served Makhno's army.

In 1921 he made Aliya to Eretz Israel and worked at the Hadassa and Bikur Holim hospitals in Jerusalem. He was active in the Medical Association and was its chairman for some time; he founded the Journal of the Medical Association Harefu'ah and was its editor until his death in 1929 in Jerusalem, at the age of 63.

His son Prof. Moshe Dolzhanski of the Hebrew University was one of the victims who fell in the "Convoy to Har Hatzofim" during the War of Independence. His daughter Tamar is a poet.

[Page 141]

Leon Rothenberg

Rothenberg was one of the well-known community workers in Ekaterinoslav. He was born in 1868 in Odessa. After graduating from Law School at the local university, he moved to Ekaterinoslav and made his home there. Because of the limitations imposed on Jews who desired to practice law, he devoted himself to one special aspect of the profession – classification of the decisions of the Russian Senate (the supreme judicial institution in Russia), as well as to publishing various law books, which proved to be very helpful to jurists.

In Ekaterinoslav, Rothenberg took part in the Zionist activity and was active in several institutions of aid and support. His main work was his function as member of the Committee of the society for the aid of the refugees, established in 1915. This committee took care of the 5,000 refugees that arrived in Ekaterinoslav during World War I. As chairman of the Committee, his work was intense, extended and ramified and carried much responsibility, in the difficult conditions of those days.

In 1922 Rothenberg left Ekaterinoslav and relocated to Moscow, and from there he went abroad. In the thirties he arrived to his daughter in Eretz Israel, and there he continued his judicial work – classification of the laws of the British Mandate government – and published several volumes titled Laws of Palestine, edited by Moshe Dukhan.

David Shmorgoner

He was one of the prominent leaders of the Ekaterinoslav community in the years before the February 1917 Revolution; a well-known attorney, of a dignified and impressive appearance, a very good speaker in the Russian language, liked by many. He took an active part in the management of several community institutions and often appeared vis-`-vis the authorities in the name of the Ekaterinoslav Jews, being able to present the requests of the Jewish population in an appropriate way. His activity was important in particular during the First World War, when he was a member, as a representative of the Jewish Aid Committee, of the government committee for the aid of the refugees. His role in this committee was to see that the Jewish refugees are not deprived in the distribution of the funds allotted to them.

In the days when the government in town changed often, he was part of the small group that cared about the well-being of the Ekaterinoslav Jews and represented them before the local authorities. He was a member of the Jewish party "Volkspartei." In the twenties he left Ekaterinoslav and moved to Moscow. There he died.

Pavel (Pinchas) Cohen

He was the founder and the principal of the Jewish High–School (Gimnasia) in Vilna, one of the first in Russia. This school was founded in 1906, with the obvious intention to overcome the discriminating and cruel law of "numerus clausus" according to which only a certain percentage of Jews were accepted to the general high schools.

This Jewish Gymnasia was different from the others of its kind by the national spirit that reigned there and by the excellent curriculum and teachers – all of which attracted Jewish students from all parts of the country.

In 1915, during World War I, this high–school, including its teachers, relocated to Ekaterinoslav, and so its doors were opened to the children of the town and surroundings. Many received their general and Jewish education there (the curriculum included Hebrew language and Jewish history). Its teachers took an active part in the Jewish life in town and the principal Mr. Cohen became an appreciated community worker, in particular in the year of the revolution, 1917.

Mr. P. Cohen, a man of initiative and practical knowledge, played an important part in the preparations for the elections to the Community Managing Committee in Ekaterinoslav, as well as to the All–Jewish Convention in Russia. He was elected to the community managing committee as representative of the Jewish Folks Party ("Volkspartei"). Thanks to his talents, he was elected as the head of its Executive.

In fact, he was the real leader of the Ekaterinoslav community, organized its committees and helped shape it – all this during the difficult years of revolutions. On his shoulders lay the responsibility to manage the community until the termination of the Soviet rule.

In the Twenties he relocated to Moscow (The Jewish High School, which had been under his direction, was transferred to the general school system and thus it lost its Jewish character). He was one of the few who signed the memorandum sent to the authorities, asking to allow the study of Hebrew language and culture in Russia.

[Page 142]

Zalman Ostrovski

In the years 1904–1906 he was one of the most active members of the Po'alei Zion Party in Russia. Known by the name "Comrade Zyama," he became famous by his popular articles about the political platform of Po'alei Zion: "Letters to the Jewish worker," which he signed "Tovarish (comrade) Zyama."

He returned to full activity in the party during the 1917 revolution and became one of the most prominent speakers (in Yiddish) in those days. He was the head of Po'alei Zion in Ekaterinoslav and fought against the "Jewish Zionist bourgeoisie."

He was also the director of the orphanage in Ekaterinoslav, founded by M. Karpas. In the late twenties, he left Po'alei Zion and joined, together with many other Jews, the Jewish Communist Party (EKP).

Dr. Boris Chanis

He was one of the last devoted community workers in Ekaterinoslav. At the end of World War I, after being released from the Russian army where he served as a military doctor, in 1918–1919 he headed the organization "The Union of the Jewish Soldiers" in Ekaterinoslav and was known by his warm attitude toward his Jewish brothers and his being ready to help at any time. In 1918 he was elected to the managing committee of the Ekaterinoslav community and was appointed as the head of the Health and Social Aid sub-committee. These were difficult years – the Jewish population in town was in great distress and there were almost no sources for earning a livelihood, due to the constant changes in the leadership of the town. Dr. Chanis was charged with organizing and managing the aid and health institutions of the community, with no regular sources of income.

Then came the great hunger of 1922, and thousands of Ekaterinoslav Jews were in danger of starvation. The community workers in town organized a local committee to help the needy and Dr. Chanis was an active member. He was appointed – by the "Committee of the Ukraine Jews" in London as well as by the "Joint" in America, the organizations that helped the Jews suffering from hunger in Russia – as their representative in Ekaterinoslav to organize the aid activity in their name.

He excelled in this function. He opened soup-kitchens, organized help for the intellectual professionals, supplied working materials to the craftsmen, opened a loan and credit fund etc. – all this in collaboration with the local committee. On behalf of the "Joint" he renovated the Jewish hospital in town, renewed the equipment, opened new clinics and kindergartens, organized a co-operative by the name of Makolet ["grocery"], opened a food warehouse to distribute food to the needy and more. All these activities saved many from death and helped others to recuperate and return to regular life. At the same time the US Jews continued their own aid activity, in many ways.

In 1924, the activity of all these institutions ended and they were closed, one by one, by the order of the authorities. A few of them were transferred to the management of the government or the municipality. Thus, ended the blessed activity of Dr. Chanis. Still, considering his former work, the authorities permitted him to keep a private medical clinic, which lasted several years. In the early thirties, his clinic was closed, and he was exiled to Siberia. From that time, we do not have, unfortunately, any information about him.

[Page 143]

Shlomo Braslavski

He was one of the most active and energetic persons in the Zionist movement in Ekaterinoslav, in the first decade and a half of the 20th century.

He was born in 1879 in Elizabethgrad. He studied in the Cheder and in the general school. As a young man he was teacher of Hebrew and Russian. After he married, he became involved in business (especially the oil business), and succeeded thanks to his commercial talents and his energy; in a short time became a rich man. After he went to live in Ekaterinoslav he joined the Zionist work and his devotion, diligence and hard work soon placed him in the first line of the local movement.

Shlomo Braslavski

He was most loyal to the Hebrew language and devoted much work to support its teaching and its institutions. He was member of the Zionist Party institutions and its delegate to various conventions and councils. His house was open to Zionist and Hebrew Cultural meetings and he contributed generously to Zionist and cultural institutions (at the 11th Zionist congress he made a very important contribution toward the foundation of the Hebrew University). He was loved by the Ekaterinoslav Jews and Zionists for his personal qualities, his open heart and his willingness to help his fellows.

With the occupation of the town by the Soviets and the stabilization of their rule, he relocated to Rostov, and since he was of the "bourgeois class" he could expect persecution and arrest. Indeed, he was not left alone: he was arrested in the synagogue, as he was preparing to deliver a eulogy in memory of his friend and partner to the Zionist work, M. Bruk. He was executed by the government on 31 October 1920. His children made Aliya to Eretz Israel.

[Page 144]

Baruch Toporovski

He was one of the veterans of the Zionist movement in Ekaterinoslav. He was a member of Hovevei Zion and worked with M. Ussishkin and later with M. Bruk.

His main activity was in the area of culture: at meetings, as well as at closed or half–open parties he lectured on Zionist topics. He participated in the Jewish press, in particular in the weeklies of the Zionist Organization, where he reviewed the community life in Ekaterinoslav. He was close to the local Jewish youth and lectured on Jewish history and on Zionism. There were many who first heard about Zionism from him. The Ekaterinoslav Zionists valued and respected him.

He wrote in Hebrew as well.

With the stabilization of the Soviet regime, his Zionist activity stopped, and we do not have any information about his death.

Avraham Berezovski

He was one of the prominent personalities in the Zionist movement in Ekaterinoslav, in the second decade of the 20th century. The son of the leader Yakov Berezovski, he received a wide general and juristic education. He was a good and popular speaker in the Russian language and a sharp debater. He was very active among young people, strived to educate them in the spirit of Zionism and fought assimilation and its negative influence on the Jewish youth.

Until the February 1917 Revolution he was forced to work mostly underground, however later he was able work openly, and then he could truly realize his talents and ability. He fought successfully for the Zionist idea at every meeting, in spite of the speakers from the leftist parties whose influence on the Jewish population increased steadily. His original ideas were studied, and many learned from him how to hold their ground in a debate. He was a proud Jew and Zionist, and, on appropriate occasions never failed to stress that. He did not believe that the revolution would give the people the freedom and happiness that they expected, and many considered him a "reactionary." He was member of the "General Zionists" party and was elected to the Zionist institutions and to the community council as their representative. He did not make Aliya. Until the thirties he continues his membership in the Zionist organization but was not active in the underground movement. He embraced tradition and began to keep the Commandments [mitzvot], in contrast to the spirit of his own home.

Pinchas Schiffman (Ben Sira)

He was one of the best Zionist leaders in Ekaterinoslav. He was born in 1874, in the town Yelsk, Minsk district. He studied in the Yeshiva and worked as a teacher.

During World War I he relocated from Lida to Ekaterinoslav and worked as a Hebrew teacher in the Yeshiva. He was invited as well to teach in the schools for the refugees that were organized at the time, gave Hebrew lessons to the members of the Hovevei Sfat Ever [lovers of the Hebrew language] circle, began to work with the local Zionists, was invited to teach at Cohen's High–School (that had just relocated from Vilna) and lectured at the Yeshiva of Rabbi Gellman.

After the February 1917 revolution, P. Schiffman's activity increased greatly. He began appearing at public meetings, supported Zionism and Hebrew teaching and was in constant struggle against the "Yiddishists," who requested recognition of the Yiddish language as the only national language of the Jewish people. He wrote, in Hebrew, several information booklets, which were printed in Ekaterinoslav and then translated to Yiddish, among them "The Balfour Declaration" and "Building the Community." These booklets, which described and explained the Zionist ideology, were very valuable and served the organization activists as publicity material. He was elected to the party committees and represented it at various conventions and councils. As a person rooted in Hebrew culture and a talented speaker, he was loved by the local Zionists and served them as teacher and guide and played a significant part in the growth of the Zionist movement in 1917–1918 in Ekaterinoslav.

As the Soviet regime consolidated and with it came the restrictions on the Zionist activity and the study of Hebrew, Schiffman's activity was minimized. However, in spite of the danger involved, he continued to teach Hebrew, whether in the synagogue or in his own home. Finally, he left Ekaterinoslav and after a few years in other locations in Poland he made Aliya to Eretz Israel in 1926. Here he continued his literary and educational work in religious schools. He died in 1945.

[Page 145]

Moshe Duchan

Moshe ben Aharon Duchan was born in 1884 in the town Verknodneprovsk, not far from Ekaterinoslav. As a child he studied in the Cheder, and after he passed the matriculation exams, he went to study Law at the University of Charkov, continued his studies in Germany and finally in Petersburg. He excelled in his studies and was offered an academic position, on condition that he convert to Christianity – which he declined naturally.

Moshe Duchan

After completing his studies, he opened a Law Office in Ekaterinoslav. He became a Zionist and continued this work in Petersburg, in the Tze'irei ZionI group. He was soon noticed and recognized for his large juristic education and general knowledge and reached a high position among the Petersburg Zionists, in particular after the 1917 revolution. He believed that the revolution was not the solution of the Jewish problem; the only solution was political Zionism. He was elected to the community council and appointed vice–chairman.

In 1918 he relocated to Ukraine. In 1919 he was appointed head of the Eretz–Israel Office in Novorusisk and later he went to Paris and represented the Ukraine Jews at the Peace Conference.

In 1920 he arrived in Eretz Israel. After passing in 1921 the Law Exams for foreign lawyers he worked at the government office as vice–manager of the Real Estate Department. He kept this position until 1937, when he resigned since he realized that as a Jew, he had no hope to make progress professionally. He has been one of the few Jews who held a high-ranking position; he introduced some order in the department (which was quite neglected up to that time) and in the British Mandate laws concerning land ownership. His book (in Hebrew) on the subject, "Real Estate Laws" in which he reviewed systematically the Ottoman laws, became a basic book in the profession. M. Duchan served also as lecturer in the Law School of the Mandate government in Jerusalem and published several books on law.

After resigning, he continued working as a lawyer specializing in real estate laws and was active in public matters. With the establishment of the State of Israel he was member of its Judicial Council. He died in 1958.

[Page 146]

Israel Idelson (Bar–Yehuda)

Israel Idelson

Israel ben Baruch Idelson (later Bar Yehuda) was one of the prominent leaders of the Tze'irei Zion movement and the Zionists in Ekaterinoslav. He was born on 15 November 1895 in the town Konotof, Tchernigov district. When his family moved to Ekaterinoslav, he went there to the local High School and after graduating he enrolled in the Superior School for mining studies. While still in high school he joined (in 1909) the Zionist Youth Study Group and later the Tze'irei Zion movement. Thanks to his devotion and energy he soon rose to a position of guide and leader in the Movement.

During the First World War, while still a student at the mining school, he worked to reinforce the organizational as well as the spiritual activity of Tze'irei Zion, in spite of the restrictions and limitations imposed by the government. At the time of the 1917 revolution, an unlimited area of political activity opened and the movement, united, energetic and of a clear ideological standpoint, was ready for action and soon became an influential power in the "Jewish street" in Ekaterinoslav. Idelson's rare qualities, his personal integrity, his comprehensive political understanding, his attitude towards his friends, his Zionist belief – all this made him the leader and main spokesman of Tze'irei Zion and his decisions were accepted by most members. Under his leadership, the movement was strengthened and the Ekaterinoslav branch became one of the strongest in Russia.

No wonder, then, that Idelson was elected member of the Presidency of the Tze'irei Zion convention that took place in 1917, and later member of the Central office of the movement. In Ekaterinoslav he was elected as the representative of Tze'irei Zion to all institutions (municipality, community, national assembly of the Ukraine Jews etc.). Idelson, whose name had been known only to a few, became one of the leaders of the Ekaterinoslav Jews and the Ukraine Zionists. Everyone listened to his reasoning and his opinions, which he never failed to strongly defend. Those were difficult times, and the decisions demanded a great deal of responsibility. His appearance was proud, radiating national consciousness and national as well as personal honor. Yet he remained a modest man, as before, his warm attitude toward his friends did not change and he listened carefully to what they had to say. His fellows in the movement appreciated and respected him; his opponents valued him and listened to his opinions.

As the Soviet regime consolidated, things changed, and the activity of the movement had to adapt to the conditions of the time – prohibitions and limitations imposed by the authorities. Idelson did his best to preserve the achievements of the movement and at the same time he fought communism, which had begun to spread in the Jewish circles. He was one of those who requested that Tze'irei Zion change their program, a suggestion that was approved during the Charkov Convention in 1920.

After many years of successful activity, he left Ekaterinoslav and relocated to Charkov. He was soon arrested and exiled to a remote place in Russia, and after he was released and received a permit to leave, he made Aliya to Eretz Israel. Here, after many years of fruitful work for the Party and after serving as minister in the Israeli government he died on 4 May 1965.

[Page 149]

In Memory of the Departed

Yakov Moiseyev z"l
by Dr. Yakov Kostrinski
Translated by Yocheved Klausner

He was a native of Ekaterinoslav, a son of assimilated parents, far from the Zionist Movement – yet Yakov Moiseyev was attracted, at the young age of 16, to the Zionists. It was at the time of Lenin's "New Economic Policy" (NEP), which brought a great change in the character of the cruel dictatorial rule in Russia, and opened, among others, a certain new horizon for some public activity in the Jewish Street as well, where the Yevsektsiya [Evsektsiya = Hebrew Section] was the only public Jewish authority recognized as the representative of the Jews.

The Zionist movement, which up to that time was forced to act under difficult underground conditions and devote most of its activity to cultural and ideological topics, turned then into a movement of a social–political character as well.

The Zionist youth movements (Tzeirei Zion, the legal and illegal Hechalutz, Hano'ar Hatzioni, Hashomer Hatza'ir) managed to break through the narrow cracks of the underground and reach the Jewish Street in the towns of Russia and Ukraine. They began spreading information to the public, orally and in writing, about the general and Jewish questions, as seen by the Soviet regime. Oral information was given on every occasion and where it was possible – in the framework of institutions, synagogues etc. Parallel to that, a ramified written activity developed as well, in the form of brochures and newspapers ("In this Hour," "Land and Work" and others).

Distribution of the brochures was made – facing mortal danger – by sending them through the government post offices to personal addresses, posting them on the walls of the houses, or placing them on the chairs and benches in the synagogues. The Zionist movement came out of the underground and turned into a lively public movement, arousing enthusiasm among the Jewish people; thus, it became a serious and dangerous rival to the Yevsektsia.

In this lively and active atmosphere, Lusia (Eliezer) Tripolski (now in Israel) began his visits at the home of the assimilated parents of the talented, quiet and modest Yakov Moiseyev. As a member of the "Organization of the Zionist

Youth" Tripolski, who was aware of the personal qualities of the young Yakov, tried to make him join the Zionist movement. At first, Yakov's parents welcomed him heartily, but when they realized what the purpose of his visits was, they began treating him with reservation, even with open mockery. However, in spite of his parents' opposition, in 1921 the young man joined the Techiya [Revival] circle and devoted himself with all his warm heart to the activity of the group: he persuaded friends to join and guided them and was lecturing among the activists. After a short time, in 1923, he joined the national Hashomer Hatza'ir, where, thanks to his talents and punctuality, he became in a short time the leader.

By the testimony of his friend and fellow student, Zvi Bukerinski (now in Israel), he excelled in his studies as well. Arguments and disputes occurred between him and the management of the school, regarding his Zionist views – the result being his expulsion from the school. His friends mentioned that he was also writing poems on national topics. His fine human qualities – "of a lively character and a warm soul," as related by his eulogizer in the book In Klem ["In the clamp"] published by A. Tzantzifer – helped him increase the scope of his Zionist work under the cruel underground conditions in the Soviet regime. Moiseyev was one of the most liked activists among the Zionist youth and was loved and much appreciated by his friends.

The arrests in Ukraine on 2 September 1924, disrupted his activity – and he never resumed it, since "the gates of the prison are wide when one enters it, but too narrow to let one out" (In Klem). On 28 February 1925 he was exiled to the village Oritzkaya in Kirgizia (not far from the town Kostanay), where he was together with his friend Yosef Singer, who was also deported there for his Zionist "sins" (to this day we have no knowledge about the fate of this dear friend). In the fall of that year he became ill. For lack of a doctor in the village he did not receive medical help of any kind, and died a few days later, in great pain, without even having been diagnosed.

Since there were no other Jews in the village, the body of Y. M. was brought to Kostanay by his devoted friend Yosef Singer and was buried in the local cemetery. A small Jewish community was in town (mostly refugees from World War I. Yakov was buried on a snowy day, 4 November 1925, at the age of 21. Several Zionist exiles were present at his funeral. Shortly afterward these exiles made Aliya to Eretz Israel, according to the agreement with the chairwoman of the "Committee for the aid of political prisoners and exiles" Mrs. Pashkova (former wife of M. Gorki), which stated: "in order to replace the three–year–exile to the far areas of Russia with the deportation to Palestina." After the grave was covered, the writer of these lines recited the Kadish (as remembered by my friend Eliyahu Moravski [Mor, now in Israel]). We parted with our friend z"l with a broken heart and the song "The Oath."

[Page 150]

It was rumored later, that among the people present were also members of the GPU, posing as Zionists…

May his soul be bound in the bond of the living.

Zalman Yupit z"l
by Chanania Reichman
Translated by Yocheved Klausner

Zalman Yupit

Zalman ben Nechemya–Leib Yupit was born in 1885 in Piryatin, Poltava district. In his childhood he received a traditional education – *Cheder* and Yeshiva – and then he continued his general secular studies.

In 1905 his family relocated to Nizhnidnieprovsk. He was recruited to the Russian army, fought in World War I and was wounded. After he recovered, he continued his service and in 1917, after the "revolution spring" he was elected and sent by the Jewish soldiers as one of their representatives to the Congress of the Russian Zionists in Petrograd.

When he was released from the army he went home and continued his activity in the Tze'irei Zion movement. He also participated in the Jewish and Russian press – he wrote feuilletons about current subjects. In addition to this activity, he was one of the senior employees of the "Joint" in Ekaterinoslav and in Charkow.

During his activity in the Zionist underground, 1922–1924, he was arrested several times. In 1927 he was arrested again and released by the end of 1929. In 1939 he was arrested again and deported to a desolated place in the Russian regions in Asia. He died in exile on 25 May 1944.

*

I met Zalman Yupit (Ziama) in 1922 in the underground Zionist movement in Ekaterinoslav. I had just joined the committee of the Tze'irei Zion party and Ziama was also a member of the committee, already a veteran and respected member of the movement.

He was a brilliant newspaperman and excelled in particular in the area of humor and satire. He was fluent in the three languages of our world at that time: Hebrew, Yiddish and Russian. He was also a virtuoso in writing verse and light poems. He was "the living soul" in all parties and festivities organized secretly in our movement. He edited the "Live Newspaper," recited feuilletons and his own verses on various subjects, improvised and composed a wealth of brilliant jokes and witty sayings.

Sometimes I think with great sorrow about his talents that were untimely lost during in exile. Had he not perished in a strange and desert land, had he been able to make Aliya, who knows what new spring of creativity would have sprouted from his heart and what blessed harvest of humor and satire his pen would have created in the reality of the homeland!

All his friends who surrounded him and enjoyed the sparks of his many talents and the treasure of his sharp mind – shall never forget his most original and special figure. May his memory be blessed

[Page 151]

Moshe Rissin z"l
by Dr. Yakov Kostrinski
Translated by Yocheved Klausner

Moshe Rissin (1889 – 1962)

A righteous and honest man, speaker of truth, "pure of hands and pure of heart", innocent, modest and of many deeds – this was the spiritual figure of Moshe Rissin.

He was a well–known personality in Zionist Ekaterinoslav, in particular in the *Tze'irei Zion* club, and was totally devoted to it. He would pay special attention to organizing regular lectures given by well–known writers as well as by local members, performances by local artists and courses in the Hebrew language, the Bible [*TANACH*] and Hebrew literature. He would take care also of the material needs of the club: cleaning, lighting and firewood to heat the rooms in the winter evenings. This was important, in particular in the view of the fact that it was so difficult to obtain firewood during the years of hunger and suffering in the "intermediate" period between the regimes in Russia, as well as during the first years of the Soviet rule.

The Tze'irei Zion club, half legal, attracted not only Zionists, but a large part of the Ekaterinoslav Jews as well, since this was the only place where one could listen to "a Jewish word" – a lecture, poetry reading, singing, a Yiddish or Hebrew play – and feel the surrounding national–Jewish atmosphere.

Considerable financial means were needed for the maintenance of the Club and M. Rissin managed to obtain them from various sources – public (the Joint and the like) and private (well–to–do people who were still in town) thanks to his many personal connections.

He paid not only the writers and artists who appeared in the Club but tried as best he could to improve their general material situation during the years of hunger and need by various financial contributions. He kept in close personal contact with the intellectuals who were permanent members of the Club and was aware of their family and financial situation. When he gave the "celebs" financial help he was very careful to preserve their dignity, by charging an official of the party with the task of delivering the money and so give the procedure a public, rather than personal nature. For example: he gave the writer Y. Fishman (who was one of the frequent lecturers at the Club) a "note" to buy matzot for Passover rather than give him directly the matzot, or a check to Dr. Y. Chazanowitz (delivered by the writer of these lines).

He talked very little about his private life, even with his close friends. It was not known in what government office he worked, since he was so totally devoted to the community. All his free time, after finishing his regular work, was devoted to children and adults. During the cold winter evenings, he would invite to the Club some of his friends – for example Mr. Levinson from Po'alei Zion Left, former resident of Ekaterinoslav, who had arrived as an emissary from Eretz Israel after the October Revolution. He lit the stove himself and prepared tea and refreshments.

He was devoted with all his heart and soul to the Zionist ideals. He was an enthusiastic follower of Achad Ha'am and considered Eretz Israel as the spiritual center [merkaz ruchani] for the Diaspora and as the salvation of the Jewish people. He was very hurt by the split that occurred in 1920 in the Tze'irei Zion and would say: Is there a difference between me and the member who left Tze'irei Zion? Both of us are slaves of the Yevsektsia and the communist regime.

After the Club was closed by the authorities, Moshe devoted his energy to developing a secret web of Hebrew courses for young people and adults and took upon himself the responsibility of its maintenance and collection of contributions for this purpose.

[Page 152]

In 1922, Moshe Rissin was a delegate of Ekaterinoslav to the third All–Russian Congress of Tze'irei Zion in Kiev, was arrested and tried together with all the delegates of the Congress – and was several months imprisoned in the well–known Kiev prison Lukianovka. After his release he returned to active work in the committee of Tze'irei Zion in Ekaterinoslav until his Aliya at the beginning of 1925.

After several years of separation, I met him in our country. When he made Aliya, he came to visit me in the agricultural experiment station of Kibbutz Gevat near Nahalal, where I worked in the research of grain cultivation as the chief assistant of Y. Vilkenski z"l. It is difficult to describe in words the joy of our meeting. His face was radiant with the happiness of having reached Eretz Israel, and especially since he managed to find good work in the main office of the Survey Department of JNF [Keren Kayemet]. This work – preparation of the soil for Jewish agricultural settlement in Eretz Israel – was his desire and aspiration while he was still living in the Diaspora. It demanded much travel during the week, sometimes to dangerous places that were far from any Jewish settlement, but he would say that the salvation of the land demands devotion and sacrifices, and he did that with much love and a feeling of fulfillment.

He was devoted to his faith and kept the commandments. His private life and his home were religious–national in character and he went to the synagogue in his neighborhood, especially on the Sabbath.

Sometimes (especially in his later years) he would volunteer to be the cantor in his synagogue and the people came to like him and his pleasant voice.

By the way, his voice was already famous during the underground years of the Zionist movement in Ekaterinoslav. Moshe Rissin was a lover of song, played with the military orchestra as a soldier in the Russian army during World War I and studied music. He was the living spirit in the underground parties, led the public in song and helped create a warm atmosphere of original Jewish and Hebrew folklore.

Moshe Rissin, of the smiling eyes, a goodhearted man, always ready to help his fellows, departed from us.

Woe for those who are lost and cannot be found.

Dr. Moshe Ofir (Zolotrevski) z"l
Translated by Yocheved Klausner

He was a member of the young generation of the Ekaterinoslav Zionists. He was born in 1901, his father was Naftali Zolotrevsli. As a high school student, he was attracted to the Zionist movement and after the 1917 revolution he began to take an active part in the Zionist organizations in town. He was active in Tze'irei Zion, was one of the founders of the Maccabi organization etc. His talents, his personal qualities and warm–heartedness made him popular and loved by his friends. He continued his Zionist activity even after the Soviet regime stabilized, and finally he managed to leave Russia and make Aliya, at the beginning of the twenties.

On his way to Eretz Israel he made a stop in Istanbul and worked in the Eretz–Israel–Office, which had just begun operations there. At the same time, he began studying Law at the Istanbul University and received the degree of PhD in Law.

In 1934 he made Aliya and here he continued his work. As a member of the Haganah he was the commander of Jaffa during the War of Independence. He was the chairman of the Israel philatelic association, was one of the founders of the organization of the former Ekaterinoslav Residents, as well as one of the first writers for this book.

He died on 29 January 1962, after a long illness.

Zvi Sheftelson z"l
by Chanania Reichman
Translated by Yocheved Klausner

Zvi ben Chaim Sheftelson, one of the active members of the Zionist underground in Ekaterinoslav, born in the early eighties of the 19th century, was an interesting and noble figure of a taciturn man, a philosopher of a beautiful soul and delicate feelings.

Fate allotted him, since his youth, a life of distress, hard work and suffering. He grew up during the great social turmoil that preceded the first revolution in Russia (in 1905). As a result, he became a revolutionary – and as I was told he was a member of a military organization that fought against the Czar regime by means of terror. Very soon, however, perhaps under the influence of the wave of pogroms in Russia, Sheftelson, disappointed by the aid of strangers, turned to Zionism.

[Page 153]

Zvi Sheftelson

Due to his material situation he could not study during his youth – and he satisfied his great hunger for an education by reading during nights, after a day of hard work from dawn to evening. This way, after years of effort, he became knowledgeable in many areas – in particular humanistic studies. He also amassed a treasure of choice books: all the money that he managed to save from his meager salary was devoted to acquiring books.

In 1922, when I met him the first time, Sheftelson was already an educated man, with knowledge in Hebrew, Yiddish and Russian literature – and the only piece of furniture in his room was a huge box full of books in these three languages.

His work–room served as a meeting place for the members of the underground organization of *Tze'irei Zion*. In the evenings, important official meetings as well as meetings of friends would take place there.

His home served also as an underground "postal office" for the party: written "notes" and oral messages were exchanged, since all active members would often come to the place, to hear "news." The constant movement to and from his apartment finally aroused suspicion – and the secret police entered his name on the "black list."

However, his turn to be arrested and exiled came much later, during one of the later waves of pursuing Zionists in Russia. He was arrested and sent to

Asia and his wife Lidia went after him – to share with him his suffering in exile. His valuable treasure – his library that had taken him years to collect – was lost.

He never complained; not when he worked so hard, not when he was in danger while active in the underground Zionist groups, not in prison and not in exile.

After many tribulations, in 1935 he was allowed to make Aliya together with his wife. They found a room in Tel Aviv, near the "Ohel Shem" theatre – and even before he found work, he found a source of learning: He visited every week the "Oneg Shabat" meetings [Friday night gatherings in honor of the Sabbath, lit. Shabat pleasure] and participated in lectures and lessons in TANACH [Bible] and Talmud, which took place at Ohel Shem.

After he found work and was able to make a decent living, he began to buy books again – and in the course of the 20 years that he lived in our country he succeeded to collect a substantial library, this time mainly in Hebrew.

In 1958 he died, at the age of 77. He worked almost to his last day. How happy he was, that he had the privilege to live in the country of his dreams, working and studying the Torah, listening every Shabat to the words of sages and spending his few free hours among his books!

Zvi Sheftelson, taciturn and of deep thought, was, as by the words of the poet Bialik "one of the modest and humble people, short in words and rich in splendor." His friends engraved these words on his tombstone – not in vain. May his memory be blessed!

Avraham Gutman z"l

by Chanania Reichman

Translated by Yocheved Klausner

He was one of the devoted, loyal and active Zionists during the difficult years of the early Soviet rule in Ekaterinoslav.

He was born in 1873 in the town Vorchanidnieprovsk (Ekaterinoslav District) and there he has received his traditional Jewish education and general education (in the municipal school).

After he married, he relocated to the near–by town Buzhidarovka and opened a lumber store. At the same time, he began his public Zionist activity.

From 1907 to 1919 he headed the local Zionist association (80 members out of the 130 Jewish families in town).

[Page 154]

Avraham Gutman

Several institutions, as the "Modern Cheder" [*cheder metukan*], the Jewish library and its reading hall etc. were registered in his name (due to the limitations imposed by the police in those times). He was arrested and kept in prison for a short time. In 1917 he was elected delegate to the Petrograd Congress, but because of the bad roads he could not reach it.

After the revolution, as civil war broke out in Russia, gangs of hooligans operated in the area, and in 1919 Gutman relocated to Ekaterinoslav. Immediately after his arrival, he resumed his Zionist activity, in spite of the restrictions by the authorities. He was an active member in the "General Zionists" organization and helped, in their behalf, the Jewish institutions that were still active in Jewish Ekaterinoslav, as Hebrew courses, Zionist youth organizations etc. His home served as a meeting place for Zionists and he also hosted festive parties and Zionist banquets. He worked as the secretary and assistant of Rabbi Immanuel Bronstein, who served, before the revolution, as the "rabbi appointed by the authorities" and later was the head of Social Aid of the Jewish community in Ekaterinoslav.

In 1925 he made Aliya to Eretz Israel (after his son went in 1921 as "the pioneer of the family") and settled with his family in Tel Aviv.

Here, as well, he soon started Public and Zionist activity. He was member of the councils of the General Zionists party [Brit Hazionim Haklali'im] and the "Association of the Russian Jews," member of the management of the Great

Synagogue in Tel Aviv and the management of Oneg Shabat and Ohel Shem, active in Brit Rishonim etc. His devoted activity continued until his death in 1942.

Dov Admoni z"l
Translated by Yocheved Klausner

Dov Admoni

Dov ben Yakov–Nathan Admoni (Boris Krasni) was a proud Jew and a devoted Zionist. I met him in 1922, in the days of the underground Zionism in Ekaterinoslav. He was about 50 years of age, member of the "General Zionists" in town, and, among others, was active helping the "Prisoners of Zion."

Since his youth he was concerned with spiritual matters, but he gave up his studies in order to start making a living, to help his family and enable his young brothers to acquire a high education.

Indeed, his sacrifice was not in vain. One of his brothers, Gregory Krasni (Admoni) became an important writer and scientist (Oriental Studies and Law) in Petersburg, wrote review articles about Hebrew and Jewish literature in the monthly "Voshod" and other Jewish journals in the Russian language, edited the TANACH [Bible] section in the "Great Jewish Encyclopedia" (16 volumes, in Russian), and after the revolution was professor of Oriental Studies at the Leningrad University.

Dov Admoni excelled in diligence and perseverance and in time became well established economically, but the October Revolution destroyed his position.

[Page 155]

In 1925 he and his wife made Aliya to Eretz Israel, where he had many family relatives. He lived in Tel Aviv and in his old age made a living working with his hands (as an artist creating stamps). But even then, his life and spirit were devoted to Zionist matters. He was a great admirer of Zev Jabotinski – and was attracted to the Revisionist Movement.

His delicate character and noble spirit made him beloved by all those who knew him.

His personal charm may perhaps best be described by the eulogy–poem that I wrote after his death in 1952.

(A poem by Chananya Reichman)

Translated by Yocheved Klausner

Dov Admoni, a friend, a most honest man!
Your noble heart burst and was suddenly silent.
But the memory of your shining figure
Will never leave our hearts.

You were not a poet, ruler of words,
Nor a singer, commander of sounds.
But your beautiful heart would secretly sing
The greatest of all songs: the song of love for living things.

You never knew hatred, and you lived your life
In the light of love: love of your fellows,
Love of your Nation, love of your homeland,
Love of the children, love of the Torah…

How you loved books! But you gave up
The beauty of study for the benefit of your brothers –
And you devoted your time to keep them away from need
And to pave the way for them, a spiritual way of light.

Your property in the Diaspora was destroyed.
Here you earned your sustenance by making seals.
But our heart is a witness: you left on it your mark,
Which Time will never erase or spoil.

Slowly you paced the paths of life,

Satisfied with little and generous to your fellows –
Forgiving, and careful not to disturb, God forbid,
Or to become a burden to a friend or acquaintance.

No blows of fate, no evil of man
Have extinguished the holy innocence of your heart –
That gentle and splendid light
Which spread around a blessed kindness of the soul.

Your shining light had a secret brilliance:
Educating, calming, refining, purifying…
And your life – an example for the near and far,
Better than one hundred preachers of morals!

Yehuda Avisar z"l

Translated by Yocheved Klausner

Yehuda Avisar (Kozlovski) was born in 1895. He spent his childhood and his youth in Nizhnidnieprovsk. At the time of the change of regimes in the Ukraine, after the 1917 revolution – a time of anarchy and activity of hooligan gangs – he was part of the Jewish self–defense in town.

In 1919 he married, and the young couple went to live in Ekaterinoslav. There he acquired his technical education and worked as an engineer in various plants – but at the same time he was active in the Zionist underground movement Tze'irei Zion.

His activity was intensified in the days of emergency, days of mass–arrests of Zionists. At first he could not devote much time to his Zionist work, due to his heavy load of professional work, but when most of the committee members were arrested he volunteered to help and was part of the committee until the day he made Aliya with his wife and children, in 1925.

He worked in the Tel Aviv city Hall and at the same time was active in the Haganah in the Tel Aviv area.

[Page 156]

Later he worked in Jaffa as deputy city engineer, and during the bloody riots in 1936–1939 he risked his life day by day as he continued to go to his office in Jaffa where Arab gangs rioted in sight of the British authorities. The Jewish institutions were reluctant to give up any position they held in Jaffa – therefore Avisar continued his work.

In 1942, at the age of 47, he joined as a volunteer the British army – to fight against Hitler, went through difficult training in Egypt, received a

Sergeant Major degree in the "Royal Engineers Corps" and fought on the Italian front.

In 1945 he was released from service in the army and returned to his old post as deputy city–engineer in Jaffa – and at the same time returned to his activity in the Haganah as head of the "Engineers Company." Later he worked in the Tel Aviv City Hall, about one year, and in 1948, when the Israel State was established, he went to work with MA'ATZ [the Section of Public Works], first in Tel Aviv and later as the District Engineer in Jerusalem. His hard work in his last position weakened his health, and in 1950 he died suddenly of a heart–attack, to the shock of all his friends. He was only 55.

*

Yehuda, of great personal charm, pleasant and polite, was loved by all his acquaintances. Several years ago, I had the opportunity to remember him in a letter in rhyme that I sent to his grandson Niv. I would like to conclude these lines with a few lines from this letter, remembering his special figure.

A poem by Chananya Reichman)

Translated by Yocheved Klausner

My eyes remember a smile full of splendor
The smile of Yehuda, whom I knew
And loved, and admired
Since my youth, my age of spring.

His good and wonderful heart
Was courageous, noble and charitable.
His life he sacrificed
For the light of Zion – an exalted and glorious vision.

In the Diaspora he was the keeper of the spark –
And in Tel-Aviv he was a defense man;
He fought in battle against the evil destroyer –
And yet he was a man who built, programmed, planned…

He volunteered – without setback
Ready to stand against any danger or foe:
Always pacing to the end of the road
To the target that he had set.

Even when the situation was difficult and painful
He remained strong, tough and stable –
And he always found the words
Of joke and courage, good sayings and proverbs.

He was polite with his subordinates;
He guided, encouraged, stimulated…
The new recruit regarded him as his father
And the veteran – his brother.

In every answer and reaction
He was wise, moderate and consistent.
Never offended his adversary
But tried to convince him respectfully.

Was kind to all his friends,
And his friends appreciated him.
His life was a magnificent example
Of a struggle that showed to others the way.

[Page 157]

Daniel Wechsler z"l

Translated by Yocheved Klausner

He was born in 1893 to his father Jonah Wechsler, a teacher and owner of a private school (pre-high-school) for Jewish children in Ekaterinoslav.

In his home, national-Jewish spirit reigned, and in this atmosphere was the young Daniel raised. Contrary to many of his young friends, who were assimilated, Daniel served as messenger in the Jewish defense groups during the 1905 pogroms and was wounded by army bullets.

In school he was one of the founders of the first Zionist association in Ekaterinoslav, Nechdei Zion [Zion grandchildren] and for several years he headed the group. At the time, the group was the center of the national and Zionist education, and most of the young people in town were members. Thanks to Daniel, the Zionist ideas spread among the Jewish high-school students in Ekaterinoslav, and they liked him for his personal qualities, his warm heart and his readiness to help his fellows.

He was one of the first members of Tze'irei Zion in Ekaterinoslav and participated in 1912 in the first Congress of Tze'irei Zion as a delegate of the movement. There he was arrested and released after a short time. He was active in the general Zionist movement in Ekaterinoslav.

As he completed his studies at the School of Mining and received the title of Engineer, he worked in Mariopol (now Zsdanov) on the Donetz River, where he acquired experience and also helped spreading the Zionist idea among the Jews in the region.

In 1924 he made Aliya, worked several years as an engineer, then worked 23 years in the Government Survey Office. During the last years of his life he worked in the Office of the Interior. He was one of the active members in the organization of former Ekaterinoslav residents and one of the originators of this book.

He died 18 August 1964 in Tel Aviv.

Asher Pevzner z"l

Translated by Yocheved Klausner

Asher was one of the members of the young generation of the Ekaterinoslav Zionists.

He was born in 1920 to his father Menachem-Mendel Pevzner, a veteran of Hovevei-Zion. He visited with his father in Eretz Israel when he was a young boy of 8.

In 1917 he joined the movement of the "Jewish Zionist Students" in Ekaterinoslav. As a young talented man of speaking ability, he soon stood out among the movement members and became one of its main spokesmen and organizers. With the help of his friends, he managed to unite the national Jewish young people in town and turn them into an active and activating power. He appeared on their behalf before the local Zionist organizations and the various youth congresses. He was also an active member of Tze'irei Zion in Ekaterinoslav.

In 1919 and 1920, during the Civil War he was in Crimea and was active in the central offices of the Hechalutz organization that had just been established and managed the Aliya office which helped people who gathered there on their way to Eretz Israel. He invested in this work most of his strength and energy.

He relocated from Crimea to Istanbul – on his way to Eretz Israel; he was asked to remain there and continue his work in the Hechalutz office and in the newly opened Aliya office.

After completing his work in Hechalutz, he moved to Prague, where he completed his studies in the School of Economics. In 1928 he made Aliya and worked in his profession of accountant. In 1945 he died after a severe illness.

David Izraeli (Rubin) z"l
Translated by Yocheved Klausner

He was born in 1886, to his father R'Binyamin the scribe [sofer STAM] and cantor. In his childhood he received a traditional education and was a member of the synagogue choir. He was an active member of the Go'alei Zion association in Ekaterinoslav, founded by M. Ussishkin.

In 1908 he made Aliya and worked in agriculture in Menachamiya. He was also a member of the "collective" in Segera, where he worked together with Ben Gourion. From there he relocated to the Kineret colony [moshava] and there he built his home and his farm.

When he reached middle-age, he began composing. He was a working-man, who knew how to combine labor with song. He composed music for chapters of the Book of Psalms, Song of Songs [Shir Hashirim] and Israeli songs.

His melodies were well received by the public and his songs were sung by various song-groups as well as on the radio.

His compositions were published by the Center of Education and Culture of the Histadrut.

He died 12 June 1965 in Kineret.

(From Tidhar Encyclopedia, Volume 13).

[Page 158]

Photocopy of a letter (in Yiddish) written 6 October 1969 by Jonah Radinov in Riga to Dr. Z. Harkavi in Jerusalem, and the translation of the letter to Hebrew, in print

To Dr. Harkavi, Jerusalem

Dear friend Dr. Z. Harkavi

I was informed that you are editing the book "The Jews of Ekaterinoslav." I would like to advise you to include the matters concerning the heroes of the Jewish partisans, who fought the Nazis in Ekaterinoslav – now Dniepropetrovsk – as well as in the forests around the town.

Two companies if partisans were organized: one was headed by the Ekaterinoslav resident Binyamin Sachanowitz, who fell in battle as a hero. The Ekaterinoslav Jews took part in all battles against the Nazis.

It would be a crime, if they were not mentioned in this book. I have a great deal of material on this subject. I am now sending to Yad Vashem a book that appeared in Dniepropetrovsk in the Ukrainian language: R. Chumiakova, Soldiers without uniform.

See also the book by Dr. Y. Karmish (at Yad Vashem, Jerusalem) and you will find there "USSR Heroes" about the Ekaterinoslav Jews.

Please write to me,
Write! I wish you good health!
In friendship
Jonah Radinov
Riga, 6 October 1969

[Page 159]

Mark (Mordechai) Schaechter z"l

Dr. Zvi Harkavi

Translated by Yocheved Klausner

The poet Mark (Mordechai) Schaechter was born in 1911 in Ekaterinoslav, to his father the doctor, Prof. Anani (Chananya) Schaechter. Until the age of Bar Mitzva he learned Hebrew with the teacher and writer Arash, the father of the Habimah actor Avital. When he grew up, he studied Medicine and in World War II he volunteered to the Army, was wounded and received a medal (War of the Homeland, Grade A).

As a young man he began publishing poems and translations of poems from Russian; 9 collections appeared during his life and three after he died.

The poet A. Pen who met him in Moscow, described him as "a distinguished lyric poet, of a quite respected position in USSR; a tall man, wearing glasses, sharp-spoken and tending to use biting humor. His creations are extensive, although sometimes restrained." Mr. S. Even-Shoshan, who spoke with him in Moscow, writes about him: "The subjects of his poems are varied, and rich in descriptions of the mood and frame of mind of the Soviet person of his generation and environment. In his letter to me he testifies that philosophic lyricism is characteristic to his writing, which also includes poems about the Russian landscape, which he loves very much. The titles of the sections in his last collection are characteristic as well: Adulthood, Poems about my Town of Birth, Nature, Latvian Diary. In this collection he included also translations from the languages spoken in USSR: Ukrainian, Georgian, Ingush and Kalmyk languages, as well as Czech and Yiddish."

According to Even-Shoshan, Schaechter was one of the 'old guard" of Russian poetry. He wrote poetry in the course of 30 years, and the collections he published were "Days and Years," "A Good Word," "Noon," etc. The collection "A Lyric Weather" appeared in 1963. A volume of his assorted poems is now in print – he prepared the collection but didn't live to enjoy the completed work.

He devoted several poems to Ekaterinoslav; the Jewish motif is felt, in spite of his restraint.

M. Scaechter showed much interest in the translation of his poems to Hebrew

Following are excerpts from his letter to me:

1. Moscow, 12 June 1963.

... It is good that the writers in your country decided to take interest in the works of Russian poets, in particular my own work. However, it seems to me that the matter is somewhat biased, and this is expressed in the choice of the poems for translation. If the work of a poet is of interest, it is important to present it in its entirety.

Concerning the plan to publish my poems in Hebrew – I would like to express my appreciation and thanks. However, as you write, you have in your possession only two of my books: "Noon" and "A Lyric Weather." I think that in order to present a complete picture as a Soviet poet, it is important to wait for the volume of a selection of my poems, to be published in the autumn of this year by the National Publishing House (in Moscow).

I would be pleased, if other poets in your country, who have in common sympathy for the Soviet poetry, would be invited to translate the poems of the collection.

Concerning the "Author's Preface" – I think it is not really necessary, although I would be glad to write a short address to the Israeli readers. I could do that in September, after the summer vacation.

2. Moscow, 3 July 1963.

... You are asking, whether to send to me the translations of "A Good Word" and "My Father's Grave, which were published in your press." This would please me very much...

My late mother loved poetry with all her heart, and was happy knowing that her son was a poet... Until her last moments she held in her hands the collection "A Good Word" and we buried her with this book on her chest...

In my work – as you write – Jewish motifs occupy a very insignificant place, compared to other subjects that are of interest to me...

Following, from his work:

My Father's Grave

Translated by Yocheved Klausner

(Hebrew; from Russian: David Yosifon)

Only an intoxicating smell of wood
And odds-and-ends, and pits to no end…
But where is the Jewish cemetery,
Where my father is buried?
We are looking for it, three days…

Therefore, Father, not a hand of metal, nor of rock
Shall guard thy peace in the grave…
But the spoils of war from the King of Demons:
A Nazi cannon I shall place in the valley
In your memory, for generations to come.

[Page 161]

At the End of the Book

by Rabbi Dr. Tzvi Harkavy

Translated by Jerrold Landau

Addenda[1]

To my article and the articles of others in this book, in no particular order.

1. I included a bibliography in my article on YEKATERINOSLAV (aside from limited articles on the topic. I have lectured and organized this): a) Research of Families, second edition, from page 51 and onward, Jerusalem, 5713 (1953). b) Community of YEKATERINOSLAV, Hatzofeh, 11 Tevet 5713 (1952). c) YEKATERINOSLAV, HaAvar (Tel Aviv), 5717 (1957) (from a monograph and my words in a gathering of the natives of our city in Tel Aviv, 3 Sivan, 5717 (1957). Printed as handouts. d) YEKATERINOSLAV and its rabbis, Maariv, 9 Marcheshvan 5725 (1964). e) House of My Father, Jerusalem, 5728 (1968) (from a broadcast on Kol Yisrael). f) YEKATERINOSLAV, "Year by Year", 5729 (1969). g) Underground Zionism in Yekaterinoslav (minutes of absorption), the institution of modern Judaism of the Hebrew University, Jerusalem, 5728 (1968). The rest of the articles on YEKATERINOSLAV are listed in my autobiography, Jerusalem, 5730 (1970). See the article in the general encyclopedia, Brokhaus–Efron in Russian; in the large Soviet encyclopedia in two edition, as well the short version; in every Jewish encyclopedia, especially those in Russian; in the Hebrew Encyclopedia in the article on Dnipropetrovsk (my material, without mentioning it) [Tz"L; founded in 1778]; in Encyclopedia Judaica (1971), edited, based on my article, as is noted there. Екатериносла́в; Ukrainian: Катериносла́в. And from here, the popular pronunciation in Yiddish: Katerinslav. This is how the Yeveskstia wrote it in in its publication, as well as YIVO, and others. During the time of Pavel (1796–1801)[2], due to his hatred of Yekaterina II "the Great", it was called Novorossiysk, and later returned to its original name – Yekaterinoslav.

2. During the 17th century, there was a Polish fortress there, which was destroyed by the Cossacks during the time of Chmielnicki [perhaps this was the Keidaki mentioned in "Fire and Sword" by Sinkewicz – Farber, with that name existing in Yekaterinoslav]. There are those that say that the city was designated by Potemkin to be the new capital of Russia instead of Peterburg (?) [M. Asherovitch, Cities and Towns in Ukraine, New York, 1948; Ch"b from page 99 and onward. I did not find another source for this theory, and it does not make sense, perhaps it was confused with Novorussia in Russia?…[3]]. #1041;. 3. Просвещени е, after 1902, approximately in Yekaterinoslav: founded in 1783, in the place of the village Лоловицы ["only the center of the city is considered in the protocols(?)"].

3. Petrovski, for whose name the city was called from June 1926, is Grigory Ivanovitch P. (1878–1958). In 1905, he was the secretary of the workers council of Yekaterinoslav; the chairman of the Bolshevik faction in the fourth Duma; 1917–1919 – Narkum (minister) of the interior of the R.S.F.S.R.; 1919–1939 – chairman of the central executive council of all–Ukraine, chairman of the central executive council of the

Soviet Union and deputy chairman of the chief soviet leadership of the president of the state (see the article in 3. Споварь, Moscow, 1964). The name of the city in Ukrainian is Днпропетро́вск.

4. The beginning of Yekaterinoslav as a district city is from 1783 (then its place was determined, where it is to this day, and some calculate its history from that date). It was designated as a regional city at that time.
In 1768 (according to Y. Trevitch, the Jews in the Former Novorussiya, 5714 – 1954 – based on sources) Jews were permitted to live in Novorussiya and to occupy themselves as they desire. The Pale of Settlement was established as a law in 1791. Yekaterinoslav was included in the Pale in 1794 by an official proclamation.

5. There were 359 Karaites in Yekaterinoslav in 1857, and they had a community until the time that I made aliya to the Land of Israel. [I left Yekaterinoslav at the end of Sivan 5686 – 1926]. The street in which they were found was called Karaimskaya.
At that time, there were 14,000 Karaites in all of Russia. It is known that the Nazis did not consider them to be Jews and did not persecute them. The Karaites collaborated with the Nazis against the Jews in Russia and Poland. Many long works have already been written, and I too have written about this. The Soviets did not leave a trace of them in Crimea, as with the Tatars who collaborated… (See "With the Tribulations of Destruction" issue 138 and onward. – According to German, Soviet and other sources. See my article "The Karaites During the Period of the Holocaust in Europe," Gesher, Kislev 5730 – 1969).

6. Regarding the 17 Jewish settlements in the Yekaterinoslav region, see the book: "Jewish Farmers in the Plains of Russia" (among the participants in the book – Rivka Guber, and see her book "Rak Shvil"). Especially page 409. There it mentions their names, connections to Yekaterinoslav, and the final fate of their Jews.

7. The sugar enterprise and largest hydroelectric power mill in Europe in its time was called "Dniprogas" [Dniprostroi" – the name of the company that built it]. Another similar power mill was built north of Dnipropetrovsk.

8. Aside from the bibliography on Yekaterinoslav in publications and what is brought here, other items and sources that I have listed throughout the years, by reading, should be noted.
Collections (of the labor archives), Tel Aviv, Sivan, 5717 (1957).
M. Asherevitch (aforementioned) – notes his connection to Lazar Kaganovitch in Yekaterinoslav.

[Page 162]

Reb Yaakov Lipshitz, Zichron Yaakov, Ch"A, from page 144 and onward – about Yekaterinoslav.
Пркднелровский край – a newspaper distributed in Yekaterinoslav, in which Jews were involved.
Letters, Rabbi Y. Nissenbaum, Jerusalem, 5727 (1967) – Letters relating to Yekaterinoslav. See the introductions there.
Yaakov Leshchinski, The Socio–Economic Development of Ukrainian Jewry, Jews in Ukraine, I, New York, 1961.
In Esp. Ст. (1917/18), p. 320: it is noted that V. Toporovski helped bring regular

members from Yekaterinoslav into E. И. З. О.
Ibid. booklet A. (1914), in the article of S. Stanislavski from Yekaterinoslav about Reb Zundel Luria the author of "Knaf Renanim."
Ibid. booklet D. (1909) the article about the history of the Cantonists.
In the books of A. L. Raphaeli–Zinzifer there is significant material on personalities from Yekaterinoslav. See the indices.

9. During the pogroms of Nov 21–23 1905, 67 Jews were killed in Yekaterinoslav, and hundreds were injured, some of whom died later. The dead included: Rabbi Yeshosua–Eliahu Neimark (the son of Rabbi Meshulam–Zalman, one of the greats of Chabad, the head of the rabbinical court of Starodov), who worked in business in Yekaterinoslav and refused to accept a rabbinical position that was offered to him several times. He was killed in Yekaterinoslav on 7 Marcheshvan, 5666 (1906). His friend – a member of Chovevei Zion, the author of "Shivat Zion," Reb Avraham–Yaakov Slutzki.
[In "Talpiot" 8, pp. 556, in the article of Rabbi Nissan Wachsman about Rabbi Avraham–Yaakov Neimark, the author of "Eshel Avraham" (Farein–Lita – Tel Aviv), he incorrectly writes that Rabbi A.Y. Slutzki was also killed in Yekaterinoslav in 5666 / 1906. It is not true: it was in Iyar 5678 (1928) in his city of Novogorod–Sibirsk!] From the hands of the collector of the photographs of the victims.

10. In–2000, the Pogroms in Ukraine (1917–1919). 200,000 Jews were killed in 700 places. Eliahu Chrikover wrote this in several books, in which he deals with the pogroms of Yekaterinoslav: The Ukrainian Pogroms in 1919, YIVO, New York, 1965, pp. 41, 56, 64, 71, 98, 99, 111, 114, 191, 192, 200, 202, 290, 296, 320, 324 (area around Yekaterinoslav: 20, 22, 213, 244, 294, 300, 301). In the index on page 366: Katerinaslav.
Prior to the aforementioned: Antisemitism and Pogroms in Ukraine, 117–1918, Berlin, 1923: Introduction – Shimon Dubnow; pp. 24, 46, 51, 100, 107, 113, 137, 148, 153, 292, 293, 306.
On Machno in Yekaterinoslav (XI.16 – XI.28.1919) see, the HeAvar 17, pp. 88, from "Barkai" (Hebrew newspaper in Odessa 1919/.20): 4.XII.19 Кр. Пр.: as well as in the Russian book of Аршинов on the "Movement" of Machno.

11. Yitzchak Sheinis, a native of Yekaterinoslav, who made aliya in 5682 (1922), a farmer in Moshav Tzipori, wrote to me (18.2.58, and I have the letter), that his relatives from Yekaterinoslav were among the settlers of the Golan in 1895. He has interesting material about that period. See "Settlement in the Upper Galilee" 5715 – 1955, p. 39 and the index. In the archives of Ussishkin in the Zionist archives of Jerusalem, there is material about cases adjudicated before Rabbi Binyamin Zakheim in Yekaterinoslav, regarding the topic. It should be published!

12. Jewish musicians lived in Yekaterinoslav, and well–known cantors conducted services. There were also composers. Artists stemmed from there.
The cantors of Yekaterinoslav: the blind prayer leader Reb Ber (?) 70–80 years ago. During my time, during the time of the First World War and thereafter, Lachman served in the Choral Synagogue until he left for Riga. He was an observant Jew, who worshiped at the synagogue daily, knowledgeable in Torah and Hebrew – unlike all the other cantors. The choir director there was Mariaskin. After Lachman came Ulshanitzki, who had musical education. He conducted a mixed choir (with the soloist Freda, who was famous for her "Al Chet." Regarding the complaint of Rabbi Reloish against the

"innovations," the cantor responded, in Psalms it is stated Lamenatzeach al Alamot[4]...) Then I moved to the synagogue on Kazachia Street, where the bima was in the center in accordance with the law [halacha]. The scholars and rabbis from among the refugees set their place of worship and study there, both in privately and with the congregation. On festivals, Rabbi Levi Schneerson, may the memory of the righteous be a blessing, preached there on festivals. Cantor Pinchuk served as cantor there for some time, standing at the bima for the entire time of his prayer, as was his manner. The composer Golinkin lived in Yekaterinoslav and dedicated a chapter about it in his book. The composer from Kfar Kinneret, David Yizraeli, who came on the Second Aliya, was from Yekaterinoslav.
Leonid Kagan (Cohen), the famous Soviet violinist, who also played in Israel, was from Dnipropetrovsk. Dina Potapovskaya – the singer of Ofira of Moscow, who also sang in Yiddish and Hebrew, was from Dnipropetrovsk. She visited and sang in Israel.
In the cards of M. Sh. Geshuri, the researcher of Jewish music, there are several cards from Yekaterinoslav. There are 300 cards of Yekaterinoslav in the hand of M. Tzinovich, a researcher of the history of the rabbis and communities of Russia–Lithuania.

13. In 5621 (1861) we find the community of Yekaterinoslav among those who greeted Reb Moshe Montefiore (in Hebrew). See "Noach Tehila: in Honor of Reb Moshe Montefiore," Yosef Cohen–Zedek, Lvov. HaOda–Haadrista – composed by Reb Avraham–Dov Dobzevitz of Yekaterinoslav.

14. At the Zionist convention in Minsk (1902) 20 delegates and 10 guests from Yekaterinoslav participated. From Yekaterinoslav itself: the engineer M. Bruk, Sh. Dubin (teacher), Orlov (teacher), S. Shapira (agent) – from the review of Ussishkin on 3.9.02 after the convention, that I found in Ussishkin's anthology (number 21/383), in the Zionist archives in Jerusalem.

15. Yisrael Ritov in his book "Chapters in the history of Tz.TZ. Tz.S.," dwells on the activities of that faction in Yekaterinoslav (see the note on page 22).

16. The monument for Eliahu Orshanski was set up according to the plan of the great sculptor Mordechai (Marek) Antokolsi. V Stasov wrote an article about this in 1878, that entered his writings. HAA, [Н. А. Куанецоиа, 1968, М. I.]

17. Orshanski wrote sharply against Hassidism – to the point where in the publications of the atheistic Yevsektsia of "Melumad" Moshe Blanki and the Professor Shachnovitz, "Amei Haaretz" his words are cited at length.

18. Regarding the Modern Cheder in Yekaterinoslav (in which Ch. A. Zuta studied in his time), there is an article in the Barkai anthology, Brooklyn, 5706 (1946).

19. In 5656 (1896), 2 Shvat, the maskil writer Yaakov–Shlomo Olshevnegar (Olshevengy) died in Yekaterinoslav at the age of 56. See the article about him in the Sokolow Yizkor book, and in the Lexicon of Hebrew Literature by Kressel. He signed: Yshbiel"l.

20. In 1920–1921, "Der Communist" was published in Yekaterinoslav. The place of publication was noted as Katerineslavy [? Tz H.]. "Kemper" preceded in (1917), Yekaterinoslav. See: The Av. Kahn Fund, New York, 1965: number 1394 issue

[Page 163]

47, and number 1445 issue 49. As well as the index in number 64 issue 54 (and in number 56. Between numbers 137–138 hint: Katerineslav).

20. In 1959, the district of Dnipropetrovsk had 72,430 Jews. The region of Dnipropetrovsk was one of 17 regions in which the Jewish population was between 30,000–150,000. It was in fourth place, after the regions of Kiev, Odessa, and Kharkov (region – before the war was Guberniya, today Oblast). Nachman List, Soviet Jews as victims of Russification and its Subjects; Hamolad 187/188, Iyar–Sivan 5724 (1964), p. 21, line 2.

21. All three daughters of Feivel Paley made aliya and died in the Land of Israel. First Esther Ussishkin (on Shushan Purim, 5712, 1952, at the age of 81) in Jerusalem; later Zina Bruck in Tel Aviv (see Haaretz, 28.8.58); (in the year 5727 – 1967) Roza Jacobson in Tel Aviv. She was the wife of the Zionist activist Dr. Avigdor Jacobson, from whom she was divorced, but kept his surname; She made aliya after concluding her course of natural studies at a university in Switzerland. She worked at scientific endeavors in Tel Aviv at the experimental division. [From her youth, she maintained friendly connections with my mother, may peace be upon her, and she assisted, through efforts and money, to bring me out of there].

22. A grove in memory of the 55,000 martyrs of the community of Yekaterinoslav was planted in the Martyrs Forest of the Jewish National Fund by the survivors of the community in the State of Israel (through my efforts). Certificate 4198, 9 Shvat 5729, signed by Yaakov Zur.
Some studies of the era in The Yekaterinslavit of Borochov (July 1900 – June 1902). Dr. Matityahu Mintz (University of Tel Aviv), Along the way – writings of research on the Jewish workers movement, Nisan 5730 – 1970.
19 pages 64 notes, Bibliography.
[Mentioned in a book published in Russian in Yekaterinoslav in 1923; M. A. Ruvach, History of S.D. in Yekaterinoslav, 1889–1903.]
Mintz cites Borochov; Poalei Zion in general was founded in Yekaterinoslav by him and by Shimon Dubin Banov, 1900. Armed self–defense was renewed in Yekaterinoslav (after having been interrupted in the 1880s) by Poalei Zion in "the Small Pogrom", Passover 1901. In general, the research is full of not well–known details on Yekaterinoslav.

23. Mark Schechter translated from Yiddish from Seven Special Poets, and others. (Russian publications in the Soviet Union on Jews, numbers: 664, 702, 704, 842, 849, 852, 875, 976, 1076 and the index).

24. Orenberg in "Murder and Folklore" includes a total of 10 chapters on the saving of 24 Jews by gentiles. In one article, he notes the saving of 30 Jews (7 families).
[С. Шварц, Антисемнтнзм в С.С.С.Р., 136–7]
There is information that German gentiles were killed by the Nazis for saving Jews and protesting their murder. Schwartz considers this as unsourced.

25. Alter Katzizna (1885–1941) was born in Vilna and lived in Yekaterinoslav. He became one of the chief spokesmen in the Yiddish literature arena in Warsaw.

26. Dr. Esther Kololchik was born in Yekaterinoslav in 1890, where she grew up. Her father, a physician, was an active Zionist who was inscribed in his time in the Golden Book of the Jewish National Fund [I found the listing and sent her a copy of the certificate as "scientific material"…]. Until the end, she worked in Leningrad on the history of the workers movement in Russia (about 50 researchers). She wrote a documentary novel "Grigory Chudnovski" (in Russian) who she knew personally still in Yekaterinoslav and loved him. (Prior to that, a novel by Zabara was written about him, of which excerpts translated from a Yiddish manuscript were published in the original in "S.H." under the name "Ordinary Mame" Обыкновенная мама.) According to her words (in a letter to me from 19.9.69) There was a hospital in Leningrad and a street in Dnipropetrovsk named after her (in Politzieskaya).

27. More on religious life in Dnipropetrovsk:
There were two rabbis in the 1930s. There were two synagogues at the beginning of the 1930s. There was a secret mikva [ritual bath] at the end of the 1930s.
In 1930, there were 30–40 students in the Chabad Yeshiva. The lads were able to study a page of Gemara on their own. The teachers were: Rabbi Dov Kornitzer, may G–d avenge his blood – a great scholar, and Rabbi Mordechai–Tzvi Chartonov. The Yeshiva changed synagogues on occasion with the knowledge of the gabbaim and shamashim. The shochet Roglin of blessed memory took on responsibility for expenses. He was imprisoned and died in jail, may G–d avenge his blood. The students were forced to leave Dnipropetrovsk.
(A. A. Gershuni, Jews and Judaism in the Soviet Union, 5730 – 1970, pp. 77, 87, 97, 106, 135).

28. *. S. Ortenberg (Einikeit, 27.6.46) determined that the number of Jews in Dnipropetrovsk at the time of the Holocaust was 150,000. He writes that the Red Army found 10–15 Jews (and some minimize this number even more) including Yeva (Chava) Chebrinichkaya – see "Soviet Homeland" 1966 (10), and my letter there (1967). I have a letter to me from the late Ukrainian poet Ivan Chomkin, whose mother Agrafana Fedorivna has a file as a righteous gentile in Yad Vashem, stating that she saved her.

29. **. More on the Jewish population of Dnipropetrovsk:
At the end of the 1930s, it was one of the five cities with the largest Jewish population (totaling 1,300,000): Moscow, Leningrad, Kiev, Kharkov, Dnipropetrovsk (Gershuni, p. 51). There were 100,000 Jews before the war. There were 50,000 in July 1946 (?).

30. More on the stories of the Holocaust of the Jews of Dnipropetrovsk:
Molotov, when he approached all governments that had strong diplomatic relations with the Soviet Union in those days, gave information on 6.1.42 of the murder of 10,500 (?) Jews of Dnipropetrovsk, and 52,000 Ukrainians, Russians and Jews (?) in Kiev. The minimization was deliberate "Without connection to a nationality"!

31. *. In Yad Vashem, Nisan 5721 (1961) (17), the table of times of events of the Holocaust (page 4, line 1) 12–13 October 1941. That is: Hoshana Rabba and Shmini Atzeret [the slaughter in Dnipropetrovsk].

32. More on Reb Levi"sh: He had a rabbinic writ in Jaffa – thus writes Rebbetzin Chana Schneerson (peace be upon her) in her memoires, as she describes the confiscations that took place in their home in Dnipropetrovsk.

About him – see A. A. Gershuni (in his book of 5730 – 1970) pp. 80, 111–112.
Rabbi Avraham–David Lavaut (the grandfather of Rebbetzin Chana Schneerson and of the mother of A. [D.] Shlonski, called by the name of his mother) wrote (and published) aside from "Beit Aharon and Additions": "Kav–Naki", laws of divorces (5625 – 1865, 5674 – 1914, 5677 – 1917) [Included a section on "Hashlamat Hasedarim"]; "Netiv Chaim" – in "Derech Chaim" of Rabbi Y. of Lissa on the Code of Jewish Law. "Likutei Levi Yitzchak" (notes on the Tanya) from the Gaon Rabbi Levi"sh, may the memory of the righteous be a blessing, was published in 5730 – 1970 in Brooklyn and immediately photocopied in Kfar Chabad. A survey on him was added to it. I have "Memoires of the Rebbetzin Chana Schneerson" in Yiddish, photocopied from the printed version (about 100 pages): dealing with the imprisonment of the Gaon Rabbi Levi"sh until the rebbetzin left

[Page 164]

The Soviet Union with a forged Polish passport. [The time has come to publicize this!] Now, "Likutei Lev"I" on the Zohar (Bereshit–Devarim) and on the Talmud has also been published. Both reached the Admor, may he live [translator's note: the Lubavitcher Rebbe] from the Soviet Union. They were written during the time of the deportation (?).

32. *. Personal addenda: the lawyer Oscar Grosenberg (known from the Beiles trial and others) was a native of Yekaterinoslav. As well as the well–known cellist Petogorsky. (See my research on Yekaterinoslav in Shb"sh, where there are details.)

33. Peretz Markish lived in the city for some years. He published six anthologies of his poems there (Abba Finkelstein in S.H." 12/1970., pp. 177–178). He wrote in the "Trep" anthology, Yekaterinoslav, 1921, in "Der Ois Der Ein" (in Hebrew "A Generation Goes and a Generation Comes" with a translation by Meitos). There are mentions of Yekaterinoslav [A. Bik noted this to me]. See "Al Hamishmar", 27 Kislev 5731 – 1970, Jews of Silence).

34. More on the artist Avani of Yekaterinoslav – see his chapter in the book by Avraham Arst "In the Midst of My Nation, in the Midst of My City," Tel Aviv, 5730 – 1970; and in the book: In the Worlds of Beker Vishlonski.

35. Regarding the Yiddish Courthouse in Yekaterinoslav, see: HaAvar, 18, p. 137. [from there – in the district of Yekaterinoslav in 1925, there were 72,719 Jews].

36. Shneur Zalman Aharonov – A scholar, published an anthology of Torah novella that was published in Warsaw (from 5660 – 1900 and onward), from Yekaterinoslav.

37. Mighty Ones of the Soviet Union from Dnipropetrovsk: Lev Gutman, Leonard Brzidovsky, and Yuru Doljanski – who fell at the hands of the Nazis. Their photos are found in Yad Vashem (from letter of Dr. Y. Karmish to me from Adar II 5730 – 1970).

38. Chana Levina – One of the best Soviet children's writers. Lives in Kharkov. Participates in S.H. A writer in Yiddish and Ukrainian. Born in Yekaterinoslav in 1900.

39. Yekaterinoslav is mentioned in "HaAvar" 17, pp. 32, 42, 88, 108.

40. David Rabinovitch was born in Yekaterinoslav on Passover, 5765 – 1905. He made aliya at the age of 4. He was active in P"T. (See Tidhar, 18, p. 5347).

41. Autobiography, Zalman Aran, Am Haoved, Tel Aviv, 1971. On pages 53–55, Z. A. describes the period of his studies in the Yeshiva of Rabbi P. Gelman in Yekaterinoslav [he has the name wrong, as Helman].

42. The family ties of Reb Chaim Cohen of blessed memory, the well–known philanthropist of Peterburg (oil business) to Yekaterinoslav: His son David was the head of the oil company in Yekaterinoslav in his time; He made aliya in 1942. His daughter Rachel Etinger lived in Yekaterinoslav and made aliya from there with her family. (HeAvar, 18).
Due to these family ties, the seminary was set up specifically in Yekaterinoslav from the estate monies of Reb Chaim Cohen of blessed memory.

43. Proclamation of anti–Semitism number 4 in Yekaterinoslav (Lenin, Iskra, February 15, 1903).

44. Mordechai the son of Hillel HaKohen dedicates several pages in his book to Yekaterinoslav (Olami, book 3, pp. 88–92).
See there about Michael (it should be Michel?) Meidanski [visited the Land of Israel with Rabbi Shmuel Mohilever, Shimon–Yehuda Stanislavski, M.M. Ussishkin, Sharyahu Payel, and Dr. Sh. Levin.

45. The physician Dr. Aryeh Ben–Gefen (Gedera) of Yekaterinoslav claims that he received a proclamation of support of Zionism from Tolstoy and approval for a Jewish state from Lenin prior to the First World War. Both had an echo in the Jewish and general newspapers in Russia and Germany and were written about in "Maariv" and others (see my autobiography).

46. Rabbi Eliahu Goldin was a teacher in the Yeshiva of Yekaterinoslav, according to the testimony of Rabbi Y. Z. Diskin of blessed memory (from a letter to me from Yekaterinoslav from 12 Marcheshvan 5728 – 1967). Olshevski, a businessman in Tel Aviv, was a student of the yeshiva.

47. The Pushinists note that Yekaterinoslav was a place of meeting for Pushkin with the Jews.

48. More on Y. Sh. Olshbang, see now: Sh. Breinman, K.S. 160, 47.

49. More on the settlement of Yekaterinoslav natives in the Golan and the founding of the Achva Moshav there – Dr. Y.Sh. Klausner, Hauma 34.

50. Rabbi Yaakov Elishevitz was a native of Yekaterinoslav. He was a shochet in Dnipropetrovsk and Moscow, and then he made aliya. See my article from 5731 (1971) on the religious situation in the Soviet Union, and on Rabbi Levin (there are several inaccuracies). Shearim, 12 Tishrei, Hamodia, 29 Kislev, Hatzofeh, 19 Tevet.

51. Reb Mordechch"l (The writer Chaim Tshemrinski) lived his final years in Yekaterinoslav, where he died on 31.1.17. His book of parables in Yiddish was published in Yekaterinoslav in 1919.

52. Regarding the physician and chalutz from Yekaterinoslav, Dr. Tzipora–Fania Lvova – see the article that I wrote. Bant, Tidhar of blessed memory, and one should amend

there: She was in Kushta (Constantinople). In "Mesila Chadasha" in Shechem she treated Arabs and Samaritans. She studied Arabic. She observed Kashrut and the Sabbath. She recited Modeh Ani when she woke up and Shema before she went to bed. She died on the 3rd day of Chanukah 5725 (1964) and was buried in Nachalat Yitzchak near Tel Aviv. Appreciations were spoken and written about her, by me as well. My article on her, and her letter to me as the edited of a book, as well as her photograph – were not included in the book.

53. The text on the gravestone of Yisrael Aryeh Leib Schneerson of Tzfat [Safed], who died on 12 Iyar 5712 (1952), mentions his brother Dovber, may G–d avenge his blood. (Regarding both of them it is written: peace be on them, heritage and rest, of fine deeds"). Their father: The rabbi and Gaon, guided by the spirit of G–d, a Kabbalist, of great deeds for Torah and the commandments, responded to many, Levi Yitzchak, the fourth generation of the honorable, holy Admor Tzemach Tzedek"…
Regarding the rebbetzin Chana Schneerson of blessing, see G. Berechia (Tz.H.) Davar, 24 Marcheshvan, 5724 (1963). As well as Dr. Ch. Zeidman, Shearim, 20 Tammuz 5729 (1969), B.Tz. Goldberg, Tag (?)

Translator's Footnotes

1. Throughout this article, the author uses Y–V as an abbreviation for Yekaterinoslav, and D–K for Dnipropetrovsk.

2. See https://en.wikipedia.org/wiki/Paul_I_of_Russia

3. See https://en.wikipedia.org/wiki/Novorossiysk

4. A play on words, as this could mean "To the conductor of young women."

INDEX